THE ARCHAEOLOGY OF CYPRUS

Errata

Page 41: Numbers shown in Plan 1 should all
be preceded by 8. List at bottom of
the page identifies objects shown in
the figures accompanying the chapter.

Page 53: A line has been omitted between lines
3 and 4. It should read:

Cypriote II and III.[48]

The Archaeology of Cyprus—Recent Developments

Vassos Karageorghis

The Archaeology of Cyprus

Recent Developments

Edited by
NOEL ROBERTSON

NOYES PRESS
PARK RIDGE, NEW JERSEY

Copyright © 1975 by Noel Robertson
Library of Congress Catalog Card Number: 75-34930
ISBN: 0-8155-5039-1

Published in the United States by
NOYES PRESS
Noyes Building
Park Ridge, New Jersey 07656

Library of Congress Cataloging in Publication Data

Main entry under title:

The Archaeology of Cyprus.

    Papers from the first international colloquium
on ancient Cyprus, held at Brock University,
October 1971.
        1. Cyprus—Antiquities—Congresses.
I. Robertson, Noel.
DS54.3.A85 *1975* 939.3'7   75-34930
ISBN 0-8155-5039-1

61,029

FOREWORD

This book is a result of the first international colloquium on ancient Cyprus which was held at Brock University, St. Catherines, Ontario, Canada in October, 1971. Some thirty-five scholars engaged in Cypriot studies gathered at Brock to pay tribute to Dr. Vassos Karageorghis, Director of the Department of Antiquities in the Republic of Cyprus, and to participate in the colloquium.

Ten of the papers delivered on that occasion, together with Dr. Karageorghis' address, are printed in this book, which has been edited by Noel Robertson, Chairman of the Department of Classics of Brock University, who has also written the introduction.

CONTENTS

Introduction

Noel Robertson

The archaeology of Cyprus is a lively and challenging field of study, in which an international band of scholars have been cooperating under the most agreeable conditions. It was not always so; the picaresque depredations of Cesnola were a scandal even to the age in which he lived, and the beginnings of disciplined study in this century were at first slow and tentative. The climate for the last several decades, though assisted by many factors, owes much to a man whose own researches are responsible for some of the most significant advances in our knowledge of ancient Cyprus—Dr. Vassos Karageorghis, since 1963 director of the Department of Antiquities in the Republic of Cyprus. In October, 1971, some thirty-five scholars engaged in Cypriot studies gathered at Brock University to pay tribute to Dr. Karageorghis, then visiting North America, and to participate in the first international colloquium on ancient Cyprus. Ten of the papers delivered on that occasion, together with Dr. Karageorghis' address, are printed here.

The papers display nearly the full range of Cypriot archaeology, and also reflect to some extent the measure of scholarly attention which has been devoted to each period. The only period which is not touched on is Neolithic; at present no study of Cypriot Neolithic will have more than transient interest, for every season of fresh excavation modifies our understanding of the subject. R. S. Merrillees deals with the Bronze Age in general; Ellen Herscher with Early and Middle

Cypriot; Sarandis Symeonoglou with the transitional period at the end of Middle Cypriot and the beginning of Late Cypriot; J. D. Muhly, Lynn Holmes, and Barry Gittlen with Late Cypriot; Javier Teixidor, J. L. Benson, and Peter Kahane with Geometric or Archaic; and Jean des Gagniers with Greek and Roman. Their work represents a very substantial contribution to Cypriot studies; and without anticipating arguments and conclusions in any detail, the general bearing of each paper may be described as follows.

R. S. Merrillees, who usefully reviews the archaeology and historiography of Bronze-Age Cyprus ("Problems in Cypriote History"), observes that the island and its people have seldom been studied for their own sake, but rather for their connexion with stronger neighbours and larger conflicts in the eastern Mediterranean. Even professed historians of Cyprus commonly treat the island as a station or an outpost controlled by some foreign power, though often enough the evidence warrants no such construction. In scouting the "invasion complex" of modern authorities, and in rejecting several purported invasions as illusory, Merrillees shows how this unbalanced approach has obscured the real achievements of native Cypriot art and industry, which for long periods flourished in quiet independence. There is much to ponder in his provocative account; those who identify *Alashiya* as Cyprus must now contend with Merrillees' arguments for *Tanaja*, another place-name in Egyptian records of the Eighteenth Dynasty.

During Early Cypriot and the first part of Middle Cypriot, the principal settlements clustered round the springs that issue from the lower slopes on both sides of the Kyrenia mountain range. One such settlement, particularly long-lived, lay near the later town of Lapithos, and from its rock-cut chamber tombs has emerged an exemplary sequence of pottery types, which Ellen Herscher here presents in some detail ("New Light from Lapithos"). The libation jugs, cooking pots, and offering bowls deposited by funerary ritual show the verve and skill of the Cypriot potter of the Bronze Age—painted and plastic decoration, bull and bird motifs, geometric designs—and enable us to trace the broad development of Cypriot culture through several centuries. The earliest affinities of the Lapithos pottery are with Vounous and other Kyrenia sites, afterwards with Dhenia and the plain that looks toward Morphou Bay, and finally with the new centres in the eastern part of the island. At the beginning of Middle Cypriot foreign imports or influences come from Minoan Crete, but by the end from Syria and Palestine. Miss Herscher's survey will provide valuable guidance until the pottery from Lapithos is at last published in full.

Towards the end of Middle Cypriot the pattern of trade and settlement began to shift in favour of the eastern plain and coast. Sarandis Symeonoglou discusses the enigmatic site of Vounari near Phlamoudhi, first occupied at this time ("Excavations at Phlamoudhi and the Form of the Sanctuary in Bronze Age Cyprus"). The settlers built on a small but striking conical hill that dominates the surrounding farmland, and their rough irregular walls might suggest a fortress, especially as the period saw a number of strongholds erected elsewhere in the eastern part of the island, which was plainly threatened by internal unrest. But certain typical features of other fortified sites are lacking at Vounari, and Symeonoglou prefers to think of an open-air rural sanctuary, perhaps resembling the famous clay model from Vounous. At any rate the hill-top structure undoubtedly belonged to the flourishing settlement at Panayia Melissa about a mile to the west, where several houses of the same period (late Middle Cypriot through the first half of Late Cypriot) have been uncovered. An archaeological survey conducted by Symeonoglou and his colleagues in the Columbia University Expedition has revealed that the rather isolated stretch of coast round Phlamoudhi, which today supports only a few hundred inhabitants, was thickly populated in ancient times, above all in the Hellenistic and Roman periods. The origins of this prosperity go back to the enterprising settlers of Vounari and Melissa.

Because Cyprus has yielded no decipherable records earlier than the first millennium, the chronology of the Bronze Age in the island depends entirely on material links, direct or indirect, with the literate civilizations of Egypt and Asia. At the end of Middle Cypriot and during the first half of Late Cypriot such links exist in plenty between Cyprus and the towns of Syria and Palestine, but just at this point our reckoning is bedevilled by the problematic dates of the first dynasty of Babylon. J. D. Muhly addresses himself to this famous conundrum ("Near Eastern Chronology and the Date of the Late Cypriot I Period"), and argues shrewdly for the "middle" chronology, which gives the year 1594 for the fall of Babylon. Drawing on the recently discovered archives of the Hittite king Hattushilish I, Muhly demonstrates that the sack of Alalakh Level VII in the mid-1600s must be ascribed to this king, whose grandson and successor Murshilish I destroyed Babylon. Since some students of Middle and Late Cypriot continue to advocate or endorse a system based on the "low" chronology of Babylon, Muhly's study deserves close attention.

After long ages of isolation Cyprus suddenly entered the lively commerce of goods and men that traversed the eastern Mediterranean in the Late Bronze Age, intermingling Mycenaeans, Canaanites, and Egyptians; and it is extremely useful to have the large body of evidence collected by Lynn Holmes ("The Foreign Trade of Cyprus during the Late Bronze Age"). As a firm supporter of the equation of *Alashiya* with either the whole or some part of Cyprus, Holmes exploits documentary references as well as material remains. Cyprus exported, along with copper, wood from her still abundant forests and also ships as a finished product. The innumerable Cypriot vessels found abroad probably contained, not opium as one authority has it, but some kind of ointment or perfume. The chief imports were luxury articles such as glass, faience, and alabaster; at the same time Cyprus admitted many less tangible but more significant influences from foreign lands. During Late Bronze I and II she had close ties with Egypt and Palestine, not quite so close with Syria, but in Late Bronze III she breaks entirely with these countries, and Aegean trade and influence, already increasing in the previous period, flood the island and transform its culture. Such are the broad outlines of the picture which Holmes fills in with a wealth of substantiated detail.

In a paper related both to Muhly's and to Holmes's, Barry M. Gittlen takes us to several key sites in Palestine—notably Hazor, Megiddo, and Lachish—in order to examine the precise context of an important class of Late Cypriot pottery, White Slip ware ("Cypriote White Slip Pottery in its Palestinian Stratigraphic Context"). He finds the evidence insufficient for any chronological differentiation between the three successive stages which have been distinguished in the stylistic development of the ware: possibly, he suggests, the three varieties came to Palestine concurrently from separate areas of Cyprus.

In historical times Citium and central Cyprus belonged to the

Phoenicians. The date at which the first Phoenician colonists arrived is controversial: some would trace them back to the tenth century, others to the ninth. Javier Teixidor takes a more astringent view ("Early Phoenician Presence in Cyprus: Analysis of Epigraphical Material"), discounting all evidence earlier than the second half of the eighth century, when the governor of *Kartihadast* dedicated a series of bronze bowls to Baal of Lebanon; and *Kartihadast*, he argues, is not Citium as commonly supposed, but an unidentified colony of Tyre elsewhere in the island. Earlier Semitic inscriptions in Cyprus are not specifically Phoenician, but rather Canaanite—the language common to Syria and Palestine at the beginning of the first millennium—and doubtless originate with Syrian residents. The circumstances of Phoenician colonization remain obscure.

During the early first millennium Cyprus developed a vigorous native art compounded of Aegean and Levantine elements. The full flowering of this art in the Archaic period is now familiar from the excavation of the cemetery of Salamis, but its earlier, formative stages are less known and less appreciated; J. L. Benson's study of one engaging aspect of Cypro-Geometric pottery, the representation of birds, is therefore all the more welcome ("Birds on Cypro-Geometric Pottery"). In the Late Bronze Age Cypriot potters had no independent tradition of depicting birds, but began to copy, rather ineptly, the birds of Mycenaean and Syrian art, and this forlorn practice continued into Geometric times. But when left to themselves, and thrown back on imagination and experiment, the Cypriots eventually produced graceful, distinctive birds which vie with the best in contemporary Greek vase-painting. Benson further offers the interesting hypothesis that in one Late Geometric workshop a new departure in bird shapes was actually inspired by Mycenaean prototypes which had come to light again.

Among the spoils carried off by Cesnola from those mysterious underground rooms at Curium which he conceived to be the treasure vaults of a temple—perhaps in reality an Archaic tomb with several chambers—was a splendid Late Geometric crater of Cycladic, probably Naxian, origin, standing nearly five feet high. In the zones of ornamental animals covering the upper half of the vase the late Peter Kahane discerns a complex symbolism which unites Near Eastern and mainland Greek motifs ("The Cesnola Krater from

Kourion in the Metropolitan Museum of Art: an Iconological Study in Greek Geometric Art"). The sacred tree flanked by two heraldic creatures and the frieze of grazing animals are emblems of fertility deriving from the Levant; the continuity of this symbolism from the Bronze into the Iron Age can be safely inferred, if not strictly demonstrated. On the other hand a third motif, represented on the vase by a tethered horse, comes from post-Mycenaean Greece and reflects funeral games and hero cults, possibly a Dorian innovation. The fusion of East and West perceived by Kahane is certainly appropriate to the island in which the crater was found and for which it was presumably created.

In recent years exploration has begun at several of the great cities which dominated Cyprus during the Greek and Roman periods. After Salamis, none of these cities holds more promise for the excavator than Soli, the capital of a rich agricultural and mining district on the south coast of Morphou Bay. Jean des Gagniers, director of the archaeological mission which has enlisted the efforts of Canadian, French, and Swiss scholars at Soli since 1964, reports on the remains uncovered thus far, spanning some two thousand years of history ("Excavations at Soloi"). The Greeks, misled by a typical pun, ascribed the foundation of Soli to the advice of Solon the lawgiver, but the Geometric tombs here described by des Gagniers show that the city antedates Solon by several centuries. Remains of Archaic and Classical date have been traced in some areas and await excavation in detail. The Roman city is already well represented in the Agora and some peripheral buildings, and in a paved avenue sixteen feet wide bordered by porticoes. Perhaps the most impressive monument of all is an Early Christian basilica, originally built (with a magnificent mosaic floor) towards 400 A.D. and maintained through successive transformations for nearly a millennium thereafter. Some of the buildings will permit a measure of restoration which ought to bring fame and fortune to this attractive site and its idyllic landscape of hills and plain and coast.

Such are the papers collected here; together they form an impressive index of scholarly endeavour. Ancient Cyprus has been well served in the present generation.

       *   *   *   *   *   *   *

The preceding account was written in happier days. The events of July and August '74, which for the people of Cyprus meant the end of peaceful, ordered life, also scattered the foreign scholars and students working in the island. The Turkish military occupation has foreclosed a number of important sites in the north, and the emergency conditions prevailing elsewhere will hamper archaeological activity and discourage new undertakings. Although the Cypriot Department of Antiquities, resolutely led by Dr. Karageorghis, continued to function even during the weeks of crisis—securing the treasures of the National Museum, and pressing forward (as a solace or a diversion) with the excavation of Kition—and although most foreign missions are prepared to resume their work at the earliest possible moment, it is clear that archaeological research has been greatly impaired. Worse still, the unsettled state of the island is likely to lead to large-scale looting of unprotected sites, such as Cyprus has seen all too often in the past. The disruption of research and the pillaging of sites are, to be sure, a small matter when set beside the enormous sum of human suffering in the island; and yet all friends and admirers of Cyprus and of its rich history must regret the permanent loss which will ensue.

The island's present misfortunes are all the more lamentable because they have abruptly reversed the high hopes and fair promise inaugurated by the brief period of independence (1960–74), a period that was, on the whole, stable, prosperous, and constructive—especially by Middle Eastern standards. The least promising solution for Cyprus is foreign control, whether by Greece or by Turkey or by both. The old attachments to Turkey or to Byzantium, which irredentists seek to revive, are as obsolete as the imperial systems that created them (and since Byzantine domination, like Turkish, was exercised from Anatolia, it offers no excuse for the impossible dream of uniting Cyprus with peninsular Greece); moreover, these attachments never brought advantage to Cyprus, unless in protecting the inhabitants from still worse oppression. In the present day Cyprus does not need foreign arbiters or champions: it is not only that the claims of Greece and Turkey are conflicting and irreconcilable, but neither is wanted by Cyprus, and neither is needed for general peace and security.

The Republic of Cyprus should not be seen as a novel and dubious construction, but as a natural return, after long ages of imperial entanglements, to the dictates of human geography. It was as an island, differing markedly in natural features and resources from the neighbouring coasts of the mainland, that Cyprus in early times produced a strong native culture which subsequently proved both adaptable to external influences and tenacious of its own distinctive qualities: these qualities were communicated to successive waves of newcomers (of whom only the literate Greeks and Phoenicians can be identified by modern historians), and the newcomers soon became authentic Cypriots. Now that economic and strategic patterns have changed so that Cyprus no longer appears a valuable prize for larger powers contending in the Mediterranean, the islanders can reassert their essential separateness, and their own best interest requires them to do so.

An oracle quoted by the geographer Strabo tells us that because the coast of Asia Minor is being continually advanced by river silt, Cyprus will some day be united with the mainland. As a physical reality the prediction is no less unlikely than undersirable. Let us hope that the oracle does not find (after the manner of such things) an unlooked-for fulfilment in the political sense.

Perspectives

Vassos Karageorghis

Dear Colleagues,

It has been a pleasantly moving experience to be with you during two days in a symposium dedicated entirely to the history and archaeology of Cyprus. The very fact that such a symposium should be held in a place outside Cyprus, in this distant but hospitable country, is an indication of how much interest exists nowadays in Cypriote studies.

I am fully aware that so many distinguished scholars have come here from many lands, not to honour my humble self, but to honour Cyprus, and it is in this spirit that I thank you all and also the Chairman and other members of the Department of Classics of Brock University for the splendid organization of this first (outside Cyprus) international gathering on Cypriote Archaeology.

This is a particularly interesting Symposium, as it has recruited scholars who are interested in one single country of the ancient world; however small the island is, it developed a sophisticated ancient culture, important enough to overpass the insular boundaries. There was a time when research on the archaeology and history of Cyprus suffered from a very close isolation, either because it was thought by the Orientalists as too Western, or by the Classicists as too Oriental. However, now that both the Aegean and the Near Eastern cultures are thought of as one unit, and indeed now that one considers almost the whole of the Mediterranean as one unified cultural area, Cyprus comes to the foreground of research, as a place where the great civilizations of the Aegean and the Near East met and influenced each other on a number of occasions. But as Dr. Merrillees very convincingly pointed out in his admirable paper, the island was not only a meeting place of great cultures, but a place with a great culture of its own.

I shall not discuss here the nature of ancient Cypriote civilization, nor try to trace the history of Cypriote Archaeology. You all have an intimate knowledge of both, and some of you have been involved in making this history through your own research over a number of years. After a very short excursion to the early stages of Cypriote archaeology I would like to examine with you the prospect of future research in the island.

The end of the nineteenth century marked the beginning of interest in the antiquities of Cyprus, with Cesnola and other amateur archaeologists hunting for treasures for private collections and foreign museums. Much damage to archaeology was done by these early "scholar-treasure hunters," but that was the fashion of archaeology during that period and one should not be unduly dismayed. Soon afterwards came the scholarly work of Max Ohnefalsch-Richter and of Sir John Myres who put an order to the chaotic state of knowledge about the archaeology of Cyprus.

During the second quarter of the twentieth century the excavations and scholarly publications of the Swedish Cyprus Expedition, under the leadership of Einar Gjerstad, marked the initial stages of the great epoch of Cypriote studies. Schaeffer, Stewart, and Dikaios are but a few names among those who dedicated themselves to the study of ancient Cyprus and who raised the standards of Cypriote research with their labours and erudition. But the story does not end with these great names, some of whom are still gracing and enlightening our sphere of studies. There is now a large group of younger scholars throughout the world who have joined our ranks, and it is with particular joy that I see so many of them here. The interest is growing all the time, and I may mention as an indication the fact that whereas about ten years ago there was only one foreign excavation in Cyprus, this year there were seventeen, and this number will certainly increase during the next few years.

There is definitely a revival of interest in the oldest stage of Cypriote culture, the Neolithic period. The pioneer work of Gjerstad and Dikaios will certainly be elucitated further by the new excavations at Philia, Ayios Epiktitos (both British excavations headed by Drs. Watkins and Peltenburg respectively) and Cape Andreas (a French excavation headed by M. Le Brun). We still have to fill a gap of 1500 years in the sequence of Neolithic culture, produced as a result of carbon 14 dating. It is hoped that at one or more of the above sites a sufficiently deep accumulation of strata will be found to enable us to study all the successive phases of Neolithic culture. No doubt new carbon 14 tests will be useful for the better dating of this very remote and robust civilization of Cyprus.

The Early Bronze Age, in spite of the vast amount of material which has been unearthed up to now, remains very incompletely known, though one should praise the monumental works of Gjerstad, Dikaios and Stewart. We certainly know a great deal about its ceramic material and also about its religious beliefs, but we have very little to illustrate its architecture and daily life. Professor Weinberg started about twenty years ago a pioneer work, with the excavation of a settlement near Kourion. We hope that he will return to resume his excavation and that others will also choose to excavate settlements, however ungratifying the results from the point of view of finds may be; the harvest will certainly be rich in information about architectural styles, town planning and daily life during this important period in the history of Cyprus, when the copper mines of the island were exploited for the first time and a vigorous trade was initiated with the Near Eastern countries.

The Middle and Late Bronze Ages are more adequately known, thanks to the work of a great number of scholars. Professor Åström has already written a synthesis about the Middle Bronze Age, and more information will be brought to light with continued excavations at sites like Phlamoudhi, where the Columbia expedition is now working under Professor Edith Porada and Professor Symeonoglou. The great work of Schaeffer and Dikaios at the important Late Bronze Age town of Enkomi is now continued by Professor Olivier Pelon, and the excavations of the Department of Antiquities of Cyprus at Kition still continue to uncover important monuments every year.

Two new Late Bronze Age sites have attracted the attention of archaeologists during the last two years, both on the northern coast, which is so little known: one is the site "Palaeokastro" at Ayia Irini, excavated by an Italian expedition from the Institute of Mycenaean and Anatolian Studies of Rome under Professor Gallavotti, and the other is site "Toumba tou Skourou," excavated by an American expedition from Harvard University under Professor Emily Vermeule.

The discovery of Aegean and Syrian imports at both these sites, dated to the sixteenth century B.C., will no doubt throw more light on the trade relations between Cyprus with the Near East on the one hand and with the Aegean on the other. Other Late Bronze Age sites which are currently being excavated include Athienou, between Nicosia and Kition, where an Israeli expedition from the University of Jerusalem under Drs. Dothan and Ben Tor discovered this year a site which may be connected with a metallurgical installation in the proximity of a sanctuary. The metallurgy of Cyprus during the Late Bronze Age may now be studied also at Kition, where important installations came to light this year in connection with the worship of two divinities in twin temples of the twelfth century B.C.

In spite of the fact that the Late Bronze Age is perhaps the most widely investigated period in the archaeology and history of Cyprus, yet it is also the one with many unsolved problems. The Cypro-Minoan script, of which we now possess a fairly large number of tablets, remains undeciphered, in spite of persistent efforts which are still going on by a small number of epigraphists, mainly by Madame Emilia Masson (France). The provenance of Mycenaean pottery found in the Levant, particularly in Cyprus, is still the subject of long discussions, in which we may now see the chemists taking an active part. The problem of the identification of Cyprus with Alasia is still a controversy, as we have ascertained from Dr. Merrillees' paper.

Some of these problems will no doubt find their solution during the next few years with continued research. In the meantime excavation work continues, and new sites are sought every year. At the well-known site near the Larnaca Salt Lake, known as Hala Sultan Tekké, Professor Åström of Göteborg University excavated this year the first trial trenches. This coastal harbour town may one day prove to be the largest and the most important of all Late Bronze Age towns of Cyprus. The German expedition of the Deutsches Archäologisches Institut at Palaepaphos, under Professor F. G. Maier, has already started finding Mycenaean remains, and one day we may see the Mycenaean or Homeric temple of Aphrodite coming to light at this site. At Salamis, the French expedition of the University of Lyon under Professors Pouilloux and Roux have brought to light evidence for the earliest habitation at Salamis, in the eleventh century B.C., a period which coincides with the last phase of the neighbouring town of Enkomi; thus the mythical foundation of Salamis by Teucer, a hero of the Trojan war, becomes now an archaeological reality.

The importance of Cyprus during the Iron Age is still to be investigated, though several city sites are being excavated at present. One day the French expedition excavating at Salamis may come across the palatial buildings which correspond to the rich tombs of the "Royal Necropolis" of the eighth and seventh centuries B.C. Other city sites, like Idalion, where excavations were started this year by an American expedition of the American School of Oriental Research under Professor G. Ernest Wright, and Tamassos, where a German team under Professor Bucholz took up two years ago the earlier investigations of Max Ohnefalsch-Richter, may one day reveal the architectural splendours of the Archaic period which we know up to now only from the evidence of the tombs.

The Classical and Hellenistic periods have not been neglected. Apart from the main city sites already mentioned above, the Classical city of Golgoi is now being investigated by a Greek expedition from the University of Salonica, under Professor G. Bakalakis. More evidence about the trade relations of Cyprus during the late Classical period was brought to light from the bottom of the sea off Kyrenia, with the discovery and exemplary investigation of a Greek merchant ship of the late fourth century B.C. by an American expedition from Pennsylvania under Professor Michael Katsev. At Salamis, the Hellenistic remains of the temple of Zeus Salaminios, one of the most venerated sanctuaries of the island, are now being uncovered by the French expedition.

Important discoveries have been made during recent years which throw ample light on the splendours of Roman Cyprus. At Paphos the Department of Antiquities and a Polish Mission under Professor Michalowski and Dr. Dasjewski brought to light two palatial buildings with splendid mosaic pavements of the end of the third century A.D. At Soloi important remains are being uncovered by a Canadian expedition from the Université Laval (Québec) under Professor des Gagniers, whose paper describes some of the recent discoveries of his mission, including the life-size bronze portrait head brought to light this summer. The same expedition is also investigating very successfully the earlier and later periods of Soloi.

At Kourion the Department of Antiquities is continuing the work initiated by an American expedition from Pennsylvania, and at Salamis an already impressive complex of public buildings has been unearthed and restored again by the Department of Antiquities.

The Early Christian period, with its basilicas and mosaics, has attracted the interest of scholars during recent years. At Yialoussa, Salamis, Amathus, and Paphos, new remains of spacious basilicas have come to light. Mosaics and frescoes of the Early Christian and Byzantine periods are constantly being looked after by restorers of the Department of Antiquities and by the Dumbarton Oaks Institute of Byzantine Studies of Harvard University.

These later monuments and sites may not provide the scientific excitement of the earlier archaeological remains, but they promote both scholarship and cultural tourism.

The above is but a short and sketchy outline of the current work in Cyprus and a brief mention of the problems connected with various periods in the archaeology of the island. It is gratifying for me to note that during my twenty years of active service in the Department of Antiquities of Cyprus I have seen the interest in the archaeology of the island grow every year. My predecessors prepared the atmosphere; it is now my pleasant duty to maintain and cultivate even further this scholarly interest. In this task I rely on the constant help of my colleagues in Cyprus and also on the cordial spirit of collaboration which exists between the Department of Antiquities and all foreign scholars who excavate or carry other research on the island. This happy atmosphere is particularly favoured by my Government, and it will be my privilege and pleasure if more of you choose Cyprus as a field for archaeological research.

Let this Symposium be the beginning for an International Organization of Cypriote Studies. We have enough disciples already, throughout the world. The younger generation of archaeologists is certainly a guarantee of our success. I may assure you that the Department of Antiquities of Cyprus will do everything to promote the idea of such a brotherhood of Cypriologists, based on a spirit of happy collaboration.

Problems in Cypriote History

Robert S. Merrillees

If I were asked why the history of Cyprus has begun increasingly to occupy the attention of scholars outside the island, and particularly in North America, I would say that there were three principal reasons. The first of these is Dr. Vassos Karageorghis, Director of the Department of Antiquities in Cyprus. His presence amongst us is a further indication of the keen interest he has taken and fostered in studies of the island's past and of the contributions he is making to its present and future. His knowledge, dedication and enthusiasm are a source of inspiration and stimulus to us all.

The second main reason lies in the nature of Cyprus itself and of its passage through time. It represents in microcosm the history of all nations and peoples, for Cyprus has, in spite of its size, known all the vicissitudes that have befallen those countries endowed with particular strategic and commercial importance by virtue of their geographical setting and the ebb and flow of political, social and economic movements. From the earliest times it was exposed to influences and pressures from overseas, followed by a prolonged sequence of foreign occupations, which ended only in the last ten years, when Cyprus regained the political independence it had lost towards the end of the Bronze Age some three thousand years ago. It is as much a measure of the resilience of the indigenous Cypriote population as of the self-centered interests of the powers which ruled the island, that the basic character of the inhabitants has remained largely unchanged

15

since it took shape in the Bronze Age, the most formative phase of the island's civilization.

No reconstruction of Cypriote history should lose sight of the basic continuity of the native character, for despite the many enforced changes and reorientations which took place in material culture during the long periods of subjugation, the islanders' spirit survived not only unimpaired but, if anything, enriched. While it appeared to accept the alien conventions introduced or imposed from abroad, it imparted to them an indelible and unmistakable Cypriote flavour, which itself contributed to a diversification of our Middle Eastern cultural heritage. The Cypriote style manifested itself above all in products of its material industry, which are so plentiful and individualistic as to provide a reliable foundation on which to erect an historical framework that is both cohesive and coherent.

The third reason for a growing interest in the island's prehistory derives from a deepening disenchantment within the academic community for the conventional study of those major civilizations whose achievements are familiar to the point of satiation. Students are coming to recognize that a better understanding of the past, as well as the present, is to be had by tracing the history of ancient societies as a whole than by writing the lives of their most prominent leaders. We have, from our reading and research, grown so accustomed to the orthodox textbook histories of Egypt and Mesopotamia, where written records have spared scholars the need to plumb the social depths below the elite and establishment, that there is an ingrown disinclination to face up to the fact that in both pre-literate and literate cultures the great bulk of the populace was unable to read or write and has left us nothing but their material possessions to show that they, too, took a part in the events of their times.

If the study of the past is to have any relevance to a better understanding of the present, then we must start to concentrate on those aspects of the ancient civilizations which will help us to see the social evolution of the twentieth century A.D. in its proper perspective, and at the same time revise our knowledge and appreciation of particular situations which have their origins in remote antiquity.

Despite the many academic and technical advantages which the island offers a potential student, Cypriote historiography has fallen victim to a succession of preoccupations and prejudices comparable in effect to the series of invasions from which the inhabitants once suffered.

It would not be untrue to say that the conventional history of Cyprus is the history of the island as a land mass, not of its indigenous inhabitants, the Cypriote people, for they were not their own political masters for the period whose history is best documented by written sources. This three thousand year interregnum was most notable for the waves of intruders, immigrants and others who passed through Cyprus on their way elsewhere or who retreated there when forced from their own preferred homeland. Because of the less than worthy motives which brought them to Cyprus, these foreign visitors kept themselves by and large aloof from the local society and contributed little or nothing to the indigenous civilization. The tangible vestiges of their presence are largely limited to buildings of one kind or another, coinage and the occasional blue-eyed child. The superimposition of these external cultures, whose dynamics had evolved outside the island and drew no inspiration from the contemporaneous civilization of the native inhabitants, left the Cypriote populace free to pursue their preferred way of life largely unaffected by the outside world.

This was not always the case. In fact, the people's cultural receptivity has been to a large extent responsible for the direction of their political development. During the Bronze Age the island was prey, due to its geographical location, to a diversity of influences from all points of the compass. Historical accident appears to be the principal factor which conclusively shaped Cypriote cultural orientation towards the West rather than the East. It so happened that the great flowering of Levantine trade in the Late Bronze Age, when Cyprus was at its most prosperous, coincided with Mycenaean commercial expansion into the East Mediterranean Basin and the penetration of Greek Bronze Age styles into the art and craftmanship of the civilizations then flourishing around the region. The consolidation of this impact on Cyprus by the arrival of the Achaeans in the thirteen century B.C. was decisive in setting a seal on the future proclivity of the island's cultural development. For Hellenism has remained for three thousand years a dominant theme in all forms of Cypriote expression and is even today a vital force in the determination of political, social and cultural policies.

Nevertheless, the qualities which characterize the Bronze Age civilization of Cyprus and give the achievements of that time their most distinctive imprint and appeal have not been submerged by the Mycenaean, Greek or Byzantine characters, or for that matter by any other overseas contacts or associations. It is significant that the traditional life style of the Cypriote people is now after independence experiencing a rapid metamorphosis through the introduction of new processes, ideas and forces, just as a civilization of the Late Bronze Age in Cyprus, under ·the impetus of a growing political and commercial internationalism in the ancient Levant, developed a degree of uniformity, refinement and prosperity unparalleled again until modern times.

I have already asserted that when seen in historical perspective the period that holds the key to a proper understanding of Cypriote cultural development through the ages is the Bronze Age. And to illustrate the points made in the introduction to this paper, I propose now to deal with writings that are mostly concerned with this era, for the attitudes which have prevailed in studies of the Bronze Age are reflected as much, if not more, in works on the times when Cyprus was not its own ruler.

The scientific foundations of Cypriote Bronze Age historiography were laid by two scholars, René Dussaud, whose volume *Les civilisations préhelléniques dans le bassin de la mer égée* first appeared in 1910 and was republished as a second edition in 1914, and by J. L. Myres in his 1914 *Handbook of the Cesnola Collection of Antiquities from Cyprus* in the Metropolitan Museum of Art, New York. It is not without interest that both these studies appeared in the years preceding the outbreak of the first World War, the last major conflict resulting from political as opposed to ideological causes. Their accounts were in fact notably free from contamination by extraneous dogma and had clearly not been drafted with the aim of making the facts fit the political theory. Yet even these two pioneers were not without the faults of their times, for they could evidently not rid themselves of a sense of cultural superiority.

For Dussaud and Myres, Cypriote history was not considered worthy of study in its own right but only in terms of the cultural milieu of which it formed part. The essence of their approach lay in the notion that Cypriote civilization was peripheral, at best provincial, and could only be sensibly appreciated from the standpoint of its foreign relations. Myres's freedom from ideological bias but attachment to cultural elitism is well illustrated by his outline of the ancient civilization of Cyprus. He expresses the unfashionable view that in modern Cyprus the difference between "Turk" and "Greek" is one of expression rather than build, and hence that it is probably safe to separate the discussion of the culture of Cyprus from all questions of race and to regard its successive occupants simply as contributors to style. At the same time, however, he declaims that in history Cyprus is interesting less in what it yielded than in what it received and is therefore a faithful, if rather dilatory record of events and tendencies in the greater world around. Yet Myres does recognize that while Cyprus experienced every phase of the neighbouring civilizations, it never wholly surrendered its own individuality or its own earlier accomplishments.

The same point is made by Dussaud in his 1914 edition, but without the intent to flatter. He notes that the local pottery is abundant and quite varied but finds it of very poor inspiration. In his opinion, it underwent Mycenaean influence which made little impact on it, so that it kept distinctly local characteristics. Yet he believed that Cypriote archaeology should be given particular attention, as not only was the island a great centre of the metal industry, but its situation made it an excellent observation post to take account of the reciprocal influences which Aegean and eastern civilizations underwent. This evaluation is a considerably more generous acknowledgment of Cyprus's historical significance than Dussaud was initially prepared to concede in his 1910 edition. There he was at pains to lay to rest any suspicion that the island could have been the "instigator" of Bronze Age civilization in the east Mediterranean, protesting, on the contrary, that it underwent stimulus from the Aegean and only in the Mycenaean period became an active centre of diffusion, especially (and no doubt ungratefully) towards the East.

The 1920s and 1930s were a barren period in Cypriote historical writing. Contributing to this sterility is Stanley Casson's book entitled *Ancient Cyprus: Its Art and Archaeology*, which appeared in London in 1937. His philosophy was both simple and simplistic. Cyprus was for him the only British possession which served to illustrate the history and activities of the Greeks! He preferred, without any attempt at justification, to see the history and art of the Cypriotes as those of Oriental Greeks rather than of Hellenised Orientals, and allowed this prejudgment to colour the whole of his narrative. John Franklin Daniel, whose premature death robbed Cypriote archaeology of its brightest American student and one of the most outstanding scholars ever to have worked in the island, published a withering review of Casson's work in the 1939 volume of the *American Journal of Archaeology*. As a penetrating indictment of all the shortcomings and errors which could be committed by an historian of Cyprus, it could scarcely be bettered.

It was not until well over thirty years after the appearance of Myres's and Dussaud's contributions that another authoritative effort was made to evaluate the Bronze Age on its own merits and in the wider context of contemporaneous developments around the Levant. In 1948 Professor C. F. A. Schaeffer, who had before the Second World War excavated part of the cemetery of Vounous and discovered the settlement at Enkomi, produced his monumental *Stratigraphie comparée et chronologie de l'Asie occidentale*. It was a timely attempt at historical synthesis and rationalization, and exhibited a breadth of learning and experience that few could emulate today. Though Schaeffer makes no sweeping generalizations about the quality of Cypriote imaginativeness, he too is obsessed by the relationship between the island and its territorial neighbours. In this case, however, he sets out to rectify what he considers a false impression of Cypriote prehistory that has been created by emphasising the predominantly European character of the island's present culture.

He maintains that it was with Turkey, Syria and Palestine that Cyprus shared its daily life in antiquity, and that it needed a massive invasion at the end of the thirteenth century B.C., followed by other migrations from the same general source over the centuries, to turn Cyprus into an advance post of Europe opposite the coast of Asia Minor. There were, he contends, powerful return blows delivered from Phoenicia, Assyria and even Egypt and Persia which brought Cyprus back temporarily into the Asian fold, before the majority of the inhabitants came to consider themselves European, or particularly Greek, as they do today. He concludes that as long as the strength of the adjacent Asian empires stayed intact, or at each time that that strength was reasserted, Cyprus became necessarily and firmly attached to Asia.

In this connection it is perhaps interesting to note that for electoral purposes within the United Nations Cyprus is a member of the 'Asian' group, whereas Greece and Turkey belong to the 'Western European and Others' group.

Of all those who have sought to define the essence of ancient Cypriote history, none has succeeded with as much insight and sensitivity as the late Professor J. R. Stewart, whose contribution to the Second Edition of the *Handbook to the Nicholson Museum* appeared coincidentally in 1948, the same year as Schaeffer's innovative work. He is the only writer of his time to have seen Cypriote civilization as a self-contained and self-respecting entity, in relation to which foreign influences must be viewed, and not vice versa. For Stewart, Cyprus was destined by its geographical situation to be a meeting place for the cultures of both the West and the East, but was not merely a melting pot, since it asserted a reflex influence on the mainland.

Stewart's basic thesis is that the importance of the cultural history of the island lay in this adaptation to native canons of foreign styles, which produced a local commentary on the contemporary art of the Eastern Mediterranean. He continues in this way:

> More than this, the island was ground upon which Cretan and Hellene could meet Asia on intimate terms, a meeting to which Greek culture ultimately owed much. In the late third and second millenia B.C. Cyprus was rich and thickly populated, owing its wealth to a widespread export of copper. The coming of the Iron Age, coinciding with the great migration, brought economic ruin and political chaos, from which a new Cyprus emerged, again wealthy and prosperous, but now more dependent on the transit trade between the riches of the resurgent east of Assyria, Babylon, Egypt and Persia, and the developing, economic power of the Greek cities than on the still considerable wealth of the copper mines. Yet, whatever changes economics or politics made, whatever artistic influence gained favour, Cyprus remained essentially herself and the products of her art retained a distinctive Cypriote character. There is perhaps more continuity of tradition in the island than anywhere else in the Middle East, and yet greater ability to borrow and adapt.

Only one year later, in 1949, the first volume of Sir George Hill's monumental work on the history of Cyprus appeared in Cambridge,

England. For all its concessions to the growth of knowledge and understanding about the dynamics of Cypriote cultural growth, it could well have been written before Dussaud and Myres transformed the study of the island's prehistory from a pastime into a discipline. Quite apart from conducting recondite post-mortems on issues long since dead and buried, Hill revealed himself as the ablest exponent of the school of thought which sees Cyprus as a kind of caravanserai for itinerant invaders and travellers, who used the island as nothing more than a stepping stone to their ultimate destination or as a convenient place of withdrawal when the primary object of their territorial ambitions was denied them.

While it is true that every ancient historian is at the mercy of his sources for the amount of detail available on a particular period or event, there can be no excuse for not introducing a compensating factor to help redress the balance between well and poorly documented phases, to make due allowance for the differences in nature of the relevant historical data, and to set the course of events in a constant and unbroken perspective. Hill's history has done none of these things. As the author himself admits, it does not pretend to be more than a compilation of facts. It offers no sketch or appreciation of Cypriote historiography, and makes no attempt to introduce an element of proportion into the text, to act as a counterweight to the overwhelming dependence on written sources of information.

The principal deficiency of Hill's *History* is to be found in the treatment of the Bronze Age, whose legacy is almost entirely archaeological as opposed to conceptual or literary. Its pottery is superabundant, its art and architecture imperfectly known, and its written records indecipherable. As a result, Hill, whose first three volumes cover the whole of the island's history up to the Turkish invasion in 1571, devotes only some seventy pages out of a total of nearly 1150 to this period, which lasted some 1500 years and represented the most inventive and original stage of Cypriote civilization. Even of these, no less than fifteen pages are taken up with the question of Alasia, twenty-five with the religion of early Cyprus, and over ten with Greek colonization.

Hill's preponderant reliance on documentary evidence to re-create the history of Bronze Age Cyprus has therefore led him to distort Cyprus's position in the affairs of the surrounding countries.

This is most graphically demonstrated by his section on the identification of Alasia where he writes "if neither Asy nor Alashiya is Cyprus, then this important island, which undoubtedly must have played a part in the history of the eastern Mediterranean in the second millenium, is unnamed in the documents, and that is hardly credible." This assertion betrays an essential misunderstanding of the part the island played in the interconnections of the period, as well as fallacious argumentation.

In the first place Hill does not justify his description of the island as "important," since he has not specified the kind of role which it is alleged to have played in the Bronze Age. He is therefore in no tenable position to be able categorically to say whether or not this "importance" would have been enough to earn it a respectable mention in the annals of neighbouring countries. The nature of Cyprus' overseas relations must, of course, be central to our assessment of the place it occupied in the estimates and records of the Bronze Age Levantines, for it seems to have seldom required less than a powerful combination of political, military and commercial forces to impinge on the consciousness of foreign cities or states.

In the case of Cyprus there is no archaeological evidence from inside or outside the island to suggest that its overseas relations were anything more than commercial, and it is even then by no means certain that the Cypriotes themselves were responsible for conducting their own trade, rather than Syrian or other intermediaries. Furthermore, it is illusory to think of Bronze Age Cyprus in terms of an integrated political or economic unit, for the dictates of topography, temperament and tradition ensured the persistence until the end of Late Cypriote II at least of a pronounced degree of cultural regionalism, of which the large coastal cities are the most striking embodiment.

But the most fundamental weakness of Hill's statement is the claim that if Cyprus is not one of the only two—and I stress two—of the dozens of ancient place names known, then reference to the island must be lacking. This is to ignore the fact that there are still numerous proper names which occur in Egyptian and Semitic records that have not yet been conclusively identified. Indeed, one such is Tanaja, which was provisionally equated with Cyprus by H. R. Hall in 1922. This word first occurs in the annals of the XVIIIth Dynasty

Pharaoh, Thutmose III, where, amongst the tribute listed for the year 42, is a silver jug of Keftiu work and four copper vases with silver handles, which were brought by the Chief of Tanaja. It is not certain from the inscripion whether the silver jug was actually made in the land of the Keftiu, which is customarily identified with Crete, or fashioned in their technique. There is another reference to Tanaja in a topographical list from the funerary temple of Amenhotep III at Thebes, coming after the name of Keftiu and associated with places round the Aegean Sea. Tanaja further occurs in a topographical list at Karnak belonging to the time of Horemheb. In this case it is preceded by the names of Tunip, Qadesh, Qatna, Ugarit, Pihilim (or Pella), and followed by a partly erased name which Simons tentatively equates with Amres, an unidentified locality in Syria, but which Vercoutter reconstructs as Cyprus, presumably reading it as Alasia. Vercoutter has also mistakenly placed Tanaja after Ugarit, instead of after Pihilim, which is an important town in Palestine.

Quite apart from the philological comparisons used by Hall to justify his argument that Tanaja is Cyprus, there is a certain amount of circumstantial evidence that even if it does not necessarily confirm, at least does not detract from this identification. In the first place, Mycenaean pottery had begun to reach Cyprus by the sixteenth century B.C., and though there is no proof that the Cypriotes manufactured metal vases in Bronze Age Greek style, such objects did find their way to Cyprus and could have been presented by a local ruler to Pharaoh. An example of these imports is a silver cup of Vapheio type from Enkomi British Tomb 92. Certainly Cypriote pottery was already reaching Egypt in considerable quantities at this time, though the means by which it was brought are still imperfectly known.

Secondly, the presence of the name associated with the name of Crete and in a list of important localities in Syria and Palestine suggests that Tanaja should be situated to the north, but cannot help us further tie down the location, because topographical lists such as these tend to lack historical authenticity. Nevertheless these facts do not exclude the possibility that Tanaja is to be connected with Cyprus. Edel has suggested that Tanaja could have been the island of Rhodes, but he ruled out Cyprus only because it was known to the ancients as Asy! We are therefore by no means obliged to allow

Cyprus to remain anonymous in Bronze Age literary records, even if it cannot be equated with Alasia or Asy.

Catling's contribution to historical writing on Cyprus, under the title "Cyprus in the Neolithic and Bronze Age Periods," is not only the most recent but also the most authoritative. What is more, his account has succeeded as history, despite its enforced dependence on purely archaeological data and its appearance in 1966 in the revised edition of the *Cambridge Ancient History*. Yet it too suffers from what I would propose to call the "invasion syndrome" and indeed epitomizes the same incongruous notion of history and culture that has pervaded nearly all works setting out to trace the sequence of events through which Cyprus passed in the Bronze Age.

Let me demonstrate the reasons for making these strictures. At several points of his narrative Catling conceptualises the spirit which he believes guided the island's cultural development. He is at his most revealing in the statement that "the *Leitmotiv* throughout the history of Cyprus is its dependence on foreign sources for the reinfusion of vitality; by the end of the Middle Bronze Age the island had been too long without outside interference." To illustrate this thesis, Catling says that "Seal usage was unknown in Cyprus before the L.C. Period, a revealing symptom of her undeveloped and isolated state." Dare I suggest, in the presence of such eminent scholars, that the ancient Cypriotes could still have been civilized during the Early and Middle Bronze Age periods without knowledge of the cylinder or stamp seal, and that far from being an indicator of backwardness, it is rather a sign that Cyprus had thus far escaped the snares of bureaucratic red tape? There can, of course, be no doubt that the use of the seal was introduced from abroad, but its advent cannot necessarily be assumed to have conferred instant cultural benefits on its unwitting recipients.

In fact, no sooner had foreign influence come to the rescue of the island's stagnating civilization than Catling has this extremely significant observation to make:

> In the five hundred years that the Late Bronze Age lasted in Cyprus the island finally entered into full association with her more developed neighbours. This brought not only a share of their greater cultural sophistication and material prosperity but also of the troubles which beset them and the disaters by which they were eventually overwhelmed. When the end of the period was reached, Cypriote material

culture had largely lost its special character, which for better or worse had distinguished it in the preceding phases of the Bronze Age, and had assumed a flavour almost entirely compounded of influences from stronger neighbours.

One's initial reaction to this statement is that Catling cannot have his archaeological cake and eat it. Historical writing demands a coherent philosophy, and there can be no place for value judgments about levels of cultural attainment when writers assume that civilization has a dynamism all of its own, eschewing human intervention, and can therefore make no intelligible contribution towards a better understanding of the social forces behind the development of Cypriote industry.

If the ancient Cypriotes were conscious of the feebleness of their own cultural motivation and of the consequent need for an influx of foreign influences to stimulate flagging inspiration, then would they have allowed their industry to be so completely overwhelmed by these external innovations that it lost all trace of its former originality? Or is Catling saying that the culture of the Cypriote people was so poverty-stricken that they succumbed without a struggle to the force or blandishments of the more aesthetically and technically advanced civilizations with which they came into contact? Whichever concept has guided Catling, its implications are belied by the material evidence, which reveals a constant and imaginative evolution of artistic styles throughout the Bronze and Iron Ages and a capacity to adopt and adapt but not be absorbed by the overseas manufactures imported. It seems to me, therefore, that Catling has approached his study of the Bronze Age from the wrong angle, and that instead of looking from the outside in, he should have done just the opposite.

Despite the accumulated knowledge of almost a hundred years of excavation, restoration and research, popular works continue to be written about Cypriote history that betray not only a culpable lack of acquaintance with the basic sources of information but also a failure to make allowance for the various standpoints from which secondary accounts have been written. The fault for this probably lies as much with the academic specialists as with the purveyors of *haute vulgarisation*, for the former have more often than not found it a near superhuman task to master their raw data and render it comprehensible for the interested but non-expert reader.

A recent and typical example of the ill-informed treatment to which Cypriote history is open is supplied by a book published in London in 1968 by H. D. Purcell and entitled simply *Cyprus*. The author correctly recognizes that the island has seldom been a goal, but rather a base or a stepping stone, that the frequent introduction of foreigners has never been of such a scale as fundamentally to alter the physique of the Bronze Age inhabitants, and that the idigenous Cypriote culture is remarkable for its survivals and continuity. But like others he has failed to follow on logically from these propositions and shows himself determined not only that Cyprus should not be or be seen in historical isolation during the Bronze Age but that the island should be subjected to a succession of foreign interventions commensurate with its crossroads status.

Drawing on the authorities I have previously quoted, as well as other, more specialized treatises, Purcell turns up an invasion under every stone, or should I say every potsherd. The first invasion is attributed to Sargon of Akkad, whose power, or at least influence, may, according to Purcell, have extended as far as Cyprus. The first stage of the Early Cypriote period is introduced at Vasilia and Philia *Drakos* by Anatolian settlers with their typical big-spouted pots of red polished ware, and Early Cypriote III coincides with the arrival of more Armenoid settlers from the mainland. In the seventeenth century, that is Middle Cypriote III, the Hittites are said to have established themselves at Nitovikla in the Karpass and been buried in tombs nearby. Purcell suggests that the Hyksos may also have raided Cyprus at the beginning of Late Cypriote I, but is uncertain whether in the time of the Egyptian Pharaoh Thutmose III, Cyprus was conquered or merely tributary. Purcell is not party to the belief that the Mycenaeans colonized Cyprus in the fifteenth or fourteenth centuries B.C. but accepts the hypothesis that Greeks from the mainland mounted a full-scale invasion of the island towards the end of the thirteenth century B.C.

I should now like briefly to examine the bases for each of these purported intrusions, with particular reference to the archaeological evidence. That Sargon of Akkad should still be credited with the feat of bringing his influence to bear on Cyprus at the end of the third millennium B.C. is a tribute to the tenacity of historical legend, if not to the process of factual verification. This claim had a respectable academic ancestry in the late nineteenth and early twentieth centuries A.D., but as long ago as 1910, Dussaud forcefully demolished the arguments which had been used by its proponents. The belief that Sargon intervened in the island's affairs can initially be traced to the translation and interpretation of place names in certain texts relating to the time of this king. The extension and refinement of our knowledge has, however, led to greater accuracy in the identification of ancient place names, and in none of the recent translations of documents relating to Sargon's reign or in authoritative historical works is there any suggestion that Sargon ever came into contact with Cyprus.

The beginnings of the Bronze Age in Cyprus present the historian, not to mention the archaeologist, with problems that cannot be further resolved until fresh evidence becomes available. In terms of nomenclature alone, there are two opening phases, Dikaios' "Initial State of Early Cypriote I," which Stewart refers to as the "Philia Culture," and Stewart's "Early Cypriote I," to which Dikaios has given no other description. Without going into unnecessary detail, the crux of the problem is the chronological priority to be accorded the so-called Philia Culture, which is a distinctive and largely homogenous assemblage of ceramic, metal and stone artifacts concentrated in the northwestern quarter of the island.

Stewart was inclined to view this culture as an inbred regional phenomenon, sharing the same ancestry as the material from Vounous, on which he based his Early Bronze Age sequence, but contemporaneous with Early Cypriote I and II as exemplified at this site. Dikaios, however, basing himself on the evident relationship between the diagnostic wares of Chalcolithic II and the Vounous Early Bronze Age culture, argued a chronologically intermediate position for the Philia Culture, so that it would provide one of the missing links between the Chalcolithic and Early Cypriote periods.

Despite the gaps that still exist in the archaeological record, it now seems that both Stewart and Dikaios are right, and that the so-called Philia Culture, which, for reasons of convenience, I have preferred to call Chalcolithic III, began after the expiry of Chalcolithic II, borrowing the ceramic styles in use before, but persisted into the Vounous Early Cypriote period, which apparently represents a more vigorous offshoot of the Philia Culture outside the area of its greatest concentration.

The most important aspect from our point of view is the innovative character of the material culture of Chalcolithic III, particularly its pottery. Though the wares show a certain technical continuity from the earlier phase, the repertory of shapes is enhanced by the addition of such distinctive types as the jug with flat base and long cut-away spout, the mosque-lamp amphora, and handleless bottles with tall expanding neck. There is near-unanimous agreement amongst leading authorities that the inspiration for these shapes, particularly the beak-spouted jug, came from western Anatolia, and that introduction of these new features could have been due to peoples arriving from Asia Minor.

Catling has gone so far as to claim that the Philia Culture resulted from the arrival from Anatolia of bands of refugees, who had escaped from the destroyers of the Early Bronze II culture in that region. They appear, according to him, to have mixed with and not to have destroyed the sparse Chalcolithic II population they encountered in the area of Morphou Bay, their first landfall, and subsequently in the Ongos and Serakhis Valleys, where they made their initial settlements. They would have been responsible for introducing metallurgical skills; new types of pottery and methods of decorating it, particularly incision; and different ways of treating the dead.

Stewart is more cautious in drawing conclusions from the pottery and other comparisons. While conceding that an intrusion from Anatolia, such as that which may have led to the end of Early Bronze II at Tarsus in Cilicia, could have had repercussions in Cyprus, he notes for argument's sake that the best ceramic parallels with Asia Minor come later in the Early Cypriote Period, but in any case considers that the development of Bronze Age civilization in the island, no matter what influences brought it about, was essentially a Cypriote affair.

The scattered and incomplete state of our knowledge makes it unwise at this stage to insist on a substantial movement of peoples from across the seas to account for the penetration of foreign cultural influences at the beginning of the Cypriote Bronze Age. There are numerous examples from the Early Cypriote period to demonstrate the Cypriote potter's unique skill in copying the forms and styles of imported artefacts, which in the context of the overwhelmingly indigenous character of the local civilization can have found their way to the island only by trade or as souvenirs.

On the other hand, though cultural regionalism is a determinative and recurrent feature of Cypriote civilization throughout the Bronze Age, no assemblage other than the Philia Culture can be traced within quite such precise territorial confines. This factor lends weight to the hypothesis that at least a certain element in the population was descended from settlers who entered from abroad and developed in association with the local inhabitants a strong degree of cultural identity and exclusivity, from which the Vounous peoples ultimately broke away. However, such speculation is no substitute for what are known in scientific jargon as "ground truths," and these only further excavation will provide.

The suggestion that Early Cypriote III saw the arrival of more so-called Armenoid settlers from Anatolia is, of course, a figment of Purcell's imagination. Not only is there an almost total lack of archaeological evidence from the Early Cypriote III period to attest the introduction or absorption of cultural influences from Asia Minor, let alone the arrival of settlers from this region, but at least along the north coast, which faces the mainland, the orientation of foreign relations lay demonstrably both to the west, particularly the Cyclades and Crete, and to the eastern Levant, but not to the north. Moreover there was no tangible break in the progressive evolution either of settlement pattern or material culture, which could be used to argue the irruption of some alien elements. The development of pottery styles in particular was continuous throughout the Early and Middle Cypriote periods.

We are mercifully spared the ravages of foreign invaders, colonists and visitors during the greater part of the Middle Cypriote period, but as if to compensate for their unaccustomed quiescence, they return with a vengeance, via the historian's pen, from the Middle Cypriote III phase onwards. The theories of Hittite installation and Hyksos incursions have recently received critical attention from Åström, Catling and myself, and at the risk of repeating what may already be very familiar to some of you, it will satisfy the requirements for completeness if I briefly summarise the main conclusions of my paper on the early history of Late Cypriote I, which appeared in *Levant* Vol. III.

The archaeological evidence reveals the development of two important factors in the civilization of the transitional Middle Cypriote/Late Cypriote periods. The first of these is a marked degree of cultural regionalism, and the other is the existence of a state of internal insecurity. The proportionate distribution of distinctive pottery styles shows that at the beginning of Late Cypriote I the island's culture had resolved itself into two major subdivisions, one characterized by the painted wares in the eastern half of the island, the other, by the monochrome wares in the northwestern quarter. While the painted pottery of the east persisted in much the same style until the end of Late Cypriote IA, the northwest invented and experimented with new wares such as Base-ring and Monochrome, which made few inroads into the culture prevailing in the rest of the island.

Secondly, a substantial number of fortifications were erected, whose geographical and topographical placement, as well as architecture, makes it clear they were intended to serve not as posts from which armed forces could sally to repel foreign invaders, but as protective establishments in which the local inhabitants could take refuge if their security were threatened. These phenomena gain extra significance from the fact that, to judge by the classification of Cypriote wares found abroad at this time, the eastern seaboard of Cyprus appears to have exercised something of a monopoly in the island's commercial relations with its neighbours.

I have suggested that because of the economic forces unleashed in the island's growth by the expansion of trade, and because of the development in the northwest of new ceramic forms and styles with their own commercial potential, internal friction was caused by the west's attempts to expand both internally and externally, leading to isolated outbreaks of hostility and the deaths of people inadvertently caught in the fighting. I have further argued that the dislocation of Levantine markets caused by the expulsion of the Hyksos from Egypt at the end of Late Cypriote IA may have undermined the east's stranglehold on overseas trade and indirectly abetted a cultural takeover by the west.

It is particularly noteworthy that the pottery culture of eastern sites underwent an abrupt change at the beginning of Late Cypriote IB, when the hallmarks of the Late Cypriote period, the Base-ring, White Slip, Monochrome and other typical wares, made their first substantial appearance, but already in a fully evolved style. There are then, as Åström has also recently noted, no grounds for contending that the Hyksos, not to speak of the Hittites, in any way directly intervened in the affairs of the island in the seventeenth or sixteenth centuries B.C.

Whether or not you accept that the Egyptian Pharaoh Thutmose III became involved in Cyprus's affairs depends first on your identification of Alasia, and secondly on your evaluation of the historical veracity of the XVIIIth Dynasty topographical lists drawn up in Pharaoh's name. As I do not consider that Alasia was Cyprus or any part of the island, or that most of the Egyptian topographical lists were much more than propagandist compilations, I do not subscribe to the claim that there was any Egyptian intervention in Cyprus during the reign of Thutmose III. In support of this position I would have quoted the *argumentum e silentio* that no substantial monuments bearing this Pharaoh's name or even deposits of Egyptian goods datable to his time have yet turned up in the island, but unfortunately the prerequisite of archaeological corroboration appears of less account than the gymnastics of comparative philology, and so I shall not press my point further. I have, nevertheless, set out my views in some detail in a paper published in the proceedings of the 1969 Congress on Cypriot Studies, and earlier in this paper I suggested a different ancient place-name for Cyprus.

Before leaving this controversial subject I should like to offer some comments on what seems to me an interesting development in the process of research into Late Bronze Age Cyprus. Karageorghis, whose masterful excavations at Kition have added a new dimension to our knowledge of the Late Cypriote period, has already hinted at the direction in which future consideration of the Alasia question is likely to head. He first takes the unorthodox position that the frequent references to Alasia in Hittite texts make the identification with Cyprus difficult, since there is no archaeological evidence for any relations between these two areas. According to him the strongest argument in favour remains the fact that Alasia exported copper to several Near Eastern countries. If, Karageorghis argues, we accept that Alasia must be located in Cyprus, we have very little evidence to offer in favour of Enkomi as the site for Alasia. Kition has also produced evidence of copper smelting and probably other cities not yet excavated may do so as well. In Karageorghis' view, Cyprus as a whole, therefore, and not any particular city on the island, may be considered as a candidate for identification with Alasia.

Despite the tact with which Karageorghis has broached this sensitive subject, he has overlooked the fact that, as far as the ancient texts are concerned, Alasia must have been a city, at most a city state, and cannot have occupied any substantial territory—certainly not an island the size of Cyprus. Yet if Karageorghis' ideas gain ground, may we expect claims from Åström that Hala Sultan Tekke, which was evidently a major Bronze Age emporium rivalling Enkomi, was more likely to be Alasia than Enkomi or Kition? Or will Professor Emily Vermeule, whose excavations at Toumba tou Skourou have begun to reveal the remains of a fairly important city, equate it with Alasia? The scope for scholarly dispute seems limitless.

The question of Mycenaean relations with Cyprus in the fourteenth and thirteenth centuries B.C. is at once the most controversial and interesting in Cypriote Bronze Age historiography, for around it have crystallised all the empirical and scientific issues that determine the course of historical reconstruction. The most important empirical issue at stake is the establishment and acceptance of a set of criteria which can be legitimately and validly used as a base on which to argue the presence of a foreign minority in an indigenous community. At one end of the scale we have Hill, who maintained that "the immense quantity of wares imported from the west which appears in Cyprus at this time, cannot have been without its accompanying settlers." At the other end, there is Catling, whose opinion is best quoted from the *Cambridge Ancient History:*

> The proposal to locate Aegean colonies in Cyprus during the fourteenth and thirteenth centuries B.C. has never surmounted the obstacle of missing evidence. Though Mycenaean pottery is present in such enormous amounts, practically every other characteristic of Mycenaean material culture is missing. An unmistakably Cypriot cultural atmosphere was dominant even at those sites where Aegean pottery has been found in greatest abundance.

Karageorghis and Dikaios also held differing opinions but are not as far apart as Hill and Catling. Karageorghis, while firmly of the belief that Mycenaean craftsmen established themselves in the major Late Cypriote coastal emporia and produced Mycenaean pottery in Cyprus indistinguishable from the Mycenaean pottery of Greece, finds no evidence for Aegean colonisation as such during the fourteenth and thirteenth centuries B.C.

Dikaios, on the other hand, arrived quite independently at conclusions not far removed from those reached by Catling. From an analysis of the Aegean pottery of this period found at Enkomi, he maintains that all the standard Mycenaean pottery was imported and that only that of inferior quality was made locally. He further observes that in Late Cypriote IIA and B, architecture, burial customs and artefacts all continued to follow Cypriote traditions, and that native Cypriote pottery represents the overwhelming majority of the wares discovered. In Late Cypriote IIC the cultural scene remains essentially the same, but certain mainland Greek architectural principles appear to have been embodied in structures belonging to this phase. This development was particularly evident in a building which contained large-scale copper workshops, reflecting, in Dikaios' view, a considerable intensification of the copper industry, probably due to the arrival of Mycenaean industrialists who may also have introduced the architectural ideas of their home country.

Finally the dogma of scientific infallibility has received a timely jolt from Karageorghis, who remains unrepentently sceptical about the implications of the clay analyses of the Mycenaean pottery found throughout the East Mediterranean region. In Catling's view the tests lead to the inevitable conclusion that the mass of Mycenaean pottery encountered outside Greece was exported from the Mycenaeans' homeland and not manufactured locally in Cyprus or elsewhere in the Levant. Karageorghis opposes this contention on methodological grounds, alleging deficiencies in the selection of sherds for analysis, which tend to invalidate the results claimed, and asserting that the problem of the pottery's origin cannot be settled by scientific testing alone without taking into account other unspecified factors.

Leaving aside the scientific diversion to this issue, and relying solely on an empirical approach to the available data, I am inclined more to Dikaios' than to the other positions outlined. I have already argued elsewhere that fine ceramics are not in themselves, no matter how great their quantity, sufficient to argue the presence of Mycenaean artisans or settlers in Cyprus, and in the absence of other complementary evidence, such as may be readily detected in the Late Cypriote III period, it must be assumed that they came only as articles of trade. On the other hand, I am well aware of the particular problems posed by the Mycenaean vases from Cyprus, whose forms were copied from the native Cypriote repertory, such as bowls with wishbone handles of Base-ring and White Slip types. Were they perhaps made to order by itinerant mainland potters who paid short visits to the island? There are numerous ways of interpreting these finds and any attempt at a cut-and-dried answer is doomed to a controversial reception.

It is only when we come to the end of the Late Cypriote II period that the evidence for the foreign invasion and settlement become incontestable. Even then it would be rash to overestimate either the degree of organization behind the arrival of these intruders or the geographical extent of their penetration. The stratigraphical and material data attesting the forcible arrival of people from overseas and their occupation of long established sites are for the most part limited to settlements on or within easy reach of the east and southeast coasts. The cities of Enkomi, Sinda and Kition appear all to have been overwhelmed in the last quarter of the thirteenth century B.C. by bands of marauders from the Aegean area. It is presumed that they were forced from their homelands by the disasters which overtook the Greek mainland, and that they descended upon the eastern part of the island as part of a wave of displaced persons, who also joined forces with the Libyans in an attack upon Egypt at the time of Merneptah. Dikaios, basing his theories on the evidence from Enkomi, considers that these invaders consisted mainly of Greek mainland stock, but included others who were presumably drawn from various parts of the Aegean or the Mediterranean generally and who incorporated their own cultural traditions into the architecture and industry of the period. Their habitation, which was characterized by fine ashlar masonry and an overwhelming predominance of Mycenaean III C:1 pottery, was in its turn interrupted by another series of hostile incursions, usually associated with the so-called Sea

Peoples, whom Rameses III repulsed from Egypt's shores about 1190
B.C.

Yet Cyprus was by no means uniformly affected by these
upheavals. In a masterly review in the 1942 volume of the *American
Journal of Archaeology*, J. F. Daniel noted Sjöqvist's belief in
Problems of the Late Cypriote Bronze Age that Cyprus was swept into
the whirlpool of the great migrations at this time but observed with
singular perspicacity that this was probably true of the eastern part of
the island, though not of Cyprus as a whole. He continues:

> Far from marking the arrival of Greek princelings, the L.C. IIIA
> invasion did much to break the continuity of the Mycenaean cultural
> tradition in eastern Cyprus. At Kourion, which was not touched by the
> invasion, the Mycenaean tradition managed to survive the L.C. IIIA
> period, and the arrival of the new Achaean colonists in the L.C. IIIB
> period did not occasion another political break.

If I were to draw any general conclusions from the preceding
analysis, it would be that Cypriote historiography, particularly of the
Bronze Age, has been afflicted by and suffered from an invasion
syndrome. This complex has been primarily induced by the reliance
of historical writers on literary sources, which in the instance of
Cyprus chronicle invasions more frequently than any other major
event or development. It has become true by osmosis for the Bronze
Age, even though we still have no way of knowing what the
Cypro-Minoan inscriptions from the island or Ras Shamra narrate and
cannot be certain which records from the mainland are relevant to the
history of Cyprus.

The syndrome has been further abetted by the island's geographical setting, which invariably conjures up the image of a meeting
place or crossroads for diverse movements of peoples and goods,
whose significance transcends that of the indigenous inhabitants and
their material culture. This has in turn compounded the impression
created by the nature of the archaeological record and led to the
belief that native Cypriote civilization is less an intrinsically separate
entity with a personality of its own than a pale reflection of the more
sophisticated cultures around it.

The wheel is thus brought full circle, for the alleged backwardness of Cypriote achievements has reinforced and encouraged the
tendency to look at the island's culture, particularly during the

Bronze Age, through Greek, Anatolian, Syrian, Palestinian or Egyptian eyes, and concentrate on and, if necessary, invent extraneous influences and forces to bring Cyprus into the mainstream of civilized progress.

The result has been a serious distortion of the history of the Cypriote people as such, for while the reality of certain foreign interventions is undeniable, due recognition and weight must be given their political, social and cultural complexity before the history of Cyprus, at least during the Bronze Age, can be seen in its proper perspective. Appropriate allowance must particularly be made for what we know of the cultural regionalism which typified the civilization of this period, and for the limitations imposed on economic exploitation and internal commerce by the island's topography, which hampered communications and fostered isolationism amongst inland communities. Until modern times, for example, it was not unknown for country folk seldom if ever to have left their villages during the whole of their lifetimes.

Other factors which must be borne in mind concern the nature of trade relations and the periodic migrations of peoples around the Levant. There are no grounds for assuming that commercial ventures were run by large shipping companies rather than by individual operators with very mixed crews and cargoes, plying safe and well-tried routes, or that invasions were the centrally organized and highly disciplined deployment of armed forces having specific political or territorial objectives, rather than the peregrinations of marauding bands displaced from their homelands by some other invasions or disaster.

If all the material evidence for external cultural influence in Cyprus and the stratigraphical data bearing witness to a marked and significant break in occupational continuity is seen against this essential historical background, it becomes obvious that we cannot talk in terms of an invasion or colonization of the island as a whole, without taking care to specify at the outset the geographical extent of the indications for the alleged foreign presence and the precise character and presumed cause of this alien penetration.

The blurb on the dust jacket of Hill's *History* has this to say of the work to which it extends superfluous protection:

"He who would become and remain a great power in the east must hold Cyprus in his hand." Sir George Hill quotes this saying on the first page of this book. The strategic importance of Cyprus is the very reason why it has had no continuous history of its own; its history is chiefly a reflection from the activities of great powers who have found Cyprus necessary to the achievement of important objectives elsewhere; so that the story of Cyprus resolves itself, in some degree, into the story of the comings and goings of its colonists and conquerors.

Until historians free themselves from the shackles of an approach tied to ideological, political or cultural frameworks and prejudices, the history of the Cypriote people will not receive its just desserts, the privilege of reconstitution on its own merits. Let us hope that a Cypriote scholar will be amongst the first to recount the history of the island in a way which will restore to the inhabitants, past and present, a proper sense of pride of the accomplishments of the indigenous civilization.

New Light from Lapithos

Ellen Herscher

The modern village of Lapithos lies on the lower slopes of the Kyrenia range, overlooking the rich north coast of Cyprus.[2] The abundant water of the area has helped make it the site of prosperous settlements since prehistoric times.[3] At the locality known as *Vrysi tou Barba* (Spring of the Old Man), habitation from the Early through the Middle Cypriote Bronze Age is attested by a large and long-known cemetery.[4] Early excavations, by John L. Myres and Leonard Buxton in 1913 and Menelaos Markides in 1917, were followed by the extensive Swedish investigations of 1927.[5] In 1931, additional tombs were opened by a team from the University Museum of the University of Pennsylvania, under the general direction of Bert Hodge Hill.[6] The staff consisted of Lucy Talcott, Virginia Grace, and the architect, Dorothy H. Cox. Tomb 806A[7] contained an imported Minoan jar, and a report on this find was published by Miss Grace.[8] This paper is a survey of the important material from the other thirty-seven tombs. Hopefully, complete publication will be forthcoming in the near future.

The cemetery is located on low, flat, rocky land, close to the sea—unusual topography for Cypriote burials of this period.[9] The tombs are close together, a chamber sometimes cutting into that of an earlier one.[10] As at Vounous, most are oriented north-south, the door of the main chamber facing north. The tomb architecture is that familiar from the Swedish excavations—a bathtub-shaped shaft

39

or "dromos" sunk vertically into the rock, from which open one to four burial chambers. Several chambers are divided into two sections by a rock-cut pier at the back,[11] and raised burial niches within the chamber are quite common.[12] Many of the dromoi also have miniature burial chambers cut into their walls; the latest tomb of the group had eighteen such "cupboards," sealed in the same manner as the large chambers and containing miniature pots, tiny rings, and other gifts suitable for infants.[13]

Three separate areas were dug, separated by about 500 meters. In general, the earliest tombs are in the area farthest west, the latest ones to the east, although no rigid ordering can be detected. The western area (Plan I) is remarkable for the extensive cuttings on the surface, which could antedate the earliest chamber tombs. These cuttings are, for the most part, shallow rectangles about a meter by one-half meter in size, laid out in a fairly regular grid. No clues to their purpose can be found in the field notes; one possible explanation is that they result from later agriculture on the site.

The Pennsylvania tombs range in date from Early Cypriote II to the end of Middle Cypriote III. The early tombs contained simple Red Polished pottery, most of it undecorated. Large jugs are the prevalent shape, followed by Red Polished II lug bowls. Early decorated pieces include a Red Polished I tulip bowl (Fig. 1)—a shape rare at Lapithos—and a Red Polished II blacktopped jar (Fig. 2).[14] Bronzes do not make a significant appearance until E.C. IIIB.

The latest tomb, number 804, is the farthest from the sea. Most of the pottery in it is Black Slip (Fig. 3) and White Painted, with White Painted V ware well represented (cf. Fig. 4.) The tankard shape, which becomes popular at the end of M.C. III, also appears in the late Red Polished ware in the tomb.[15] The seventy-four bronzes from Tomb 804 represent a quarter of all bronzes found during the season.

Although the Vrysi tou Barba cemetery went out of use with the beginning of Late Cypriote, the pottery demonstrates clear connections with the later wares from other sites and provides evidence suggesting continuous development of the Cypriote pottery sequence.[16] For example, the teapot shape, common in late Red Polished ware, changes in White Painted IV ware to approach the shape of some Proto-White Slip bowls (Fig. 5).[17] Proto-White

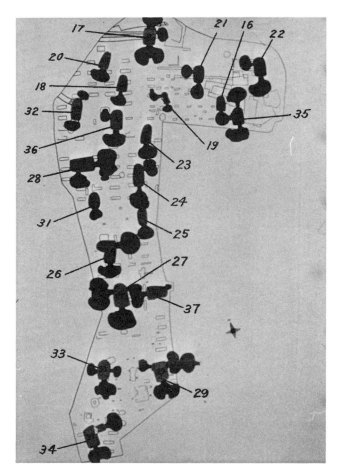

Plan I

Plan: the western area, Tombs 816-838.
Objects

1) 811A.15 (UM 69-35-252)
2) 823.7 (UM 69-35-529)
3) 804A.44 (UM 32-27-95)
4) 804A.24 (UM 32-27-87)
5) 804A.27 (UM 32-27-81)
6) 802A.13 (UM 32-27-20)
7) 803A.6 (UM 32-27-49)
8) 802A.5 (UM 32-27-16)
9) 829A.14 (UM 32-27-534)
10) 804A.80 (UM 32-27-97)
11) 813B.5 (UM 32-27-473)

12) 829C.3 (UM 32-27-542)
13) 802A.29 (Cyprus Museum)
14) 813.43 (UM 32-27-460)
15) 803A.5 (UM 69-35-69)
16) 803B.4 (UM 32-27-59)
17) 803A.18 (UM 69-35-74)
18) 829C.25 (Cyprus Museum)
19) 804A.54 (UM 32-27-79)
20) 802A.3 (UM 32-27-19)
21) 804A.5 (UM 32-27-88)
22) 813A.40 (UM 32-27-457)

Figure 1

Figure 2

Figure 3   Figure 4   Figure 5

Figure 6

Slip decorative syntax is also foreshadowed in a late White Painted
deep bowl (Fig. 6), where the horizontal bands are divided by
verticals at the front and under the handle.[18] The characteristic
White Slip ware arrangement of bands appears as incision on a Red
Slip jar (Fig. 7). A unique Black Polished miniature bottle (Fig. 8) is
decorated like Black Slip III juglets from Stephania.[19] Wishbone
handles occur on Red Slip and Black Slip bowls from Tomb 4.[20]

The potters' marks from Lapithos have been discussed
previously by Miss Grace and Paul Åström, and the new examples
simply lend quantitative weight to their observations.[21] All occur on
Red Polished II black-topped lug bowls and date to late E.C. III and
M.C. I. Except for the U-shaped mark from Tomb 806A, all are
horizontal or vertical grooves used singly or in twos or threes. One
exceptional example (13A.2) has the mark incised *after* firing, to the
left rather than the right of the lug. The same type of bowl with the
lug *punctured* at the top or bottom is frequent (Fig. 9), and this
should probably also be considered a type of potters' mark. The
exact meaning of these marks remains inscrutable, but it is
noteworthy that Tomb 806A, the largest and richest tomb of late
E.C. III date, contained more examples than all the other tombs
combined. In contrast, Tomb 829C, a rich burial of *early* E.C. III,
had only one such mark. Many of the Lapithos signs are represented
at Vounous also, but there exist major differences, such as the lack
of the "X" at Vrysi tou Barba.[22] These differences, combined with
the extreme homogeneity of the Lapithos marks in comparison to
those from other sites, suggest that the system used had only local
significance.

A study of the White Painted ware has proven somewhat more
illuminating for the activities of the pot-makers. By M.C. I, there
seem to be some specialists in the craft, who are distinguishable by
their style of painting.[23] At least seven different individuals can be
identified, who produced material for both the Swedish and
Pennsylvania tombs. It appears that the makers of Red Polished
ware remained separate, but other workshops were making both
White Painted and Black Slip wares.

The Pennsylvania excavation has provided some new evidence
for the religious practices of the settlement, although Lapithos still
has produced nothing to compare with the fantastic creations from

Figure 7

Figure 8

Figure 9

Figure 10

Figure 11

Vounous. The one Red Polished plank idol found was in fragmentary condition, and the only other figurine is a late Red Polished bull (Fig. 10). He is hollow, with a hole at his rear, and is designed to stand on his face in order to be filled. Many vessels bear designs which Stewart and others have suggested may have religous meaning. Such interpretations are impossible to prove, but perhaps the most likely candidate from our material is a small Red Polished amphora with a disk and crescent on either side[24] (Fig. 11. Their positions are reversed on the opposite side). A similar amphora is known from Kalopsidha, also dating to the end of E.C. III.[25] The crescent motif also appears on large Red Polished jugs from Lapithos; its use as a religious symbol is clearly attested at later periods in Cyprus and may be continuous.[26]

A Red Polished bird (802A.3 : UM 32-27-19) is probably broken from a large milkbowl of the Vounous type,[27] but most ritual vessels are large, round-bottomed jugs (e.g., Fig. 12). Small plank figurines protruding from the sides of gourd juglets are fairly well-known,[28] but here it has totally emerged to stand on the handle. A more elaborate vase from the same tomb (829C)[29] presents a scene of a man and woman worshipping while libations are being poured into small basins. Behind them is the familiar bird of Cypriote religion.

The elements of man, bird, and bull are combined on a late double-necked jug (Fig. 13). The style of the bull on the front is close to those in the Vounous model cult scene,[30] and a bird drinking between two jug necks also occurs at Vounous.[31] (This Vounous jug also includes human beings and a bull, represented in relief on the opposite side.) However, the figures on the Lapithos jug are atrophied and stylized, barely recognizable as representational.

Beginning in late E.C. III, the so-called "cooking pots" begin to appear.[32] None of them show evidence of burning, however, and the recently discovered bull shrine models seem to suggest that they in fact had a ritual purpose.[33] The shape of the vessel represented in the models is distinctive, and such usage would account for the jars in fine fabric[34] and those with elaborate decoration, such as relief and incision (Fig. 14),[35] ornate handles (810 A.2 : UM 32-27-442) and the painted jars known from other sites.[36]

Changes in the types of vessels placed in burials may indicate

Figure 12

Figure 13

Figure 14

Figure 16

Figure 15

changes in religious practices. The large ritualistic jugs, suitable for pouring libations, are found only in the tombs dating until early E.C. III. At this point the cooking pots appear and continue in vogue through M.C. I. Meanwhile small hemispherical bowls are increasing, until they are the main tomb offerings of M.C. III. Remains of food were found in a bowl in Tomb 806A,[37] and perhaps a gradual change in ritual has taken place, from elaborate libations to funeral meals.

Considering the size and rich contents of the Vrysi tou Barba cemetery, it is remarkable that no settlement associated with it has been found.[38] But in any case, it is clear that the population was shifting southward, up the slopes of the mountains, at the end of the Middle Cypriote period. The latest tomb excavated by Pennsylvania (Tomb 804) is the farthest south, while the major *Late* Cypriote cemetery in the area is located up under the modern village.[39]

The same kind of shifts are reflected in Lapithos' relations with its neighbors. The earlier pottery demonstrates close connections with Vounous down the coast, but by Middle Cypriote the contacts are inland, over the mountains, so that a true Lapithos-Dhenia sphere can be observed. The incised decoration of the Red Polished ware is extremely regular, with concentric circles the predominating motif.[40] The Red Polished II jug with long curving cutaway neck is a distinctive shape, usually elaborately decorated (Fig. 15).[41] Miniature Black Polished ware is best represented at Dhenia, with Lapithos yielding related examples (see Fig. 8).[42] The common White Painted II and III jug at both sites is decorated with alternating panels of cross-hatching and vertical wavy lines (Fig. 16),[43] maintaining the same basic scheme even in more complicated variations. In the later White Painted wares, the Stringhole Style and the tubular-spouted juglet are characteristic.[44] Although the Middle Cypriote settlement at Dhenia has not been located either, its proximity to the Morphou Bay river system and the passes north around the Kyrenia Range, must account for its close communications with Vrysi tou Barba.[45]

Connections with other areas of Cyprus are not so evident in the Pennsylvania tombs. Very few pieces have parallels at Vasilia,[46] and there are no examples of the Karpas-style Red-on-Black ware. Perhaps from the region around Ajios Jakovos come two pieces with peg bases—a Red Slip jug (812A.32 : UM 32-27-453) and a Black Slip amphora (Fig. 17).[47] The amphora has two depressed circles on each side, a potters' mark common on Black Slip II ware in Middle

Definite relations with the Aegean are attested by the imported Middle Minoan I jar from Tomb 806A and the Cretan type daggers and razors known previously from the site.[49] Miss Grace has pointed out parallels from Pyrgos for a bowl from Tomb 806B.[50] A Red Polished III duck askos (Fig. 18), dated to E.C. IIIA, is a rare shape, believed to be ultimately of Aegean origin.[51] Cypriote distribution of the shape is limited to Lapithos and perhaps Dhenia. Aegean connections have also been suggested for a certain type of deep bowl with high vertical handle (Fig. 19);[52] the shape appears in Middle Helladic matt-painted ware and minyan ware. There is some similarity between the painted decoration also, but this is more common in White Painted III and IV ware, so that Middle Helladic matt-painted would seem *not* to be a factor in the formation of the Middle Cypriote White-Painted sequence.

Stewart believed these high-handled bowls came originally from Anatolia,[53] and some examples with less pronounced rims approach this prototype (e.g., 804G.10: UM 32-27-182). However, a more definitely Anatolian type is the torpedo-shaped askos (Fig. 20), which appears in late E.C. III.[54] On the other hand, examples from Troy and Yortan usually have three feet rather than a column base.

Black-topped bowls are sometimes considered to be an Egyptian invention, and indeed one bowl (803A.10 : UM 69-35-72) from the Pennsylvania excavation approaches Nubian C-Group bowls very closely. But the best Cypriote bowls are of a fine, hard fabric not found in Egypt, and their mottled surfaces are more like the intentional decorative effects of Cretan Vasiliki ware. Yet arguing against any strict reliance on models or prototypes are several bowls with only their lower interior blackened.

Middle Cypriote trade with Syria-Palestine is abundantly indicated by the presence in the East of White Painted ware, especially juglets in the Pendent Line Style.[55] One trefoil lip juglet from Pennsylvania Tomb 804 (Fig. 21), which can be called Pendent Line Style although it lacks the usual wavy lines, seems to have been influenced by the painted ware more common in the Near East, which is sometimes decorated with groups of vertical straight

Figure 17

Figure 18

Figure 19

Figure 20

lines.[56] This juglet is not an import, however, because its fabric and characteristic base decoration are typical of the local ware. Eastern motifs are also copied on a black-topped bowl (Fig. 22), where the potter has imitated the effect of the strips of bone inlay with incised concentric circles which are common in Palestine at this time.[57]

Finally, we turn to the earliest Syrian import known in Cyprus, the enigmatic jug from Vounous.[58] Although the Pennsylvania excavation provides no new evidence for the *source* of this jar, it does indicate that the type was known more widely in Cyprus.[59] The unusual amphora (806A.36) actually copies the shape and size of the Vounous jar, substituting the round-pointed base so dear to the Early Cypriote heart. This adaptation of the foreign along indigenous native lines is one of the most enduring characteristics of Cypriote culture.

This survey of the material in Philadelphia may help dispel some of the "dark clouds" concerning it, until the full publication is available. The very great amount of material from Lapithos now available for study should hopefully lead to an understanding of the area to an extent not possible at any other site.

NOTES

1. It is a pleasure to join Brock University in honoring Dr. Vassos Karageorghis, who first introduced me to the earth of Cyprus. I wish to thank Dr. Rodney S. Young, Curator of the Mediterranean Section of the University Museum, and to Dr. Kyriakos Nicolaou, Curator of the Cyprus Museum, for the opportunity and permission to study this material.

2. *The Swedish Cyprus Expedition*, Finds and Results of the excavations in Cyprus 1927–1931 (hereafter *SCE*) vol. I (Stockholm, 1934), Fig. 20.

3. John L. Myres, "Excavations in Cyprus, 1913," *BSA* 41 (1940–45): H. W. Catling, "Patterns of Settlement in Bronze Age Cyprus," *Op. Ath.* 4 (1962): 133.

4. M. Ohnefalsch-Richter, *Kypros, die Bibel und Homer* (Berlin, 1893), p. 380, Pl. XXXVI: J. L. Myres and M. Ohnefalsch-Richter, *A Catalogue of the Cyprus Museum* (Oxford, 1899), pp. 7–8.

5. Myres, "Excavations in Cyprus," pp. 78–85: E. Gjerstad, *Studies on Prehistoric Cyprus* (Uppsala, 1962), pp. 73-81 (hereafter *SPC*); *SCE* I, pp. 33 ff. Recent salvage excavations at the site: V. Karageorghis, *BCH* 93 (1969): 469–71; K. Nicolaou, *AJA* (1970):76, Pl. 22, Fig. 23.

6. Preliminary report: University Museum *Bulletin* 3 (March 1932) no. 5, pp. 118–21, Pl. VI.

Figure 21

Figure 22

7. In order to simplify terminology and avoid confusion with other excavations at Lapithos, it has been decided to number the Pennsylvania tombs in sequence, beginning with number 801 (i.e., 801 through 838). Therefore, Lap. 806A is the new designation for what has usually been referred to as "Lapithos (Pennsylvania) 6A."

8. V. Grace, "A Cypriote Tomb and Minoan Evidence for its Date," *AJA* 44 (1940): 10–52.

9. *SCE* I, Plan III.1; *SPC*, pp. 49–50.

10. E.g., 824B cuts into the dromos of 823, 825 into 826A, 829C into 838, 837 into the dromos of 827; 835B and 816 are intentionally identical; cf. *SCE* I, Plan V.1.

11. E.g., 812A, 813, 817A and B, 827B, 829A, 834A; cf. *SCE* I, Fig. 43.1 (313A); Fig. 50 (318); Tomb 33 had two such piers, one of them carved with a simple decoration.

12. E.g., 802B, 804A, 805, 806A–C, 809C and D, 810C, 828B, 835A and C; cf. *SCE* I, Fig. 24.4–7 (302); Fig. 34 (309); Tomb 804B had a *lowered* burial niche ("cist").

13. Tomb 804F contained bits of a child's forehead bone, indicating that these small chambers were in fact infant burials.

14. There are several of these jars from the tombs, all almost exactly alike. A similar one was found by Professor Weinberg at Phaneromeni. The shape in general has a long history and is often found with a lid. Cf. James R. Stewart, "The Early Cypriote Bronze Age," *SCE* IV:1A (Lund, 1962) Fig. CXXVIII.2, 3; J. R. Stewart, *Corpus of Early Cypriote Material* (in preparation as SIMA III; I have used the partially revised manuscript in Göteborg, Sweden. Hereafter SIMA III). Type IXB; P. Åström, *The Middle Cypriote Bronze Age* (Lund, 1957) (hereafter *MCBA*), Fig. XVI.7,8.

15. Cf. the many tankards in L.702, the latest tomb excavated by the Swedes, dated to the last half of M.C. III. Discussed in *MCBA*, 192.

16. For a general discussion of the continuity of the ceramics and the gradual appearance of new types, see Catling, "Bronze Age Cyprus," pp. 136–7; Åström and G. R. H. Wright, "Two Bronze Age Tombs at Dhenia in Cyprus," *Op. Ath.* 4 (1962): 275.

17. See. the discussion by M.R. Popham, "The Proto-White Slip Pottery of Cyprus," *Op. Ath.* 4 (1962): 277–97, esp. pp. 278–9.

18. Ibid., pp. 282–5, Fig. 1.8; Fig. 3.

19. J. B. Hennessy, *Stephania, A Middle and Late Bronze Cemetery in Cyprus*, (London: 1964). Particularly Stephania 3.1 (Pl. XXIV); 7.11 (Pl. XXXVIII); 14A.51 (Pl. LXI).

20. 804F.8 (UM 32-27-180) and 804F.9 (UM 32-27-181); cf. *MCBA*, pp. 192, 216.

21. GRACE, "Cypriote Tomb," pp. 40–43; P. Åström, *Excavations at Kalopsidha and Ayios Iakovos in Cyprus*, SIMA II (Lund, 1966), pp. 150 and passim, 189–90.

22. Cf. the corpus in Åström, ibid, pp. 149–92.

23. Åström has noted this: *MCBA*, p. 274; Stewart believed there was specialization

in Early Cypriote: see *SCE* IV:1A, p. 291; *contra* (household manufacture continuing into Middle Cypriote); Åström, SIMA II, p. 189 ff; I am dealing with this subject more fully in a forthcoming article.

24. Worship of the sun and crescent moon: cf. *SCE* IV:1A, p. 293.

25. Åström, SIMA II, p. 10; Fig. 5 (CM inv. 1940/V-27/1).

26. E.g., Salamis (Cellarka) Tomb 84: V. Karageorghis, *Excavations in the Ne-cropolis of Salamis* II (Nicosia, 1970), p. 126; Fig. LXXI; Pl. CLXI.

27. P. Dikaios, *The Excavations at Vounous-Bellapais in Cyprus, 1931–2, (Ar-chaeologia* vol. 88; Oxford, 1940), Pl. X b,c.

28. Cf. *SCE* IV:1A, Fig. XCIV.3, 4; Fig. XCV.10; C. Schaeffer, *Missions en Chypre, 1932–1935* (Paris, 1936), *p. 36, Pl. XIV.*

29. Grace, "Cypriote Tomb," Fig. 27.

30. Dikaios, *Vounous-Bellapais*, Pl. VII–VIII; other free-standing bulls on jug bodies: Karageorghis, *BCH* 95 (1971):364, Fig. 65, 66; the second example also has disks and crescents in relief.

31. Dikaios, *Vounous-Bellapais*, Pls. XIX.d and XX. (Vo. 19.10); another double-neck jug, with a bird and a bull between the necks and a cup on the shoulder: Karageorghis, *BCH* 94 (1970):194, Fig. 3 (CM inv. 1969/V-7/5).

32. *SCE* IV: 1A, Fig. CXXII. 1-16; SIMA III, Types VIIIB and C.

33. Karageorghis, "Two Religious Documents of the Early Cypriote Bronze Age," *RDAC*, 1970, Pl. I; idem, *BCH* 95 (1971):344, Fig. 16.

34. Åström, SIMA II, p. 36; Fig. 8, row 1:1,2 (from Kalopsidha Tomb 36?: Famagusta Mus. inv. M. A. 23a); also a miniature example: L.319B.26.

35. *SCE* IV:1A, Fig. CXIX.

36. Vo 54; Schaeffer, *Missions*, Pl. XII.1; CM inv. 1967/X–27/4: *BCH* 92 (1968):267, 269; Fig. 14.a-b.

37. Grace, "Cypriote Tomb," p. 22.

38. Possibilities, see Catling, "Bronze Age Cyprus," pp. 151, 158. (Teratsouthkia, Mandra tis Zos, Asproyi).

39. Ibid., pp. 142, 165; *SCE* IV; 1A, pp. 298–9; population shifts in the east: Åström, SIMA II, pp. 139–40.

40. See Åström and Wright, "Tombs at Dhenia," Pl. VII.

41. Cf. ibid., p. 263, Fig. 10 (Dh. 6.88); Pl. I.7 (Dh.G.W. 1); *SCE* IV:1A, Fig. LXVI.2–4 (DH. 1.91).

42. Also 813B.9 (UM 32–27–470); cf. *SCE* IV:1A, Fig. CLII.1–7; CLIII.1–7.

43. Dhenia: Åström and Wright, "Tombs at Dhenia," Pl. I.16; Pl. II; Fig. 7; *Handbook to the Nicholson Museum²*, (Sydney: 1948), p. 142, Fig. 28; P. Åström, "Cypriote Pottery in the Allen Memorial Art Museum,"*Allen Memorial Art Museum*

Bulletin 17 (1960), Fig. 8 (#35.37).

44. Cf. Åström and Wright, "Tombs at Dhenia," Pl. I.13, 14; III. 8; IV.1,2.

45. Cf. Catling, "Bronze Age Cyprus" p. 139.

46. J.F. Stewart, "Notes on Cyprus," *Op. Ath.* 6 (1965): 157–60, esp. p. 159.

47. Red Slip II jug (812A.32: UM 32–27–453): cf. A.J. 6.2, 6.12, 6.13 (*SCE* I, Pl. LXI);
    Black Slip II amphora (803A.18: UM 69–35–74-: cf. A.J. 6.3, 6.5, 6.16 (*SCE* I, Pl. LXI); 7.12, 7.16 (Pl. LX.4); 12.27 (Pl. LXIII.4).

48. Åström, SIMA II, pp. 168–70.

49. Grace, "Cypriote Tomb," pp. 24–27. H.W. Catling and V. Karageorghis, "Minoika in Cyprus," *BSA* 55 (1960).

50. Grace, "Cypriote Tomb," p. 15 and n.1-Fig. 9.

51. *SCE* IV: 1A, p. 277; SIMA III, pp. 301-7, Type III Ba; *MCBA*, pp. 207-8; cf. S. Marinatos, *Excavations at Thera* III (Athens, 1970), Fig. 37.

52. *MCBA*, p. 207.

53. "Cappadocian": *SCE* IV:1A, p. 277; *Corpus*, pp. 950–4, Type M3a.

54. *SCE* IV: 1A, p. 278; SIMA III, pp. 328-30; Type III E^{1}a.

55. Åström, SIMA II, pp. 139–40; *MCBA*, pp. 209–25, esp. pp. 212–15; M. Popham, "Two Cypriot Sherds from Crete," *BSA* 58 (1963): 89–91, including note by Åström; Y. Yadin, et al., *Hazor* III/IV (Jerusalem, 1961), Plates CCLXXXVII.3; CCXC.8; CCCXII.5.

56. E.g., A. Scharff, *Das vorgeschichtliche Gräberfeld von Abusir el-Meleq* (Leipzig, 1926), Taf. 76.4, 5; G. Loud, *Megiddo* II (Chicago, 1948), Pl. 34.13; 41.32; 42.1; 51.5; C. Schaeffer, *Ugaritica* II (Paris, 1949), p. 247, Fig. 104.5; 249, Fig. 105.37; p. 259, Fig. 110.28; *Hazor* III/IV, Pl. CCCXII.1.

57. E.g., W.F. Petrie, *Ancient Gaza* I (London:1931) Pl. XXIII.17; P.L.O. Guy, *Megiddo Tombs* (Chicago, 1938), p. 186, n. 246; Pl. 108, 111; *Megiddo* II, Pl. 194.13, 14; *Hazor* I (1958), p. 152; Pl. CLXVI.8; CXLII.18; *Hazor* II (1959) p. 92; *Hazor* III/IV, Pl. CCLX.32; the form in Palestine lasts from the eighteenth through the fifteenth centuries B.C., and has a wide geographic distribution: J.R. Stewart, *Tell el'Ajjul* (Sydney, 1949) (privately circulated), p. 11; H. Schliemann, *Ilios: The City and Country of the Trojans* (London, 1880), pp. 425, 427, 566; C. Blegan, *Troy and the Trojans* (London, 1963), p. 94; Pl. 30; *AJA* 36 (1932), p. 111; Fig. 14 (a Middle Helladic grave at Eleusis); later occurrances in Cyprus: Schaeffer, *Missions*, p. 81; Fig. 41.5 (Enkomi 6); Hennessey, *Stephania*, Pl. LIX.34; VIII.c,d (Steph. 14A.32, 34).

58. E. and J. Stewart, *Vounous 1937—38* (Lund, 1950) Pl. XCIV.a; *SCE* IV:1A, p. 276; Fig. CLVI. 9; SIMA III, pp. 1442-3; Most recent discussion: R. Amiran, "The Much-Discussed Vounous Foreign Vessel Again," *RDAC* 1971: 1–6, with biblio.

59. Grace, "Cypriote Tomb," Pl. VIII.36.

Excavations at Phlamoudhi and the Form of the Sanctuary in Bronze Age Cyprus

Sarantis Symeonoglou

Last spring, when I was invited to present this paper, I had intended to assemble all available evidence on the form of the sanctuary in the Late Bronze Age to see whether some solution might be found to the problem we are faced with in our excavations at Vounari, near Phlamoudhi.[1] At that time, there was, to my knowledge, only one recent study on the subject—a short article published by Olivier Masson.[2] However, since then Vassos Karageorghis has written on two clay models of shrines,[3] and Paul Åström is summarizing the architectural remains of sanctuaries in his comprehensive study of the Late Bronze Age.[4]

The evidence collected and discussed by these scholars represents all one can know at this point about the sanctuaries of Late Bronze Age Cyprus, and this "all one can know" is not very much with regard to architecture, as the remains are scanty. This is the reason why Vounari presents the problems it does—at Vounari we have little besides architectural remains, and not very extensive ones at that. By the end of our 1970 season, I believed that we had uncovered not the fortified settlement we had expected to find, but a sanctuary. As the two new studies completely exhaust the subject of sanctuaries, and as the second season's work at Vounari still leaves us with the perplexing problem of what it is, I will modify my approach and compare Vounari with all similar types of structure known in Cyprus.

The goal of the Columbia University Expedition was to excavate a settlement of the Middle to Late Cypriote period. The site of Vounari near the village of Phlamoudhi looked very promising.[5] Phlamoudhi is located on the north coast of Cyprus in an area cut off from the southern part of the island by the Kyrenia range (Fig. 1). The village is difficult to approach, even from the coast: the mountains come right down to the sea in the west, and there are several difficult passes to the east. Even today one feels isolated from the rest of the world here; the nearest villages are Akanthou, 10 miles east, and Davlos, 4 miles west. The countryside is very beautiful with green mountains and a fertile plain with rolling hills. The mainstay of the village economy is the carob, but experimental farming has led to the production of a variety of goods and has proved the area to be quite rich. This area was visited in antiquity by Strabo, who mentions an Aphrodision on the north coast, 70 stadia from Salamis; he calls this area the "Coast of the Achaeans."[6]

At close range, the Vounari hill looks like a typical tell, circular, with an average diameter of 180 feet, only 10 meters high, covered with building stones and the pottery of the period, which interested us particularly. However, the archaeological pick quickly showed us that the remains were limited to the top of the hill, an area of only 60 x 60 feet, too small to be a settlement, and that the shape of the hill was not a result of human habitation but a geological phenomenon. This hill consists entirely of clay or argil, a very soft material—so soft that it contributed to the destruction of the structures built on it.

In our two seasons of excavation, we have found more or less featureless substructures of buildings. The buildings themselves must have been rather substantial, because in each of our trenches we excavated layer upon layer of large stones to depths of 3 to 6 feet. We calculate that at least 400 cubic meters of large stones were excavated. The weight of this alone would have sufficed to contribute to the collapse of the sides of the hill, particularly as the structures had no proper foundations—for the most part, no foundations at all. For this reason, the entire east side of a large building collapsed with part of the hill. We found no traces of buildings on the north side as yet and only poorly-preserved remains on the south and west.

The architectural remains at the top of the hill may be tentatively divided into two main phases on the basis of different types of

construction (stratigraphy has not yet been clarified, and would not, in any case, offer clear-cut divisions of strata). Of the earlier phase is a roughly rectangular structure (Fig. 2, walls D, E, F) about 7 x 5 meters, the west wall of which seems slightly rounded, though this may be simply the result of poor construction, or buckling after the collapse of the wall. This wall seems thicker than the others and its interior face has not yet been found. The south wall is not preserved at all—it might have been incorporated into the south wall of the later building (Fig. 2, wall C). The north wall (wall D) presents an opening like that of a doorway. This building was so poorly constructed and is so badly preserved that we still cannot be sure that the wall we have on the west belongs to the same structure as these other walls. Their only connection is the type of construction: each of these walls was built with the same kind of stone, a rough gypsum, without mortar. Larger stones were used for the faces and smaller stones as a filling.

This structure was built directly on virgin soil, no floor was found which can be associated with it, but we did find a thin layer of ashes in the eastern part of the room. A rather thick layer of ashes was traced beneath the north wall, particularly under the parts that seem to form a doorway. This probably represents an earlier level.

The later structure was a comparatively ambitious undertaking. Thus far, we have uncovered the south wall of this building (Fig. 2, wall C) which is preserved to a length of 11 meters. Its original length was approximately 16–17 meters. The west wall of the building (wall G) is also preserved, but has an inclination which makes excavation difficult. This season we uncovered the thick northern portion of the west wall (wall H) and thus we calculate that the width of the building is at least as much as 12 meters. The method of construction shows far more skill than the earlier building. Some provision was made for foundations. The outer face was built with flat stones and mortar was used to strengthen the walls. It is rather peculiar that the south wall has no inner face, whereas the west wall has.

Another unusual feature which happens to enhance the architectural remains of the site is seen in the buttresses on the south wall. Of the three, two were fully excavated. They are of the same length but were built at irregular intervals. They are not bonded to the south wall, but display the same type of construction: flat stones and mortar. Just in front of this wall was a sort of corridor or passageway

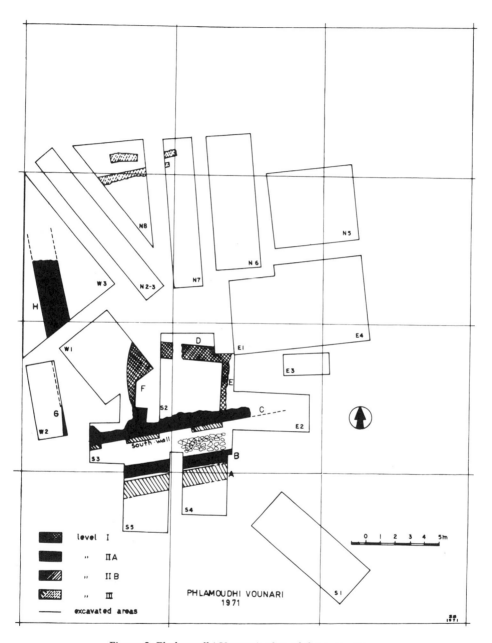

Figure 2: Phalmoudhi Vounari: plan of the excavation.

which had a floor of packed earth. Beneath this floor we found one layer of loosely set stones, parallel to the unbuttressed part of the south wall. These stones were probably set to create a substructure for the floor.

Parallel to the long south wall and south of it, run two perimeter walls which probably surrounded the central building. The pottery associated with them indicates that the southernmost wall (Fig. 2, wall A) is of later date. Both were built using flat stones and mortar. We cannot possibly expect to uncover these two walls completely, because both east and west ends have collapsed.

The Iron Age remains give no clear picture as yet and are concentrated on the north side of the hill.

Walls D, E, F seem to be the remains of the earliest structure at Vounari; we may call it Level I. The structure was roughly rectangular, though we cannot reconstruct its exact plan. The three walls belong to the same period. When this building was destroyed, for reasons unknown to us, the ancient people decided to erect a much larger one in its place. They leveled the debris as best they could and built on top of it. At the central part of the hill, the stones of Level I were abundant and provided a relatively solid foundation. The south wall was built against these stones and at first did not have buttresses. On the west, and probably the east side also, free-standing walls were erected. The first perimeter wall, the one closer to the south wall, was erected at the same time. I believe that it was during this period of building activity that the layer of stones was set to form the floor or passageway, and I will call this Level IIA. At a later time, when this building was damaged, the south wall was strengthened by the three buttresses. This addition resulted in a narrower corridor, and so another perimeter wall was built further south. These constitute the remains of Level IIB.

It is not easy to date these levels on the basis of the pottery found at the site. The characteristic pottery of MC III, Red-on-Black and Red-on-Red, so very common at Vounari, probably survived well into LC I. However, we can arrive at the terminal dates: the earliest pottery we have is Red-on-Black, White Painted III–IV, and a fragment of the earliest phase of Tell-el-Yahudiyeh Ware.[7] The latest pottery at the site seems to be White Slip II, and possibly Base Ring II. Of the fine wares, the most numerous pieces are Red-on-Black,

Red-on-Red, Black Slip II, and to a lesser degree, Monochrome. There is also some White Painted V and VI. The range of wares indicates that the Bronze Age life span of the structures at Vounari was MC III to LC II, ca. 1700 to 1400 B.C.

By the end of our first season, we were convinced that what we had found at Vounari was a sanctuary. However, this season's work did not yield any objects which would prove beyond doubt that the site was, in fact, sacred, and for this reason we began to have some doubts. We decided that it would be most useful to know what other ancient remains were to be found in the area of Phlamoudhi that might shed some light on the interpretation of our finds at Vounari. We also wanted to locate the Bronze Age settlement, as that was still the prime goal of our expedition. We conducted an exhaustive survey in the area of Phlamoudhi and discovered a total of eleven rather large settlement sites of all periods from Neolithic to Byzantine; we have another ten smaller settlements or small installations; there are four sites tentatively identified as sanctuaries, and ten cemeteries. There may well be more cemeteries in the area, but they were not the object of our survey and we did not identify them all. This gives us a total of thirty-six sites within an area of 3 x 3½ miles, a surprising density of habitation in such an isolated area. Most of these settlements date from the Cypro-Archaic to the Roman period, with heaviest concentration in the Hellenistic period. Nevertheless, it is remarkable to consider how these ancient communities organized and supported themselves, while the same area today supports a population of only 200 people.

During the course of our survey, we were surprised to find on several occasions that Vounari, despite its small size, is a prominent hill which stands out even from the rest of the hilly landscape in a most impressive way.

The site of Sapilou[8] yielded two Bronze Age potsherds during our survey, but trial trenches revealed a Hellenistic-Roman site which may have been a small installation in the Bronze Age, but certainly not the settlement we were after. One Bronze Age sherd was found at Geroschoinia and it must be considered a stray. At Melissa (Fig. 1) our trial trenches proved to be much more fruitful. We immediately found architectural remains of LC I and we decided to conduct a small excavation, parallel to our work at Vounari.

Melissa lies a mile and a quarter west of Vounari and just under one mile from the coast. The Bronze Age remains were found on the gentle slope of a rather prominent hill at an altitude of ca. 80 meters (240 feet) above sea level, the same altitude as Vounari. There are two streams (or rivers) on either side of Melissa. The one on the west side still flows and it was here that a large Byzantine settlement was established which remained until the sixteenth or seventeenth century. There are smaller remains of habitation from the Cypro-Archaic to perhaps the Roman period.

Our excavation was limited to an area of ten square meters and it might be helpful to summarize the results before returning to the problem of Vounari. We found a large building (Fig. 3), the walls of which are preserved in some places to a height of 1.70 meters. At the eastern part of the excavation there is a large room, probably 10 meters long and 3 meters wide (Room II); along the east and south sides of that room is a low wall which might have served as a bench. At the southeast corner of this room, a small addition was built, probably at a later time; this additional wall is not bonded to the earlier wall. This extension incorporated an unusual architectural feature—a drain or spout, the function of which can be explained if the room had been open to the sky. This might well have been the case as no material indicating the existence of a roof was found inside this room.[9] This room yielded only LC I pottery and a large number of bone fragments. It was filled with building material, pieces of mud brick, disintegrated mudbrick, and other materials.

At the western part of the excavation, two rooms were found, built vertical to the long room. The northern one (Room I) is at least 6.5 meters long and 2.5 meters wide. We have clear evidence in this room of two phases, represented by different types of construction and two different floors. The north wall of this room is built with larger and flatter stones than those used in the rest of the building, and includes a large ashlar block. This room belongs to the second phase of the building.

The two architectural phases of the building can be dated on the basis of the broken pottery purposely imbedded in the floors. The earlier phase can be dated to LC Ia; the second, to LC Ib. In absolute dates, the building was constructed ca. 1525 B.C. and renovated ca. 1450 B.C. In this room we found a large quantity of LC pottery.

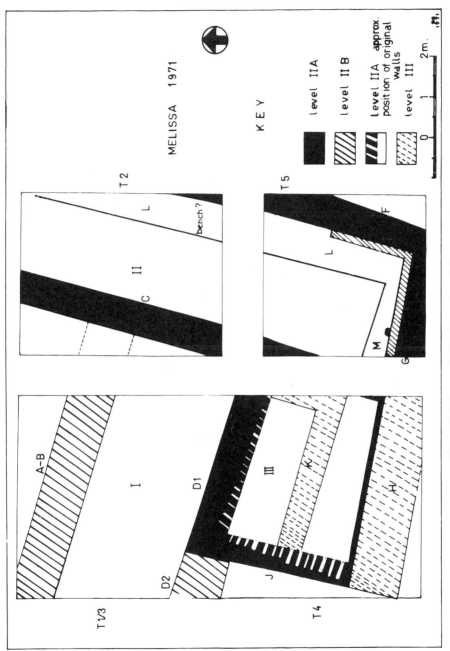

Figure 3: Phlamoudhi Melissa: plan of the excavation.

Almost every type of LC I pottery is represented with some interesting local varieties. Imported pottery was found also. We were particularly interested in the find of some Bichrome wheel-made pottery, and a Mycenaean vase which was found in the level of the destruction of this building. It is a piriform jar with an abstract foliate band, dating to the LH IIIA: 2 period, probably ca. 1350 B.C. or a little later. We also found part of a krater handle and some potsherds which seem to be local imitations of Mycenaean pottery. The same room yielded fragments of three or four pithoi and a large stone bowl. Many fragments of animal bones were scattered on the floors. There were traces of fire on the floors of both phases. The fire solidified some of the mudbricks belonging to the upper structure and we were able to isolate one of them, a large brick measuring about 50 x 36 x 12 cm. Such bricks are known from other Cypriote sites and were found in situ at Idalion.[10]

The other room (Fig. 3, Room III) is not preserved very well, because another structure was erected on top of it in the Cypro-Archaic period. It is 4 x 2.5 meters and the type of construction indicates that it belongs to the first phase of the building.

We were unable to locate any doors in this building. This, in addition to the thick walls and the large quantity of building material found in the rooms, indicates the existence of a second story, in which case these rooms might have been reached by wooden staircases leading from the upper story.

The building at Melissa may turn out to be an important structure in the history of Cypriote architecture of the Late Bronze Age. Similar buildings of LC I are known only from Enkomi thus far; for example, the buildings excavated by Dikaios in Area I of levels Ia and Ib.[11] We observe in the plan of the building in level Ia that there are several rooms which do not show evidence of doorways. In level Ia of area III Dikaios excavated a large building which he called a fortress.[12] The plan of this building also shows some rooms with no remains of doorways, but there are traces of staircases and the excavator suggested that these were made of wood. There appears to be some similarity between the arrangement of these rooms at Enkomi and the arrangement shown in our plan of Melissa, although it is too early at this stage of our excavation to establish any connections. But we were indeed surprised to find such a large building of the LC I period at Melissa, an isolated area of provincial character.

The results of both the detailed survey and the excavation at Melissa leave us with no doubt that we have found the Bronze Age settlement we were searching for, and it is the only Bronze Age settlement in the vicinity of Phlamoudhi. Therefore, on the basis of the information we have, it seems most useful to assume that the inhabitants of Melissa were responsible for the building activity at Vounari.

Having made this assumption, I would consider that the ambitious architectural undertaking of Level II A at Vounari was contemporary with the earlier phase of the structure uncovered at Melissa, and that the same people were involved in the construction. In both places, the same type of stone and mortar is used. Therefore, on the basis of the evidence from Melissa, we can tentatively date Level II A of Vounari to the LC Ia period. Level II B is also paralleled by similar construction activity at Melissa. The unbounded buttresses of Vounari have, at Melissa, the striking parallel of the addition to the wall inside the large room (the wall with the stone spout), and the wall which enabled us to distinguish a second phase; both are unbonded to earlier walls at Melissa. On the basis of these observations, we could date Level II B at Vounari to LC Ib–LC II A/B. Level I at Vounari could then be dated in all probability to the MC III period, and this is in accordance with the pottery found there, which, though lacking decisive characteristics for dating, has consistently an "early look."

The function of the structures at Vounari still remains a complicated problem on account of their poor state of preservation and the lack of parallels in Cypriote archaeology. With the exception of the corridor outside the south wall, we have no floor which can be associated with these buildings, we have no evidence as to what was built upon the sub-structures, and the finds are few and not characteristic. The south wall probably supported a kind of platform. Remains of this platform were found only in the center of the hill (trench S2) and do not extend to the adjoining trenches (W1 and E1). Whatever this platform supported, it did not cover all the interior space of the Level IIA building. The original lengths of the buttressed wall and the west wall are approximately 17 meters and 14 meters respectively. My previous calculations, on the basis of the first season's work, had given slightly smaller dimensions. The larger size of the structure leads us to entertain the possibility that we have on Vounari a fortress. We had rejected this idea after the first season because of the small size of the excavated remains.

Such mini-fortresses or military stations are known from two other sites which are of exactly the same period as Vounari. The one closest in size is the fortress at Nikolidhes-Glyka Vrysis which is just a bit bigger, measuring 23 x 14 meters.[13] Outside the fortress is a court and a building which includes workshops and a store. The interior of the fortress is divided into sections by transverse walls. The exterior walls have four projecting buttresses at each corner. None of these features can be observed at Vounari.

The other example is the fortress at Nitovikla, measuring approximately 40 x 35 meters.[14] In its III A phase (LC Ia) the fortress consisted of a double wall, probably connected with a flat roof. There was a large courtyard, in the middle of which was found a square rubble altar.

Although the architectural plan of Vounari does not show much similarity with that of these other fortresses, there are some factors which would favor such an interpretation nevertheless: the existence of such small defenses elsewhere in Cyprus; the shape of the hill and its defensibility; the enormous quantity of stones we excavated; and the lack of finds. The following considerations argue against the fortress interpretation and support the idea of a sanctuary: the absence of an inner face at the south wall; the existence of the platform and the lack of architectural divisions inside the walls; the lack of water on the hill and in the immediate vicinity; the purpose of having such a small fortress so far from the settlement. In this regard, an important consideration is that during the Iron Age the hill was used as a sanctuary and it is unlikely that a sanctuary would have been established at the site of a fortress.

With the exception of A. Iakovos, all known LC sanctuaries are situated within a settlement. The mountaintop sanctuary seems unknown to Bronze Age Cyprus, although this generalization is based on flimsy evidence. In the period we are now discussing, MC III to LC II B, only three sacred places are known—one is the rubble altar at Nitovikla which I just mentioned.[15] The others are at A. Iakovos and Myrtou-Pighades. At Myrtou-Pighades we have an open-air sanctuary within a settlement.[16] The remains of the LC IIA period are not very well preserved, but we do have the remains of a podium inside a room.[17] Later, in LC IIC:1, this was replaced by a large altar which stood at one end of a courtyard.[18]

At A. Iakovos there was an open-air sanctuary on a low hill.[19] A roughly circular area was divided by a low wall; on one side were two rubble altars and on the other a terra-cotta basin with two pits cut in the rock. The excavators suggest that there was a wooden perimeter wall.

The other Late Bronze Age sanctuaries are all later, dating to LC III and located within a settlement, like the one at Idalion.[20] No sanctuary has yet been found which can be compared to the well-known model from Vounous,[21] which clearly depicts a sacred enclosure, well protected by a wall, with divinities, and worshippers with offerings in the performance of a religious ritual. On the wall opposite the entrance one can see a group of divine images. This feature can also be seen in the two terra-cotta models recently acquired by the Cyprus Museum and published by V. Karageorghis.[22] The Vounous model seems to represent a country sanctuary of a circular form. It is possible that such sanctuaries existed at the top of prominent hills in either circular or rectangular architectural plan.

To focus once more on the problem of Vounari—the Bronze Age finds from the site do not offer a solution: we found at least twenty saddle querns, stone rubbing tools, mortars and pestles, a stone axe, a stone object which might be an anchor, a lead weight with numerals on it, and a pendant of terra-cotta, a bronze arrow head, and a few other bronze fragments, scraps of flint, and animal bones. Of particular interest was the find of a female figurine which can be dated to the beginning of the Late Cypriote period (Fig. 4).[23]

In summary, we cannot exclude the possibility that Vounari was a very small fortress with an unusual plan in the Bronze Age, but on the basis of the available evidence, both from the site itself and from the area in general, I believe it more likely that we have at Vounari a sanctuary, a well-built and well-protected one, such as that seen in the model from Vounous.

NOTES

1. Plans of the excavations at Vounari and Melissa published in this article are preliminary. They were drawn by the author on the basis of measurements made by the architect, Angel Coronado. I consider that interpretation of the architectural remains is necessary in order to present, insofar as is possible, a coherent picture of the poorly preserved structures found at Vounari. The interpretation is tentative, based on the work of two seasons at Vounari and one short one at Melissa. My prime concern in this paper has been to determine the function of the buildings at Vounari.

2. O. Masson, "Religious Beliefs and Sanctuaries in Prehistoric Times," *Archaeologia Viva*, vol. II no. 3 (1969), pp. 53–56. Other relevant publications are: R. Dussaud, "Culte funeraire et culte chthonien à Chypre à l'àge du Bronze," *Syria* XIII (1932): 223–226; P. Dikaios, "Les cultes prehistoriques dans l'île de Chypre," *Syria* XIII (1932): 345–354; E. Sjöqvist, "Die Kulturgeschichte eines cyprischen Temenos," *Archiv für Religions-Wissenschaft*, vol. 30, pp. 319 ff.

3. V. Karageorghis, "Two Religious Documents of the Early Cypriote Bronze Age," *RDAC*, 1970, pp. 10–13.

4. The book is not yet out; I am grateful to Paul Åström for sending me some of his proofs.

5. The surface indications on the Vounari hill pointed to the existence of a fortified settlement; cf. H. Catling, "Patterns of Settlement in Bronze Age Cyprus," *Op. Ath.* 4 (1962): 159.

6. Strabo, XIV, 682 mentions the "Coast of the Achaeans" in relation to an Aphrodision on the north coast "where the island is narrow, 70 stadia from Salamis." This Aphrodision is located, in all probability, at the site of Neraidhes, near Akanthou (our Fig. 1); see O. Masson, *Les inscriptions chypriotes syllabiques* (Paris: E. de Boccard, 1961), pp. 323 ff. with a discussion of this subject.

7. This pottery is now called El-Lisht ware by R. Merrillees (unpublished article).

8. We did not find any Bronze Age remains at Sapilou, which is described as a settlement by H. Catling, "Patterns of Settlement," p. 168.

9. The only parallel I can recall to such a drain is in the so-called "Court of the Stone Spout" at Knossos, A. Evans, *The Palace of Minos*, vol. III, Fig. 263.

10. *SCE* II, p. 483, wall 101, Fig. 211.

11. P. Dikaios, *Enkomi; Excavations 1948–1958*, vol. I (Mainz: Ph. von Zabern, 1969), pp. 153 ff., vol. III B, Pls. 267, 268.

12. Ibid., vol. I, pp. 16 ff., vol. III B, Pls. 243–4.

13. E. Gjerstad, *Studies on Prehistoric Cyprus* (Uppsala, 1926), pp. 6, 37 ff.; P. Dikaios, *Kypriakai Spoudai*, vol. 24 (1960), p. 11, Pl. 34a.

14. *SCE* I, pp. 394 ff.; Fig. 145, Plan XV.

15. *SCE* I, p. 398, Figs. 145, 158.

16. J. du Plat-Taylor, *Myrtou-Pighades* (Oxford: Ashmolean Museum, 1957), pp. 163 ff. Fig. 3.

17. Ibid. p. 9, Fig. 6.

18. Ibid., pp. 10 ff., Figs. 7–11.

19. *SCE* I, pp. 350 ff., Pl. XIII.

20. *SCE* I, Fig. 228, Plans XVI–XVIII.

21. P. Dikaios, *The Excavations at Vounous-Bellapais in Cyprus, 1931–32; Archaeologia* vol. 88 (Oxford, 1940), pp. 118 ff., 173, Pls. VII–VIII; cf. E. and J. Stewart, *Vounous 1937–38* (Lund, 1950).

22. Karageorghis, "Religious Documents," Pls. I-V.

23. E.g. L. Åström, *Studies on the Arts and Crafts of the Late Cypriote Bronze Age* (Lund, 1967), female figure type II: 2-3, p. 42, Fig. 70:4, and p. 112.

Figure 4: Vounari: lower half of a terracotta female figurine.

Near Eastern Chronology and the Date of the Late Cypriot I Period

James D. Muhly

Anyone who attempts to deal with the chronology of the Eastern Mediterranean in the second millennium B.C. must come to grips with the work of two men of powerful intellect and dominant personality, W. F. Albright[1] and Albrecht Goetze.[2] Both scholars were much interested in matters of chronology, held diametrically opposed positions on almost every question, and engaged one another in a lifetime of hotly fought debate. Death finally claimed both contestants during the summer of 1971 and this paper will try to be in some small way a tribute to the work of both men. What I hope to do here is to show that the points upon which both men agreed can be combined with new evidence to arrive at a conclusion which is in the nature of a compromise position midway between the High Chronology of Goetze and the Low Chronology of Albright.

Though the wide-ranging scholarship of both men stood out in this age of increasingly narrow specialization, Goetze was the leading authority in Anatolian studies while Albright was the acknowledged dean of Palestinian archaeologists. Like the imperial armies of old marching down from the north and up from the south, the conflicting chronologies clashed in the Turkish Hatay, at the site of Tell Atchana, ancient Alalakh, located at the bend of the Orontes River in the ʿAmuq plain. Sir Leonard Woolley excavated at Alalakh from 1937 to 1949, with a long interruption in between, and the final excavation report was published in 1955.[3] Two years earlier Woolley had published a popular report on the excavations entitled *A Forgotten Kingdom*.[4]

Woolley went to Alalakh looking for connections with the Aegean world, especially with Minoan Crete.[5] He was convinced that the eastward traffic of the Minoans would be aimed at the ports of North Syria and the site of Tell Atchana seemed a likely candidate. Claims were soon forthcoming for Alalakh as the source of Minoan architecture and Minoan fresco painting.[6] One of the factors which made such claims possible was Woolley's high chronology, for he began Alalakh level XVII at c. 3400 B.C.

Woolley did his best to find Minoan prototypes at Alalakh, but not a single one of his parallels has stood up to critical investigation.[7] Even the original premise of the excavation has proved to be incorrect, for recent research has presented Alalakh as a site serving the inland plain, not the coast.[8] One of the most important factors in the re-evaluation of the evidence from Alalakh is the question of the duration of habitation at Alalakh. In spite of Woolley's inflated chronology, based in large part upon a faulty evaluation of the glyptic evidence, it was soon agreed that Alalakh was strictly a second millennium site, having been occupied from c. 2000 to c. 1200 B.C.[9]

Of the eighteen levels at Alalakh attention has centered around levels VII and IV, the two periods for which Alalakh has produced written documentary evidence. The tablets of Alalakh, published by Donald Wiseman in 1953[10] and widely discussed ever since, have provided evidence which is of the utmost importance for our understanding of the ancient world in the second millennium B.C. During the period represented by level VII Alalakh, the capital of the kingdom of Mukiš, was the vassal of the kingdom of Yamhad, the latter having Aleppo as its capital.[11] By the time of the tablets from level IV Alalakh had become the westernmost limit of the empire of Šaušatar, the king of Mitanni.[12] Sometime just before this must be the period described in the famous statue inscription of Idrimi of Alalakh, whose inscribed statue has a good claim to being the ugliest work of art to have survived from the Ancient Near East.[13]

For the present, level VII alone must claim our attention. Since the time of the preliminary reports by Sidney Smith there has been a long and rather acrimonious controversy regarding the rulers mentioned in the tablets from Alalakh VII.[14] In a brilliant paper published in the *Journal of Cuneiform Studies* for 1954, the late Benno

Landsberger established that the tablets from level VII were to be placed not at the time of Hammurapi of Babylon, but during a period of five generations of the dynasty of Yamhad, all subsequent to Hammurapi.[15] This dating—to the latter part of the First Dynasty of Babylon—was confirmed by Helene Kantor two years later.[16]

Now the palace of level VII, the palace of Yarim-Lim of Alalakh, was destroyed in a great conflagration and regarding the date of this destruction there was an abundance of archaeological evidence. Alalakh VIII is a continuation of earlier levels and is typical Middle Bronze with a strong Cilician orientation. Things change in Alalakh VII and VI. Stratum VII has ceramic parallels with Hama H (in part), Ras Shamra II/2, and Megiddo XII-X.[17] Alalakh VI is to be compared with Hama G and Megiddo IX.[18] The characteristic Bichrome ware first appears in level VI[19] while a black impressed ware related to Tell el Yahudiyeh ware seems to be most characteristic of level V.[20] In general terms Mesopotamian archaeologists would place Alalakh VI-V in the late seventeenth and sixteenth centuries B.C. Thus the destruction of Alalakh VII should be placed in the mid-seventeenth century B.C., and in this both Albright and Goetze managed to agree, though Goetze favored a slightly higher date of c. 1650[21] to Albright's c. 1630 B.C.[22]

There is one other significant area of agreement. Landsberger not only established the proper relative position of the tablets from Alalakh VII, he also worked out the first correlation between Alalakh and the Hittite Old Kingdom. He recognized that the Zukraši mentioned as a general in the army (UGULA UKU.UŠ) in AT 6 was the same who appeared with the same title in the service of the king of Aleppo in a Hittite text (29/k - KBo VII 14) dealing with a Syrian war against the ruler of Ḫaššu.[23] Albright accepted this identification and even remarked that "Since both spelling of the name and title are identical at Alalakh and Hattusas, Landsberger's combination is certain."[24] AT 6 is the will of Ammitaqum of Alalakh set up before Yarim-Lim III of Aleppo who, with his son Hammurapi II, represent the last two rulers of Aleppo.[25] The events in KBo VII 14 are thus probably related, according to Goetze, to those described in KUB XXXI 5 which mentions both Yarim-Lim III and Hammurapi II.[26] The Hittite wars in Syria are also described in the famous Akkadian text known as the *Siege of Uršu* (KBo I 11).[27]

So far, so good: everyone seems to be in the same camp. Why then all the controversy? To see the problem we must move south, down the Euphrates to Babylon. In one of those great dramatic events of history the Hittite king Muršiliš I made an abrupt razzia down the Euphrates, sacked Babylon, carried off the statues of Marduk and his consort Sarpanitum to the city of Hana, and returned with the booty of Babylon to his home capital in central Anatolia only to be greeted by the hand of an assassin.[28] This Hittite raid on Babylon is attested both in Hittite and in Babylonian sources. It marks the end of the reign of Samsuditana, the last king of the Hammurapi dynasty, and hence is taken as marking the close of the Old Babylonian Period.[29] A crucial event in the history of the Ancient Near East, but when did it take place? That is what the controversy is all about.[30]

Our absolute chronology for Mesopotamian history is ultimately based upon a text known as the Venus Tablets of Ammisaduqa, who was the penultimate ruler of the Hammurapi dynasty.[31] Observations of the planet Venus in the eighth year of his reign give us a series of astronomically fixed dates. Not just one series of dates but a sequence of dates, for we are dealing with a recurrent phenomenon.[32] Taking what we know about the general history of the period and the length of reign for each king as given in the Babylonian Kinglists, we come up with three possible dates for the fall of Babylon: 1650, 1594, or 1530. Hence the High, Middle, and Low Chronologies. Which one is correct? Goetze said the high date, Sidney Smith the middle, and Albright the low one. For the past sixty years scholars have been looking for a way out of this bind.[33] I think one is now at hand.

Muršiliš I, the destroyer of Babylon, used to be the first Hittite king really known to history. In 1957 all that changed, for in that year the German excavators found at Boğazköy the bilingual annals of Hattušiliš I, the grandfather and predecessor of Muršiliš.[34] These annals, written in Hittite and Akkadian, record the campaigns of six years in the reign of Hattušiliš.[35] These campaigns are, for the most part, to be located in northern Syria. On the second such campaign Hattušiliš sacked and destroyed the city of Alalakh.[36] Is this destruction to be associated with the end of Alalakh level VII? If so, our problems are solved. If the destruction of Alalakh VII is placed, on the basis of archaeological evidence, in the mid-seventeenth century

B.C. then, since we know that Muršiliš was the immediate successor of Hattušiliš, the Hittite raid on Babylon must be dated in 1594 B.C. and the Middle Chronology is proved correct.

Can we prove that Hattušiliš is to be associated with Alalakh VII? I believe that we can. To do so we must return to Zukraši. The correlation established by Landsberger showed that the Syrian war described in the Hittite text (KBo VII 14) came at the time of Alalakh VII. Other Hittite texts described the same series of campaigns and referred to the same rulers of Alalakh. In his annals Hattušiliš refers to a campaign against Uršu[37] and even such a supporter of the Low Chronology as Kurt Bittel now assigns the *Siege of Uršu* text to the reign of Hattušiliš I.[38] Quite apart from reference to the destruction of Alalakh, Goetze had already also assigned the Zukraši text to the reign of Hattušiliš I.[39] There is no reason to change this dating. Now Hattušiliš explicitly refers to his destruction of Alalakh; this can only be the Alalakh of Zukraši, Alalakh VII. In fact Hattušiliš actually describes the war against Ḥaššu in his 'sixth' year, and this is also the rebel city mentioned in the Zukraši text.[40]

Neither Goetze nor Albright had discussed this problem in detail, but we can see that they saw the threat to their own chronological systems. Goetze thought that Alalakh VII was destroyed by Muršiliš, even though Muršiliš never mentions Alalakh and Hattušiliš does.[41] Albright, writing before the discovery of the annals of Hattušiliš already saw that the Zukraši correlation presented a serious problem. In order to explain it he was forced to reconstruct a new and entirely hypothetical generation of Hittite kings before the time of Hattušiliš I. Thus, referring to Zukraši, Albright says:

> . . . the events referred to in this Hittite text must have occurred not far from 1670 B.C., according to the low chronology, i.e., not only before Labarnas but also before the latter's grandfather Tudhaliyas I who is at present the earliest known Hittite king in the direct line of ancestry.[42]

There is no evidence for such a line of rulers. Nothing we know about Hittite history justifies the creation of such a dynasty.

There is one final point. Perhaps the Zukraši text is a late archaizing composition or perhaps the annals of Hattušiliš represent late legendary history. This is not the case. It can be shown that both texts were composed in the Old Kingdom.[43] They are contemporary historical texts. Babylon was sacked by the Hittites in 1594 B.C. Today no other date fits the known historical evidence.

Somehow Cypriot archaeologists have gotten the idea that the Alalakh level involved in this chronological dispute was Alalakh VI. This idea seems to go back at least to Basil Hennessy's publication of the cemetery at Stephania. Thus:

> The occurrence of Bichrome Wheel-made ware at Alalakh in level VI need not mean an occurrence before 1550 at this site. Following Albright's chronology the date for the destruction of Babylon by Mursilis I and the presumed associated destruction of level VI at Alalakh is 1531 not 1550. . . . The twenty years are important. It is worth remarking that only the low chronology of Albright and Cornelius can fit the Cypriot evidence for level VI at Alalakh.[44]

Bichrome ware there is indeed in level VI and it is right where it should be. I feel that Albright would not have welcomed such a confirmation of his chronology. Unfortunately this confusion over Alalakh has found its way into the current archaeological literature. Frankly, the statement by Hennessy does not seem to be valid even on its own terms, as Bichrome ware is apparently already present in MC III levels at Enkomi.[45] Alalakh V has also entered the picture because of an alleged MM III sherd found in that stratum.[46] I have my doubts about the sherd but, even at face value, such a find is not much evidence for anything. Certainly not for a low chronology.

With the destruction of Babylon securely placed, Hammurapi can be dated to 1792-1750 B.C. and the Mari letters in the first half of the 18th century B.C. There is time here for but one example of how this affects current thinking. P. Dikaios has recently stated that the Mari references to copper from Alašiya can be explained by the fact that copper was being smelted at Enkomi already in MC III.[47] But what have the two things to do with one another? They are separated by about a hundred years.

In recent years there have been repeated attempts to lower the second millennium chronology for the entire eastern Mediterranean world, including Egypt. The studies of Dr. Paul Åström are notable in this regard, especially his paper at the Second Cretological Congress held in 1966.[48] Time does not permit a complete discussion of all the points raised in that study. Two must suffice. First, the Old Babylonian cylinder from Tholos B at Platanos.[49] The important thing to remember is that Old Babylonian does not mean Hammurapi or later. In fact the cylinder seal is early Old Babylonian.[50] The latest pottery in the tomb is MM IB.[51] This means that MM IB can be late 19th century, not late 18th century as argued by Åström. Platanos provides no evidence for the Low Chronology. Åström's low date is, in fact, based upon the Low Chronology.

From the Tomb of the Seafarer at Karmi in northern Cyprus comes a cup in MM IB Kamares ware in a MC IB context.[52] Again this only shows that the two may be contemporary and are to be dated in the late nineteenth or early eighteenth century B.C. Åström's date in the late eighteenth is again based upon the assumption that the Low Chronology is the correct one. From Lerna V, marking the beginning of the Middle Bronze Age, come sherds of MM IA pottery, again indicating a date somewhere around 1900 B.C.[53] Åström concludes that: "We can now equate Middle Minoan IB and Middle Cypriot I with Syrian Middle Bronze IIA."[54] Syrian MB IIA is the time of the Royal Tombs at Byblos and of Zimri-Lim of Mari.[55] The date has to be the early eighteenth century B.C., the time of the XIIIth Dynasty in Egypt.

For the following period Miss Kantor has securely established the synchronism between the Second Intermediate Period in Egypt, MM III in Crete, and the MB IIB period in Palestine.[56] Moreover, Miss Kantor also shows that the end of the Second Intermediate Period overlaps with the beginning of Late Bronze I in Western Asia. Dr. Merrillees has now come to the same conclusion for Cyprus, for he argues that the end of LC IA coincides with the end of the Second Intermediate Period.[57] As Ahmose, the founder of the XVIIIth Dynasty, comes to the throne sometime in the second quarter of the sixteenth century B.C.,[58] the beginning of the Late Cypriot period must come around 1600 B.C.[59]

It must be remembered that pottery, in itself, does not and cannot provide independent evidence for absolute chronology. All chronological systems in the second millennium B.C. are based ultimately upon the written records from Egypt and Western Asia. Arne Furumark saw this very clearly in his studies on the chronology of Mycenaean pottery.[60] Other scholars have tended to lose sight of this very important fact. There is at present no justification for lowering the general chronological system now most widely used, which is based upon the Middle Chronology and the destruction of Babylon in 1594 B.C.[61] We cannot tinker with this system in any piecemeal fashion. It is an intricate clockwork mechanism, even though it does not always operate exactly like clockwork all of the time. If we alter one part of it, we must be prepared to adjust the entire system accordingly. That I am not prepared to do.[62]

NOTES

1. W. F. Albright, "An Indirect Synchronism between Egypt and Mesopotamia, ca. 1730 B.C.," *BASOR*, **99** (1945): 9-18; idem, "Stratigraphic Confirmation of the Low Mesopotamian Chronology," *BASOR*, 144 (1956): 26-30; idem, "Further Observations on the Chronology of Alalakh," *BASOR*, 146 (1957): 26-34.

2. A. Goetze, "The Problem of Chronology and Early Hittite History," *BASOR*, **122** (1951): **18-25**; idem, "The Predecessors of Šuppiluliumaš of Ḫatti," *JAOS*, 72 (1952): 67-72; idem, "Alalah and Hittite Chronology," ***BASOR, 146 (1957): 20-26***; idem, "On the Chronology of the Second Millennium B.C.," *JCS*, 11 (1957): 53-61; 63-73.

3. Sir Leonard Woolley, *Alalakh: An Account of the Excavations at Tell Atchana in the Hatay, 1937-1949*, Reports of the Research Committee of the Society of Antiquaries of London, XVIII (London, 1955).

4. Sir Leonard Woolley, *A Forgotten Kingdom* (Penguin Books: 1953).

5. Sir Leonard Woolley, *Alalakh*, p. 1.

6. See, for example, W. Culican, *The First Merchant Venturers: The Ancient Levant in History and Commerce*, Library of the Earliest Civilizations (London, **1966**), p. 29 ff. See addenda.

7. See the excellent discussion by W. S. Smith, *Interconnections in the Ancient Near East* (New Haven, 1965), esp. p. 104. For the assumed Syrian origin of Minoan palace architecture see J. W. Graham, "The Relation of the Minoan Palaces to the Near Eastern Palaces of the Second Millennium B.C.," in *Mycenaean Studies*, ed. E. L. Bennett, Jr. (Madison, 1964), pp. 195-215; idem, "The Cretan Palace: Sixty Seven Years of Exploration," in *A Land Called Crete*, Smith College Studies in History, XLV (Northampton, Mass., 1968), pp. 17-34, esp. p. 30.

8. See H. Seyrig, "Seleucus I and the Foundations of Hellenistic Syria," in *The Role of the Phoenicians in the Interaction of Mediterranean Civilizations*, ed. W. A. Ward (Beirut, 1968), pp. 53-63, esp. p. 57; idem, "Antiquités syriennes, 92: Séleucus I et la fondation de la monarchie syrienne," *Syria*, 47 (1970): 290-311, esp. 297.

9. See the review of Woolley's *Alalakh* by M. J. Mellink, *AJA*, 61 (1957): 395-400 (with comments by E. Porada). The revised chronology has been accepted by almost all scholars, though occasionally a higher chronology is encountered, as in D. J. Wiseman, "Alalakh," in *Archaeology and Old Testament Study*, ed. D. W. Thomas (London, 1967), pp. 118-135.

10. D. J. Wiseman, *The Alalakh Tablets*, British Inst. of Arch. at Ankara, Occas. Publ., 2 (London, 1953), hereafter *AT*.

11. Cf. H. Klengel, *Geschichte Syriens im 2. Jahrtausend v. u. Z.*, Teil 1 - *Nordsyrien*, Deut. Akad. d. Wiss. zu Berlin, Inst. für Orientf., Veröff., 40 (Berlin, 1965), pp. 203-218.

12. Ibid, pp. 219-249. Also M. S. Drower, "Syria, c. 1550-1400 B.C.," in *CAH*², II/10 (Cambridge, 1970), Part 1, p. 16 ff. For the kings of Mitanni see A. Kammenhuber, *Die Arier im Vorderen Orient* (Heidelberg, 1968), pp. 61-87; E. Weidner, "Assyrien und Hanigalbat," in *Ugaritica VI*, (Paris, 1969), pp. 519-532. See addenda.

13. S. Smith, *The Statue of Idri-Mi*, British Inst. of Arch. at Ankara, Occas. Publ. 1 (London, 1949) and see reviews by A. Goetze, *JCS*, 4 (1950): 226-230 and W. F. Albright, *BASOR*, 118 (1950): 11-20. For a recent translation of the text see A. Leo Oppenheim, in *ANET*³ (Princeton, 1969), pp. 557-558. For the statue itself, see A. Moortgat, *The Art of Ancient Mesopotamia* (London, 1969), p. 111 and Pl. 235. There has been considerable discussion concerning the historical background of the Idrimi inscription. See M. Dietrich and O. Loretz, *OLZ*, 61 (1966): 554-560. See addenda.

14. Sidney Smith presented his own interpretation in *Alalakh and Chronology* (London, 1940).

15. B. Landsberger, "Assyrische Königsliste und 'dunkles Zeitalter'," *JCS*, 8 (1954): 31-45; 47-73; 106-133. Sidney Smith had proposed that the Alalakh texts were contemporary with Hammurapi of Babylon and the Mari letters.

16. H. J. Kantor, "Syro-Palestinian Ivories," *JNES*, 15 (1956): 153-174, esp. p. 158 f., n.22.

17. Ibid.

18. For questions of chronology, see K. M. Kenyon, "The Middle and Late Bronze Age Strata at Megiddo," *Levant*, 1 (1969): 25-60; O. Negbi, *The Hoards of Gold-work from Tell el-'Ajjul*, SIMA, XXV (Gothenburg, 1970), pp. 27 f.; 33 f.

19. Sir Leonard Woolley, *Alalakh*, p. 386 (this is the pottery Woolley calls Ajjul ware). For Bichrome ware see R. S. Merrillees, "Evidence for the Bichrome Wheel-made Ware in Egypt," *AJBA*, I/3 (1970): 3-27, esp. p. 16 f.

20. Sir Leonard Woolley, *Alalakh*, p. 342 f. For this pottery see P. Åström, *The Middle Cypriot Bronze Age*, (Lund, 1957), p. 239.

21. A. Goetze, *BASOR*, 146 (1957): 25.

22. W.F. Albright, *BASOR*, 144 (1956): 28 f.; *BASOR*, 146 (1957): 30. It must be emphasized that this date is an archaeological one, based chiefly upon ceramic chronology. It is not based upon the documentary references to be discussed below. Too often in the past, especially in the field of Biblical archaeology, destruction levels have been dated upon the basis of a historical reference to that site's destruction, usually at the hands of an Egyptian pharaoh such as Tuthmosis III. Sometimes even the identification of the archaeological site is based upon such a correlation. This is simply putting the cart before the horse.

23. B. Landsberger, *JCS*, 8 (1954): 52. For the Hittite text see R. Werner, *Orientalia*, 25 (1956): 168 f. (review of KBo VII); H. Klengel, *Geschichte Syriens*, I (1965), p. 147. For Hittite texts related to KBo VII 14 see H. Klengel, p. 146 f.; A. Goetze, *JCS*, 18 (1964): 89 (to KBo XII 13).

24. W. F. Albright, *BASOR*, 144 (1956), p. 28, n. 9.

25. For Aleppo see H. Klengel, *Geschichte Syriens*, I, p. 157 f. This chronology makes Hammurapi II the contemporary of the Hittite king Muršiliš I. See A. Goetze, *BASOR*, 146 (1957): 23; idem, *JCS*, 11 (1957): 69 f.

26. A. Goetze, *BASOR*, 146 (1957): 22. See note 23.

27. Ibid., p. 20 and n. 12. For the text see H. G. Güterbock, "Die historische Tradition und ihre literarische Gestaltung bei Babyloniern und Hethitern, II," *ZA*, 44 (1938): 45-149, esp. pp. 113-132. For the Hittites in Syria see H. Klengel, "Syrien in der hethitischen Historiographie," *Klio*, 51 (1969): 5-14.

28. O. R. Gurney, "Anatolia, c. 1750-1600 B.C.," in *CAH*², II/6 (Cambridge, 1962), p. 24 f.; A. Goetze, *JCS*, 11 (1957): 55 f.

29. C. J. Gadd, "Hammurabi and the End of his Dynasty," in *CAH*,² II/5 (Cambridge, 1965), p. 53.

30. I do not wish to imply that this is the only point at issue in current chronological disputes; only that this is the most dramatic illustration of the various chronologies currently under consideration. Early Kassite chronology is another important factor, for which see A. Goetze, "The Kassites and Near Eastern Chronology," *JCS*, 18 (1964): 97-101.

31. S. Langdon & J. K. Fotheringham, *The Venus Tablets of Ammizaduqa* (Oxford, 1928), and see review by O. Neugebauer, *OLZ*, 32 (1929): 913-921; S. Smith, *Alalakh and Chronology*, p. 25 f.

32. A. Sachs, "Absolute dating from Mesopotamian records," in T. E. Allibone, et al., *The Impact of the Natural Sciences on Archaeology, a Symposium* (Oxford, 1970), pp. 19-22.

33. For an excellent summary of the basic arguments and problems involved see H. Tadmor, "The Chronology of the Ancient Near East in the Second Millenium B.C.E.," in *The Patriarchs*, ed. B. Mazar, The World History of the Jewish People, 1/2 (Rutgers, N.J., 1971), pp. 63-101; 260-269. The three basic systems of chronology are usually expressed in terms of the dates for the reign of Hammurapi of Babylon: High - 1848-1806; Middle - 1792-1750; and Low - 1728-1686.

34. Texts in KBo X 1-3. Preliminary publication by H. Otten, *apud* K. Bittel, "Vorläufiger Bericht über die Ausgrabungen in Boğazköy im Jahre 1957," *MDOG*, 91 (1958): 73-84, esp. p. 75 f. See now F. Imparati & C. Saporetti, "L'autobiografia di Hattusili I," *Studi Classici e Orientali*, 14 (1965): 40-85 (but "autobiography" is a very strange description of this text).

35. See the summary by O. R. Gurney, "Anatolia," p. 14 f.; H. Klengel, *Geschichte Syriens, Teil 3: Historische Geographie und allgemeine Darstellung*, (Berlin, 1970), p. 166 f.

36. Hittite (KBo X 2 I 15-16)

URU

MU.IM.MA-*an-ni-ma I.NA*   *A-la-al-ḫa pa-a-[u]n na-an ḫar-ni-in-ku-un*

Akkadian (KBo X 1 Vs. 6-7)

URU

. . . *a-na ba-la-at a-na*   *Al-ḫa-al-ḫa al-li-ik-ma ú-ḫal-liq-šu*

"The next year I went to Alalakh, and I destroyed it."

37. Also in the "second" year. In the Hittite version the name appears as *Wa-ar-šu-wa*, while the Akkadian gives the more familiar *Ur-šu*.

38. K. Bittel, *Hattusha, the Capital of the Hittites* (Oxford, 1970), p. 49. W. F. Albright, *BASOR*, 144 (1956): 28, n. 9, also placed this text in the mid-seventeenth century B.C.

39. A. Goetze, *BASOR*, 146 (1957): 26; idem, *JCS*, 11 (1957): 70.

40. For Ḫaššu, see H. Klengel, *Geschichte Syriens*, 1 (1965), pp. 269-274; 3 (1970), pp. 32f., 168 f.; H. G. Güterbock, "Sargon of Akkad Mentioned by Ḫattušili of Ḫatti," *JCS*, 18 (1964): 1-6, esp. p. 4. For the association of the Ḫaššu mentioned by Hattušiliš I with the Ḫaššu mentioned in the Zukraši text see also O. R. Gurney, in *CAH²*, II/6, p. 19.

41. A. Goetze, *JCS*, 16 (1962): 24-30, esp. p. 27 (review of KBo X).

42. W. F. Albright, *BASOR*, 146 (1957): 30.

43. For KBo VII 14 see A. Goetze, *BASOR*, 146 (1957): 26; R. Werner, *Orientalia*, **25 (1956): 168. For KBo X 1-2 see H. Otten, *MDOG* 91 (1958): 75, 84. See addenda.**

44. J. B. Hennessy, *Stephania. A Middle and Late Bronze-Age Cemetery in Cyprus* (London, 1963), p. 53f.

45. P. Dikaios, *Enkomi, Excavations 1948-1958*, vol. II (Mainz am Rhein, 1971), p. 44.

46. For the assumed Minoan sherd see Sir Leonard Woolley, *Alalakh*, Pl. CXXIX,1.

47. P. Dikaios, *Enkomi*, p. 500.

48. P. Åström, "New Evidence for Middle Minoan Chronology," in *Acta of the 2nd Cretological Congress, 1967*, vol. I (Athens, 1968), pp. 120-127. See also the earlier study by Åström, "Remarks on Middle Minoan chronology," in *Acta of the 1st Cretological Congress, 1961*, vol. I (Iraklion, 1962), Κρητικὰ Χρονικά, 15-16), pp. 137-150.

49. P. Åström, in *Acta of the 2nd Cretological Congress*, p. 120 f. This seal has been very widely discussed. See S. Smith, "Middle Minoan I-II and Babylonian Chronology," *AJA*, 49(1945): 1-24, esp. p. 7 f.; V.E.G. Kenna, "Ancient Crete and the Use of the Cylinder Seal," *AJA*, 72(1968): 321-336, esp. p. 324f.; K. Branigan & P. Robinson, "The Mesara Tholoi and Middle Minoan Chronology," *SMEA*, 5(1968): 12-30 (especially the comment by Robinson on p. 29, dating the Platanos cylinder seal ". . . approximately 75-100 years before Hammurabi."). The chronology of

Åström has also been discussed in W.A. Ward, *Egypt and the East Mediterranean World 2200-1900* B.C. *Studies in Egyptian Foreign Relations during the First Intermediate Period* (Beirut, 1971). Ward also rejects the low chronology of Åström. Paul Åström discusses the problem again in "Some aspects of the Late Cypriot I Period," *RDAC*, (1972), pp. 46-57.

50. I have had the opportunity to discuss this problem with Briggs Buchanan who first suggested the dating proposed here.

51. . For a general chronology see K. Branigan, *The Tombs of Mesara. A Study of Funerary Architecture and Ritual in Southern Crete, 2800–1700* B.C. (London, 1970).

52. J. Stewart, "The Tomb of the Seafarer at Karmi in Cyprus," *Op. Ath.*, 4(1962): 197-204. The Kamares ware cup is illustrated in V. Karageorghis, *The Ancient Civilization of Cyprus, An Archaeological Adventure* (New York, 1969), Pl. 55. The tomb also contained a triangular-riveted dagger and a blue faience bead. For Karmi see also P. Åström, *Acta 2nd Cret. Cong.*, p. 121 f.

53. For Lerna sherds see J. Caskey, "The Early Helladic Period in the Argolid," *Hesperia*, 29 (1960): 285-303, esp. p. 299.

54. P. Åström, *Acta 2nd Cret. Cong.*, p. 122.

55. See W. F. Albright, "The Eighteenth-Century Princes of Byblos and the Chronology of Middle Bronze," *BASOR*, 176 (1964): 38-46; K. A. Kitchen, "Byblos, Egypt and Mari in the Early Second Millennium B.C.," *Orientalia*, 36 (1967): 39-54; B. Mazar, "The Middle Bronze Age in Palestine," *IEJ*, 18 (1968): 65-97.

56. H. J. Kantor, "The Relative Chronology of Egypt and its Foreign Correlations before the Late Bronze Age," in *Chronologies in Old World Archaeology*, ed. R. Ehrich (Chicago, 1965), pp. 1-46, esp. p. 23.

57. R. S. Merrillees, "The Early History of Late Cypriote I," *Levant*, 3 (1971): 56-79, esp. p. 73.

58. The chronology of the Egyptian XVIIIth Dynasty is, at present, a very controversial subject and there have been a number of recent studies advocating a significantly lower chronology. Cf. E. Hornung, *Untersuchungen zur Chronologie und Geschichte des Neuen Reiches*, Ägyptologische Abhandlungen, Vol. XI (Wiesbaden, 1964); D.B. Redford, *History and Chronology of the Eighteenth Dynasty of Egypt: Seven Studies* (Toronto, 1967); idem, "On the Chronology of the Egyptian Eighteenth Dynasty," *JNES*, 25 (1966): 113-124; J. von Beckerath, "Methode und Ergebnisse ägyptischer Chronologie," *OLZ*, 62 (1967): 5–13; W. Helck, "Überlegungen zur Geschichte der 18. Dynastie," *Oriens Antiquus*, 8 (1969): 281–327.

59. See the discussion in P. Dikaios, *Enkomi*, Vol. II, pp. 477 f., esp. p. 479.

60. See the section on 'Absolute Chronology' in A. Furumark, *The Chronology of Mycenaean Pottery* (Stockholm, 1941).

61. One of the factors in the predominance of the Middle Chronology has been its adoption by the new third edition of the *Cambridge Ancient History*. The Low Chronology is still being used, especially in Germany. See B. Hrouda, *Vorderasien, I: Mesopotamien, Babylonien, Iran und Anatolien*, Handbuch der Archäologie, 2

(Munich, 1971), pp. 20-24. For the importance of the evidence from Alalakh see also
P. Garelli, *Le Proche-Orient asiatique, des origines aux invasions des peuples de la
mer* (Paris, 1969), pp. 229 f. See addenda.

62. In his posthumously published article on "The Historical Framework of
Palestinian Archaeology Between 2100 and 1600 B.C.," *BASOR*, 209 (1973): 12-18,
esp. p. 17, W. F. Albright now states that Alalakh VII was destroyed by Hattušiliš I
about 1575 B.C. and that Muršiliš I sacked Babylon "rather early in the reign of
Samsu-ditana, probably about 1550 B.C." This represents Albright's attempt to deal
with the new Hittite evidence and it cannot be accepted. Albright has forgotten that
his previous date for the destruction of Alalakh, c. 1630 B.C., was based upon
archaeological evidence and cannot be lowered some sixty years without revising the
ceramic chronology of Syria and Palestine. As for Babylon, Albright assumes that the
Hittite raid came early in the reign of Samsu-ditana, who continued to reign as king
of Babylonia for some twenty years. It is true that our sources make no direct
connection between the Hittite raid and the end of the First Dynasty of Babylon, but
the data we have for the reign of Samsu-ditana, chiefly dated texts and year formulae,
continue to mention Marduk and Sarpanitum and there is certainly no indication that
the city has been sacked and its chief gods carried off into captivity. There is also the
tradition, recorded in late texts, that Marduk and Sarpanitum spent twenty-four
years in captivity in the land of Hana (variant, in the land of the Hittites) before being
brought back to Babylon by the Kassite king, Agum II (see R. Borger, "Gott Marduk
und Gott-König Šulgi als Propheten. Zwei prophetische Texte," *Bi. Or.*, 28 [1971]:
3-24). This interval must represent the period between the Hittite raid and the time
when the Kassites established themselves in Babylon, an interval during which
Gulkishar, king of the Sealand, was perhaps in control of Babylon. The MBA in Syria
seems to come to an end with a series of destructions all of which can perhaps be
associated with the campaigns of the Hittites. See M.C. Astour, "Tell Mardih and
Ebla," *UF*, 3 (1971): 9-19, p. 18; P. Matthiae, "Tell Mardikh," Archéologia, 69
(1974): 16-31, p. 20. See addenda.

ADDENDA

To note 6: The problem of Syrian influence upon Minoan Crete has now been discussed in detail by M. C. Astour, "Ugarit and the Aegean. A Brief Summary of
Archaeological and Epigraphic Evidence," in *Orient and Occident (Festschrift
Cyrus H. Gordon)*, Neukirchen-Vluyn, 1973 (AOAT, 22), pp. 17-27. Again, chron-
ology plays a major role in many of the arguments, for Astour has Alalakh VII built
about 1650 B.C. and destroyed by Hattusilis I about 1570 B.C. (ibid, p. 22 and 62).
This makes the frescoes from Alalakh earlier than those from Knossos, which are to
be dated no earlier than 1600 B.C. Quite apart from the chronology of Alalakh, which
I believe is too low, it should be pointed out that the beginning of fresco painting at
Knossos is more probably placed at about 1700 B.C. (cf. S. Hood, *The Minoans*,
London, 1971, p. 78).

To note 12: See also E. von Weiher, "Mitanni," in *Festschrift Heinrich Otten*, Wiesbaden, 1973, pp. 321-326; idem, "Hanigalbat," in *RLA*, IV/2-3 (Berlin-New York,

1973): 105-107. On the 'Mitannian' question see W. Wüst, "Indo-Arier in Vorderen-Orient. Notizen zu einem unkonventionellen Buch," *Die Sprache*, 20 (1974): 136-163.

To note 13: See also A. Kempinski and N. Ne'eman, "The Idrimi Inscription Reconsidered," in *Excavations and Studies: Essays in Honour of Prof. Shemuel Yeivin*, ed. Y. Aharoni, Tel Aviv, 1973, pp. 211- 220 (in Hebrew, with English summary, pp. XXVI–XXVII).

To note 43: Regarding the Annals of Hattusilis I it must be admitted that we know the text only in late copies, probably going back no earlier than the reign of Mursilis II. See S. R. Bin-Nun, "The Anatolian Background of the Tawananna's Position in the Hittite Kingdom," *RHA*, 30, (1972–73): 54-80, p. 72 and n. 105; H. Otten, "Hattusili I," in *RLA*, IV/2-3 (Berlin-New York, 1973): 173.

To note 61: H. Otten, "Hethiter, Geschichte," in *RLA*, IV/4-5 (Berlin-New York, 1975): 371-372, still places Hattusilis I about 1550 B.C. and gives 1530 as the date for Mursilis' raid on Babylon.

To note 62: Hittite chronology has now been discussed again by O. R. Gurney, "The Hittite Line of Kings and Chronology," in *Anatolian Studies Presented to Hans Gustav Güterbock*, Istanbul, 1974, pp. 105-111. On the basis of genealogy and the count of generations, Gurney concludes that, while the evidence is inconclusive, the Middle Chronology is "...the only one that cannot be invalidated by any such new data...." (p. 111). The historical background of Syria in the seventeenth century B.C. is discussed by N. Na'aman, "Syria at the Transition from the Old Babylonian Period to the Middle Babylonian Period," *Ugarit-Forschungen*, 6 (1974): 265-274.

The Foreign Trade of Cyprus during the Late Bronze Age

Y. Lynn Holmes

In the midst of the rich and powerful nations of the Late Bronze Age,[1] the island of Cyprus has almost been forgotten. Perhaps because of its separation from important land bodies, inadequate knowledge of Late Bronze Age navigation, and ignorance about its appearance in Late Bronze Age texts, Cyprus has been relegated to the position of an unimportant island. To understand the correct role of Cyprus during this period, one must consider the textual and archaeological evidence of Cypriot foreign trade, since this material demonstrates the extensive contact Cyprus had with surrounding countries and the important place Cyprus held during the Late Bronze Age. Thus this paper will attempt to collect and evaluate evidence of Cypriot exports and imports during this period.

It should be noted in the beginning that the Late Bronze Age textual evidence will come from the so-called 'Alashiya texts,' since these texts have been shown to refer to either part or all of the island of Cyprus.[2] Therefore, some Amarna Letters and hieroglyphic texts from Egypt, Hittite texts from Anatolia and the Mari texts from Syria will be used to understand Cypriot foreign trade. Throughout this paper, the textual evidence will be consulted, and this will then be compared with the available archaeological evidence.

The textual evidence clearly indicates that the main export of Late Bronze Age Cyprus was copper. In the Amarna Letters it is only copper which is sent in such large quantities as 200 talents[3] and 500 talents[4] and that is referred to in some nine passages.[5] On one occasion the Cypriot king even apologized about sending such small amounts of copper[6] and then promised to send the Egyptian king "all the copper that you desire."[7] An Egyptian text from the Temple of Ramses II at Luxor gives a list of mining regions, and here Cyprus appears as a place which produced copper "in millions, in endless masses, in hundreds and thousands."[8] A Hittite text which tells of a sea battle between Cyprus and the Hittites also lists copper as one of the objects which Cyprus must give.[9] It is interesting that copper appears in no other Hittite tribute list. A second Hittite text, called the 'Ritual on the Occasion of Founding a New House,' includes in its special list copper and bronze from Cyprus.[10] Although they come from the seventeenth century, it should be mentioned that Dossin has recorded the appearance of Cypriot copper in four texts dealing with foundries in the palace at Mari.[11] From these texts it is evident that Cyprus had an abundance of copper and that it was exporting it in large amounts to the countries around it.

The question must be asked: was Cyprus capable of producing such large amounts of copper? From Late Bronze Age Cyprus archaeologists have discovered slag heaps of copper at eleven sites,[12] molds for copper from two sites,[13] and copper workshops with tools and fragments of furnaces and crucibles from four sites.[14] There is even evidence of Late Bronze Age mining at the site of Apliki.[15] This is adequate proof that the copper mines of Cyprus were being worked and that the material from these mines was being processed in many Cypriot cities.[16] Although no absolute proof of Cypriot copper in foreign countries is available, evidence presented here clearly shows that Cyprus was capable of providing the copper that is referred to in the ancient texts.[17]

Another important Cypriot export was wood. According to the Amarna Letters, the king of Cyprus sends to the Egyptian king wood,[18] and the Cypriot official sends to Shumitti and the Egyptian official two ship loads of wood and a piece of boxwood.[19] Along with this wood,[20] the Cypriot king also promises to make ships in great number for the Egyptian ruler.[21] These passages indicate that Cyprus was not only exporting timber, but was likewise manufacturing and exporting ships. The abundant timber on the mountains of Western Cyprus could certainly have provided an adequate supply of wood for these tasks.[22]

Oil is a promised item in the Amarna Letters,[23] while Papyrus Anastasi mentions 'Fidi liquid', 'Inbu liquid',[24] and 'oil of Aoupa(?)'[25] as Egyptian imports from Cyprus. Seemingly oils and liquids were important Cypriot exports, but evidence for this exists only in the innumerable Cypriot vessels of potential oil-bearing shapes which have been found in Egypt, Syria, and Palestine.

Other products indicated as Cypriot exports include elephants' tusks,[26] horses,[27] linens,[28] cyperus seed,[29] gold,[30] and the unclear element *GA-YA-TUM*.[31]

Although archaeological evidence is lacking to prove most of these textual assertions, material is available to show that Cyprus was exporting vast amounts of pottery during the Late Bronze Age. This pottery included Base-ring I and II wares, White Slip I and II wares, White Shaved wares, Early Monochrome wares and Bucchero wares.[32] In Egypt varying quantities of Cypriot pottery have been found at some fifty sites scattered all over Egypt.[33] These pottery exports were at their peak in LB I, dropped considerably in LB II and stopped altogether in LB III. It is interesting that Cypriot vessels and sherds usually appear in tombs and are frequently represented by only one Cypriot vessel to a tomb.

Many Cypriot vessels were shipped to Palestine during the LB I and LB II periods, but they ceased to appear at the end of LB II. They have been found at about twenty-five sites and appear in greater numbers there than in any area outside Cyprus.[34] The results of these excavations demonstrate that much more Cypriot pottery was imported in LB II than in LB I, but that the markets were almost the same in both periods. As was the case in Egypt, many of these vessels were found in tombs, but in Palestine there were also extensive quantities in the towns themselves.

In Syria Cypriot pottery was found in large quantities at Ras Shamra and its port Minet el-Beida and in much smaller quantities at about fifteen sites scattered in western Syria.[35] Although Sjöqvist thought that there was a Cypriot colony in Ras Shamra,[36] and other scholars have suggested that most of the Cypro-Egyptian trade was carried on via Ras Shamra, it seems rather strange that much less Cypriot pottery has been found in Syria than in Egypt and Palestine.[37] In fact, no sizeable quantities of Cypriot pottery have been found anywhere in Syria except at Ras Shamra and its port city Minet el-Beida, and even there the numbers were not as great as in several sites in Palestine. It is also interesting that there is no increase in the amount of Cypriot material in Syria from LB I to LB II. Based on this evidence, the writer finds it very difficult to conceive of a Cypriot colony in Ras Shamra during LB II.

As for Cypriot pottery in Anatolia, Sjöqvist notes that not one single Cypriot sherd has been discovered from LB I contexts, but during LB II stray sherds have been uncovered at Tarsus, Troy, Boghazkoi, Bulghar Maden,[38] Kabarsa, and Mersin.[39] During LB III only one Cypriot jug of Bucchero ware has so far been found.[40]

On the Aegean isles and the Greek Mainland Cypriot pottery exportation was equally limited. One Base-ring I bull vase has been found at Ialysos in Rhodes, one bowl of White Slip I on Thera, six sherds of White Slip I at Phylakopi on Melos, and three vases of what seem to be Cypriot sub-Mycenaean ware at Athens.[41] On Crete more Cypriot pottery has been found than in any other western locality, but it is limited to a White Slip bowl from Khania, two sherds of Cypriot 'White-Painted Pendant Line Style' from Zakro, one White Slip I sherd from Knossos, and two White Slip II sherds from Katsamba.[42]

Having discussed the vast amount of Cypriot pottery which was exported, especially to Syria, Palestine and Egypt, one should be reminded that the Base-ring I and II vessels, the types that appear most often on foreign soil, are not extremely well-made and that their decorations are far from beautiful, so it seems rather strange that these vessels would be valued for their own sake. It is more likely that value came from their contents.[43] Sjöqvist has suggested that these contents were scents or ointments,[44] but Merrillees believes that it was opium.[45] Based on the fact that oil and other liquids were known exports from Cyprus to Egypt, the writer is more inclined to support Sjöqvist's theory. It is therefore quite probable that one of the prime Cypriot exports was some type of oil or ointment which was shipped in Cypriot vessels.

When one moves from raw materials and pottery and tries to pinpoint other Cypriot exports, he runs into the complex problem of distinguishing foreign imports from local copies. There are really only a few suggested exports, and among these are some unusual faience goblets modeled in the shape of a woman's head or face which come from Syria-Palestine. Dussaud has suggested that these were made in

Cyprus.[46] Porada states that several elaborately engraved Cypriot seals were found in Syria and Ashur,[47] and Kenna suggests that several Cypriot cylinder seals have been found in Crete.[48] Åström thinks that unusual, terra-cotta, female figurines from Syria-Palestine are exports from Cyprus,[49] as well as some stone tripods which have been found in Ialysos and Attica.[50] In considering this evidence, one arrives at the conclusion that Late Bronze Age Cyprus was exporting few manufactured goods other than pottery.

When attention is turned to Cypriot imports, one discovers that there are only a few examples of textual evidence in the Amarna Letters. In these texts the Cypriot king and official request from Egypt such luxury items as fancy furniture,[51] a chariot,[52] horses,[53] linens,[54] ebony,[55] oil,[56] silver,[57] an ox,[58] and ivory.[59] To find archaeological evidence in Cyprus for the importation of such luxury goods is of course almost impossible, but if one examines the jewelry, ivory and stone products, glass, faience, glyptics, and ostrich eggs found in Cyprus, some idea can be obtained of the luxury in its Late Bronze Age. Perhaps it would be worthwhile to mention the luxury items which have been designated as Cypriot imports.

Suggested jewelry imports from Egypt are an engraved ring with the cartouche of Thotmose III,[60] a massive silver finger ring with a scaraboid bezel on which was the name of Amenhotep IV,[61] a plain finger ring with oval, engraved bezel,[62] bronze decorated rings,[63] the Enkomi pectoral,[64] and some scarab-shaped and frog-shaped beads.[65] Jewelry of a Syro-Palestinian origin is less in number and includes a silver earring with a pendant soldered to it[66] and the gold bands which appear so frequently in Cypriot tombs.[67] Jewelry of Aegean origin also appears in small quantities and encompasses such things as amber beads,[68] bronze fibulae, golden fibulae, and vase-headed pins.[69]

It should be mentioned that much of the above jewelry is gold and that much more of the Cypriot jewelry of supposedly local manufacture is also of gold. Where did Cyprus obtain all this gold? Even though a Hittite text includes gold as one of the tributes from Cyprus, there are actually only a few poor gold deposits known on this island.[70] Therefore, the great quantities of gold jewelry which have been found in Cypriot tombs, mainly of the LB II period, had either to be imported as manufactured items or as raw material to be worked by Cypriot craftsmen. Since extensive Egyptian influence appears on gold jewelry of the LB II period, since Egypt was decidedly the main supplier of gold in the Near East at this time,[71] and since Cyprus was carrying on extensive trade with Egypt at this time, the writer would suggest that the raw gold, if not much of the gold jewelry itself, was imported from Egypt.

Other luxurious metal goods of designated foreign origins are a bronze lion from Syria-Palestine;[72] and an inlaid silver bowl,[73] a beak-spouted brass oinochoe, a bronze-decorated amphora,[74] a pair of bronze hydrias[75] and tripods with four-sided stands, all from the Aegean.[76]

Another luxury item was ivory. Although many ivory objects have been found in Cyprus during the Late Bronze Age, few can be given exact origins. In fact only one object, an Egyptian oval plaque carved in high relief, has really been specified.[77] On other ivory objects there appears Egyptian, Syro-Palestinian, and Aegean influence, but there is no clear proof as to their origin. A greater percent of these show Syro-Palestinian influence, and some were probably imported from there. Since there were elephants in Syria until very late times, it has been suggested that much of the ivory used in Cyprus came from Syria.[78]

Glass was also an item which appears in Cyprus and which is often specified as an Egyptian import. Examples include pomegranate-shaped jars, glass jugs of base-ring shape, three two-handled flasks with conical bottom, a footed flask with festoon decoration, a vase with no handle and a flat bottom, and a vase with a single handle.[79] Although no glass objects from Anatolia or the Aegean appear in Cyprus, a glass mold-pressed Astarte figurine seems to be of Syro-Palestinian origin.[80] As this evidence shows, most of the glass imports in Cyprus came from Egypt, so it is not surprising that Flossing would affirm that all glass found in Cyprus was exported from Egypt.[81]

Egyptian influence is also strong in faience objects, and two slender faience jars are actually thought to be imports from Egypt.[82]

Some very interesting Cypriot imports in the form of eleven Mycenaean terra-cotta figurines have been found in LB III sites.[83] Products of the glyptic industry are also frequent imports into Cyprus. There are many scarabs that appear to be of authentic Rameside origin[84] and numerous others which bear the name of Egyptian rulers of earlier periods.[85] It is quite possible that these may have been imported from Egypt. There are also many scarabs that are certainly non-Egyptian but at the same time show great Egyptian influence.[86] Concerning cylinder seals, one discovers an overwhelming Syro-Palestinian influence and at times even imports from Syria-Palestine. Imports are usually represented by seals of earlier periods, but they generally show up in LB levels. Porada notes that there are four examples of the LB Syrian seals, some elaborate Mitannian seals, an even larger number of Common Style Mitannian Seals and five examples of Old Babylonian seals.[87] It should be mentioned that, although no absolute importation of Aegean glyptics can be demonstrated, it is quite clear that Cypriot cylinder seals and especially stamp seals of conoid shape were strongly influenced by Aegean traditions.[88] One Hittite seal was also found in Cyprus.[89]

Another luxury import was alabaster. Although there is alabaster of fair quality in the lowland parts of Cyprus and in most Mediterranean coastlands, the fine quality alabaster came only from Egypt. It is therefore not surprising that many alabaster jars, jugs and amphorae from Cyprus have been classified as Egyptian products.[90]

Ostrich eggs which have been found in Enkomi and Kition are also luxury items that probably came from Egypt.[91]

Moving from the luxury items into something which might be considered more practical—metal tools and weapons—one finds little available evidence. As for tools, Catling notes that many of the Aegean tool groups are entirely missing in Cyprus and that actually there is a curious dearth of all tools before 1200 B.C. After 1200 B.C. the tools take on an Aegean flavor and appear in greater number.[92] Weapons also appear in small numbers, and almost all of these are from a LB III date and are of Aegean origin. These imports include eight examples of the 'Naue II' type sword,[93] a socketed spear,[94] two sets of greaves, the Kaloriziki shield,[95] and numerous double axes.[96] Exceptions to this are iron swords from LB III Idalion and Kaloriziki which are possibly from Syria-Palestine.[97] In connection with these metal objects, it should be mentioned that Aegean influence and imports are strangely lacking in LB I and LB II, and it is only during LB III that this begins to change. Influence and imports from other areas are altogether lacking. Even in this later period, Aegean influence and imports are not extremely great, and it is likely that they are the result of Aegean migrations to Cyprus rather than through trade.

In contrast to other foreign objects, Cyprus imported pottery in great quantities. Strangely enough, no known Egyptian pottery[98] and only one sherd of Anatolian pottery[99] has been found in Cyprus during the Late Bronze Age. Syro-Palestinian pottery, however, was imported into Cyprus in sizeable amounts during LB I and very small amounts during LB II and LB III. Also much Aegean pottery appears during LB II and smaller amounts during LB I and LB III.

Concerning Syro-Palestinian ceramics, examples of Red Lustrous ware,[100] Bichrome ware,[101] Black Lustrous ware,[102] Black Punctured ware,[103] Plain White Wheel-made ware[104] and 'Syrian jars'[105] appear in Cyprus during LB I. Most of these vessels come from the eastern part of the island and cease to appear after LB I. Even though the Syro-Palestinian imports are very meager during the two latter parts of the Late Bronze Age, they do occur. Benson points to two craters from LB III Kourion,[106] and Wace identifies several Syrian jars and a crater from LB II Verghias being of Syro-Palestinian origin.[107]

When one looks at the Aegean pottery imports in Cyprus, he discovers that a sizeable number of Minoan vessels and sherds have been found in some ten LB II and LB III sites on the island. Whereas in most parts of the Near East Minoan pottery ceased to be imported after 1400 B.C., in Cyprus this pottery appears in its greatest quantities after this time. Thus it seems that Cyprus was the main recipient of what Minoan eastward trade there was after the fall of Knossos.[108] Since most of these vessels possessed a style and form which would make importation unlikely for their own sake, Catling and Karageorghis have suggested that they were imported for some type of liquid which came from Crete.[109]

In approaching the Mycenaean pottery found in Cyprus, the problem becomes more complex, because the amount of Mycenaean pottery there is so great and the types are more varied. Before LB II Mycenaean imports are represented by only a few scattered vases or sherds at about six sites, and this seems to point to rather meager connections between Cyprus and the Mycenaean world.[110] During LB II, however, Mycenaean III A:2 and Mycenaean III B pottery appear in over sixty sites scattered all over Cyprus, with some of these sites containing only a few sherds and others having fifty or more vessels.[111] Because of this vast amount of pottery, it is probable that there was extensive local manufacturing of these wares either by Mycenaean potters who moved to Cyprus or by natives who had learned the Mycenaean art.[112] At the end of LB II, there was an abrupt end to the Mycenaean III B pottery and the sudden introduction of small amounts of Mycenaean III C:1 pottery of the 'Close Style.' After a period of years in which little Aegean pottery is in evidence, there was the appearance of Mycenaean III C:2 pottery of the 'Granary Style.' Because these two types of pottery are so closely connected with the Achaean migration into Cyprus, they probably should not be considered as imports, since they were brought with the colonist and were then locally made.[113]

Having considered this evidence, what conclusions can be drawn? Relating to Cypro-Egyptian trade, the writer has concluded that there was rather close trade contact between Cyprus and Egypt during the Late Bronze Age, particularly LB II. This is manifested by some direct imports of jewelry, glass, faience, alabaster, scarabs and gold; by extensive Egyptian influence on all local Cypriot arts and crafts; and by the exportation of Cypriot copper, wood, ships, oils and pottery. It should be noted that Åström thinks that there are not many Cypriot objects of Egyptian origin and that even most of the original Egyptian objects spread to Palestine and came from there to Cyprus, sometimes in a modified form.[114] If, however, one considers the close Cypro-Egyptian contact depicted in the Amarna letters, the vast amount of Cypriot pottery in Egypt and the Egyptian objects imported into Cyprus,[115] he must conclude that there was extensive direct trade between Cyprus and Egypt.

There was also extensive connection between Cyprus and Syria-Palestine as is indicated by the importation of pottery, seals and ivory into Cyprus and the exportation of pottery and probably copper and oils from Cyprus. Syro-Palestinian influence also appears on many local Cypriot arts and crafts. These contacts are particularly strong with Ras Shamra and Gaza, but they point to intense trade rather than colonization. Probably Gaza and Ras Shamra were the main ports where Cypriot boats landed, and it was from these ports that Cypriot materials were sent through the surrounding countryside. This close trade existed throughout LB I and LB II but came to an end at the beginning of LB III.

As for trade with Anatolia, the conclusions are very simple, since there is almost no material evidence of contact between Cyprus and

Anatolia during the Late Bronze Age. This lack of communication between these two areas is certainly very strange considering their close geographical locations. This may, however, be explained by the fact that all of the main cities, particularly those smelting metal, were on the southern part of Cyprus.

From the Aegean evidence it is clear that there was relatively little contact between Cyprus and the Aegean during LB I, since the only available proof is small amounts of pottery. In contrast the LB II period displays vast amounts of Mycenaean pottery and small quantities of Minoan pottery in Cyprus and points to extensive trade and local manufacture of these goods. It should be mentioned, however, that except for the pottery Mycenaean imports and influences are generally lacking. Cypriot exports to the Aegean during this period included small amounts of pottery and probably copper. This situation changed entirely in LB III when two new types of Mycenaean pottery appeared and along with them came a considerable amount of metalwork, jewelry, glyptics, ivory work and terra-cottas of Mycenaean origin or under Mycenaean influence. This points to colonization rather than just commercial relationships, and consequently many scholars have connected the legends of the Achaean migrations with this period.[116]

In summary, the LB I period saw Cyprus begin significant shipments of pottery to Egypt and Syria-Palestine. Conversely, sizeable amounts of Syro-Palestinian pottery appear in Cyprus, and some degree of Egyptian and Syro-Palestinian influence appears on Cypriot arts and crafts. During the last part of this period, small amounts of Mycenaean pottery begin appearing in Cyprus, and a few Cypriot vessels appear in the Aegean. While experiencing great wealth and prosperity during LB II, Cyprus continued to export pottery to Egypt and Syria, increased its exports to Palestine and even sent small amounts to Anatolia. At this time there is also the appearance of large amounts of Mycenaean pottery and lesser quantities of Minoan pottery in Cyprus. Some imports and influence from Egypt and Syria-Palestine continue on glyptics, ivory work, jewelry, glass and faience, and now there is the introduction of small amounts of Minoan and Mycenaean influence on these crafts. With the coming of LB III Cypriot pottery and luxury trade with Egypt and Syria-Palestine came to an end, and even the influence of these two areas on the material culture of Cyprus diminished. In contrast to this, Aegean objects and influence appear in Cyprus in their greatest extent and point to the arrival of settlers rather than to trade. All of these things indicate that Cyprus was not just an unimportant island, but rather a wealthy and prosperous nation which was an active participant in the commercial activities of the Late Bronze Age world.

NOTES

1. In this paper the Late Bronze Age will cover the periods from 1550 to 1075 B.C. This will generally be represented in the paper as LB. As for the breakdown during this period LB I will be from 1550-1400, LB II from 1400-1200, and LB III from 1200-1075.

2. See Y. Lynn Holmes, "The Location of Alashiya," *JAOS*, 91(1971): 426-429.

3. EA 33:16

4. EA 35:10

5. EA 33:16, 18; 34:18; 35:10; 36:5-7; 40:7, 13.

6. EA 35:12

7. EA 35:17

8. See W. Max Müller, *Egyptological Researches* (Washington: The Carnegie Institution, 1910), p. 19. It should also be noted that this text includes silver as a product of Cyprus. As Wainwright has observed, "The scribe who composed this text has shown himself a somewhat unsafe guide in his allocation of the various materials mentioned by him." See G. A. Wainwright, "Alashia-Alasa and Asy," *Klio*, 14(1914-15): 26. Thus this reference of silver from Alashiya may well be put into question, since the Amarna Letters show the Cypriot king asking Egypt for silver and since Cyprus has no good silver deposits.

9. KBo XII 38 i 5, 13, 15, 17, 19. This text deals with a sea battle between the Hittite king, Suppiluliuma II, and ships of Alashiya (Cyprus), and it tells how the two forces met three times with the result that the Alashiyan ships were defeated. The Hittite king then landed his troops, fought a vast number of Alashiyan troops on dry land, defeated them, and imposed a tribute on them. For discussions on this text, see H. Otten, "Neue Quellen zum Ausklang des Hethitischen Reiches," *MDOG*, 90(1963): 1-23; G. Steiner, "Neue Alasija-Texte," *Kadmos*, 1(1962): 130-138; and Hans G. Guterbock, "The Hittite Conquest of Cyprus Reconsidered," *JNES*, 26(1967): 73-81.

10. KBo IV 1 obv. i 39-40. The objects to be placed under the foundation stone with copper and bronze included gold from Pirundummeya, silver from Kuzza, lapis lazuli from Mt. Tagniyara, alabaster from Kanisha, quartz(?) from the earth, black meteorite iron from heaven. A complete translation of this text is given by Goetze in ANET, pp. 356-357.

11. G. Dossin, "Les Archives economiques du palais de Mari," *Syria*, 20(1939): 111.

12. These sites included Enkomi, Apliki, Hala Sultan Tekke, Nicosia, Kition, Athienau, Mathiati, Lythrandas, Arpera, Ayios Sozomenos and Lapithos. See Porphyrios Dikaios, "Excavations and Historical Background: Enkomi in Cyprus," *Journal of Historical Studies*, (1967): 41-49; Vassos Karageorghis, "Ten Years of Archaeology in Cyprus, 1953-1962," *AA*, (1963): 528; Kyriakos Nicolaou, "Archaeological News from Cyprus, 1968," *AJA*, 74(1970): 73.

13. H. W. Catling, *Cypriot Bronzework in the Mycenaean World* (Oxford: Clarendon Press, 1964), p. 21. These sites were Klavdhia and Enkomi.

14. These four sites are Enkomi, Apliki, Golgi and Kition. See Porphyrios Dikaios, "The Context of the Enkomi Tablets," *Kadmos*, 2(1963): 40; Claude F. A. Schaeffer, *Enkomi-Alasia: Nouvelles missions en Chypre 1946-1950* (Paris: Librairie C. Klincksieck, 1952), p. 412; A. H. S. Megaw, "Archaeology in Cyprus, 1958," *Archaeological Reports for 1958*, (1959), p. 27; Karageorghis, "Ten Years of Archaeology," p. 521; Kyriakos Nicolaou, "Archaeological News," p. 73.

15. Porphyrios Dikaios, *A Guide to the Cyprus Museum* (Nicosia: Chr. Nicolaou and Sons Ltd., 1961), pp. 117-118.

16. It should be noted that O. Davies tried to prove that there was no evidence for copper mining in Cyprus before the Classical period. See O. Davies, "The Copper Mines of Cyprus," *BSA*, 30(1928-30): 74 f. Davies did not argue with the evidence from the Classical period because the evidence is very clear from archaeological and textual material.

17. It should be mentioned that Dikaios has pointed to some copper which was found in Ras Shamra in 1934 and has stated that its analysis shows it to be from Cyprus. Catling, however, has presented evidence to disprove the validity of this analysis. See Dikaios, *Guide to the Cyprus Museum*, p. 117 and Catling, *Cypriot Bronzework*, pp. 20-25. There is also the possibility that some of the copper ingots scattered around the Mediterranean came from Cyprus. The origin of these ingots is a rather difficult thing to figure out, but Catling has suggested that they probably developed in Crete as an administrative measure in the palaces and were then adapted by the Mycenaeans who brought them to Cyprus when they came there in LB III. Catling's Type III ingot is not found anywhere except in Cyprus and its date was after 1200. It is quite possible that these ingots may have been made in and exported from Cyprus. See Catling, *Cypriot Bronzework*, pp. 266-272 and George F. Bass, *Cape Gelidonya: A Bronze Age Shipwreck* (Philadelphia: The American Philosophical Society, 1967), pp. 52-83.

18. EA 35:28

19. EA 40:6-8, 12-15

20. EA 36:12-13

21. EA 36:16

22. It should also be mentioned that the Hittite text describing the sea battle between the Hittite king and the Cypriot king points out that Cyprus had a navy. See note 9.

23. EA 34:51

24. Papyrus Anastasi IV, Pl. 15 lines 2-4. These are mentioned in connection with liquids from Hatti, Babylon, Amurru, Naharayim and an unidentified place(thys). For the text and discussion of this passage, see G. Maspero, "Le Pays d'Alasia," *Recuil de travaux relatifs*, 10(1888): 209.

25. Papyrus Anastasi IV Pl. 17 lines 7-9.

26. EA 40:7, 12-15. It is interesting that although ivory is sent to Shumitti and the Egyptian official, in the same letter ivory is requested from the Egyptian official. See EA 40:11.

27. Papyrus Anastasi IV, Pl. 17 lines 7-9. In EA 34:22 and 37:9 the Cypriot king requests that horses be sent to him.

28. I BoT I 31:4. Goetze thinks this is a tribute list of an unnamed Hittite queen. The 37 linens are in a list along with objects from Amurru, Hurri, Ankuwa and Pashura. For a complete discussion of this text, see A. Goetze, "The Inventory I BoT I 31," *JCS*, 10(1965): 32-38.

29. Ventris and Chadwicks record Text 102 as: *tu-wi-no ku-pi-ri-jo ku-pa-ro*, "120 l. of cyperus seed from Cyprus." Michael Ventris and John Chadwick, *Documents in Mycenaean Greek* (Cambridge: University Press, 1959), p. 223.

30. KBo XII 38 i 5, 13, 15, 17, 19. Cyprus has only a few poor gold deposits so it is likely that this gold was imported into Cyprus and then shipped to Hatti as a tribute.

31. KBo XII 38 i 13, 15, 17, 19. There is disagreement about this element as to whether it means a grain or whether it is the measure for an unknown precious element. See A. Goetze, "A Critical Review of Keilschriftexte aus Boghazkoi IX and X and Keilschrifturkunden aus Boghazkoi VIII," *JCS*, 18(1964), p. 90.

32. For the characteristics of all these wares see Erik Sjöqvist, *Problems of the Late Cypriote Bronze Age* (Stockholm: The Swedish Cyprus Expedition, 1940), pp. 34-43.

33. These sites include Meydum, Riqqeh, Saft el-Henneh, Suwa, Tell el-Yehudïyeh, Sedmant, Saqqara, Abusir el-Melek, Mazghuneh, Haragh, Kahun, Gurob, Ehnasya, el-Arabah, Nabesha, Balabish, Qau, Zawiet el-Maietin, Abydos, Zawiet el-Aryan, Refeh, Tell el-Amarna, el-Arish, Ali Mara, Tell el-Rataba, Heliopolis, El-Giza, Abusir, Beni Hasan, Deir Tasa, el-Sawama, el-Lahun, Hu, Dendra, Deir el-Ballas, Thebes, Esna, el-Dakka, Aniba, Semna, el-Shallal, Quban and Buhen. Complete discussions on these sites giving exactly which and how many pieces of pottery were there can be obtained from Sjöqvist's *Late Cypriote Bronze Age*, pp. 156-161, 174-175, and 179-180; R. S. Merrillees, *The Cypriote Bronze Age Pottery Found in Egypt* (Lund: Studies in Mediterranean Archaeology, 1968); and Y. Lynn Holmes, *The Foreign Relations of Cyprus during the Late Bronze Age* (Unpublished Ph. D. dissertation, Brandeis University, 1969). University Microfilms: Ann Arbor, Michigan, 1969, pp. 7-12.

34. These sites include Megiddo, Beisan, Tell Abu Hawam, Gezer, Ain Shems, Tell el-Hesy, Jericho, Tell beit Mirsim, Tell Zakariya, Beth-Pelet, Tell ed-Duweir, Tell Jemmeh, Askalon, Tell Ta'annek, Tell el-Harbaj, Tell Amr, the 'Government's House Tomb' in Jerusalem, Gibeon, Shechem, Ashdod, Amman, Hazor and Gaza.

Complete discussions on these sites giving exactly which and how many pieces of pottery were there can be obtained from Sjöqvist's *Late Cypriote Bronze Age*, pp. 152-156, 160-161, 169-174 and 176-180; and Holmes's *Foreign Relations*, pp. 34-47.

35. These sites include Atchana (Alalakh), Qatna, Majdalouna, Khirbet Selim, Karayieh, Mamireh, Khan Sherkun, Beqa'a, Aktanit, Tell Simiriyan, Sabouni, Deir el-Ades, Qalaat, Tell Judeidah and Chatal Huyuk. Complete discussions on these sites giving exactly what and how many pieces of pottery were there can be obtained from Sjöqvist's *Late Cypriote Bronze Age*, pp. 151-152, 160-161, 168-169, 175-176 and 180; and Holmes's *Foreign Relations*, pp. 34-47.

36. Sjöqvist, *Late Cypriote Bronze Age*, p. 183.

37. Lena Åström, *Studies on the Arts and Crafts of the Late Cypriote Bronze Age* (Lund: Berlingska Boktryckeriet, 1967), p. 150.

38. Sjöqvist, *Late Cypriote Bronze Age*, pp. 175, 180, 183 and Dikaios, *A Guide to the Cyprus Museum*, p. 33.

39. M. V. Seton-Williams, "Cilician Survey," *AS*, 4(1954): 133 and John Garstang, et. al., "Explorations in Cilicia; The Neilson Expedition: Fifth Interim Report Excavations at Mersin: 1938-39," *AAA*, 26(1940): 131.

40. Sjöqvist, *Late Cypriote Bronze Age*, p. 263. This was found in connection with Mycenaean pottery of the 'Granary Style'.

41. Ibid., p. 160; Einar Gjerstad, *Studies on Prehistoric Cyprus* (Uppsala: A. B. **Lundeqvistska** Bokhandeln, 1926), p. 324; R. W. Hutchinson, "Three Vases in Cambridge: An Attribution to Cyprus," *AAA*, 21(1934): 28.

42. M. Popham, "Two Cypriote Sherds from Crete," *BSA*, 58(1963): 89-91; A. H. L. Megaw, "Archaeology in Greece, 1965-66," *Archaeological Reports for 1965-66*, (1966), p. 24; E. H. Hall, *Excavations in Eastern Crete: Vrokastro* (Philadelphia: University of Pennsylvania Museum, 1914), p. 183.

43. Additional evidence for this theory has been given by Merrillees who points out that in Egypt one can distinguish a gradual development from Base-ring I to Base-ring II. Since the same shape was continually used despite the transformation of its external appearance, Merrillees concludes that it was the contents which remained unaltered and desirable on the Egyptian market. See R. S. Merrillees, "Opium Trade in the Bronze Age Levant," *Antiquity*, 36(1962): 288.

44. Sjöqvist, *Late Cypriote Bronze Age*, p. 79.

45. Merrillees states that the form of the Base-ring I and II vessels in Egypt is very much like the head of an opium poppy whose dried out shell could easily have been used in its own right as a container. With this theory as his basis, he goes on to mention that opium was introduced into Egypt during the time that Base-ring I was being imported and that the decline of Base-ring II corresponds with the emergence of faience copies of poppy heads in Egypt. Merrillees hints that the opium was grown in Cyprus, but he never really says so nor does he offer any other origin for the opium. He likewise never produces evidence that opium was found in these vessels. See Merrillees, "Opium Trade," p. 288.

46. These faces were applied in relief to the side of a goblet. They have been found at Ur, Ashur, Mari, Ras Shamra and Tell Abu Hawam, as well as thirteenth century Enkomi in Cyprus. See Karageorghis, "Ten Years of Archaeology," p. 67; Åström, *Arts and Crafts*, pp. 122-123; H. R. Hall, "Minoan Fayence in Mesopotamia," *JHS*, 48(1928): 67-73.

47. Edith Porada, "The Cylinder Seals of the Late Cypriote Bronze Age," *AJA*, 52(1948): 182.

48. There is a broken cylinder seal at Knossos from about 1375, which Kenna thinks to be a Cypriot seal of the fine class. This seal shows the typical Cypriot motifs of a goddess with a flounced skirt holding a doe upside down, a bullman, and a script sign engraved in the right hand corner after the seal had been engraved. Kenna says that a Cypriot cylinder also comes fromMallia in Crete and two others from unknown sites in Crete. See V. E. G. Kenna, "Crete and the Use of the Cylinder Seal," *AJA*, 82(1968): 330-334.

49. These figurines possessed flat heads, small ears and attached pellets as eyes. Very few examples of this type have been found outside Cyprus, so Åström has concluded that the examples (one each) found at Tell Abu Hawam V, Tell el-Hesy and Ta'annek are Cypriot exports. Myres understood the matter somewhat differently by suggesting that the objects were actually Cypriot imports from Syria. See Åström, *Arts and Crafts*, p. 112; John Myres, *Handbook of the Cesnola Collection of Antiquities from Cyprus* (New York, 1914), p. 335.

50. Åström, *Arts and Crafts*, p. 128.

51. EA 34:20, 28

52. EA 34:21

53. EA 34:22; 37:9

54. EA 34:22-23, 25, 47

55. EA 34:21

56. EA 34:24; 35:24-25

57. EA 35:19-20, 43-44; 37:18

58. EA 35:24

59. EA 40:11. There are also five talents of something merely written as 5 *biltu*. It is very interesting to note that while horses, oils, linens and ivory were being sent from Cyprus to other countries, the Cypriots also requested that these things be sent to them. Perhaps these things were thought to be royal gifts which should be exchanged between all courts.

60. This comes from the sanctuary at Dhima. See Einar Gjerstad, et al., *The Swedish Cyprus Expedition: Finds and Results of the Excavations in Cyprus 1927-1931* (Stockholm: The Swedish Cyprus Expedition, 1934), I, p. 360 (hereafter *SCE*).

61. On the bezel is engraved in hieroglyphs, "Nefer-Kheperu-Ra (Amenhotep IV), beloved of Ra and Ptah, lord of vigor and truth." See H. R. Hall, *Catalogue of Egyptian Scarabs, etc. in the British Museum* (London: The British Museum, 1913), I, p. 276.

62. There are several of these in Cyprus and Åström suggests that they are Eighteenth Dynasty Egyptian. See Åström, *Arts and Crafts*, p. 93.

63. All of these are from Enkomi. Catling, *Cypriot Bronzework*, p. 235.

64. Åström, *Arts and Crafts*, p. 107.

65. Ibid., pp. 134-135.

66. Ibid., p. 94. There are five examples of this which come from Gaza during the Eighteenth and Nineteenth Dynasty.

67. Ibid., p. 108. Examples of this appear in Beth-Shan, Megiddo, Gaza Hama and Beth-Pelet.

68. Ibid., p. 144.

69. Catling, *Cypriot Bronzework*, p. 246.

70. This was related to the writer in a personal conversation by Vassos Karageorghis.

71. For information about this, see the Amarna Letters from the kings of Assyria, Mitanni and Babylon in which they ask for much gold. See also Wolfgang Helck, *Die Beziehungen Ägyptens zu Vorderasien im 3. und 2. Jahrtausend v. Chr.* (Wiesbaden: Otto Harrassowitz, 1962) and Vassos Karageorghis, *The Ancient Civilization of Cyprus* (New York: Cowles Educational Corporation, 1969), p. 145.

72. Catling, *Cypriot Bronzework*, p. 320.

73. This comes from a LB I tomb at Enkomi and closely resembles one found in a Mycenaean tomb at Dendra in the Greek Argolid. Åström suggests that the same artist made both bowls on the mainland and exported the more elaborate one to Cyprus. See Åström, *Arts and Crafts*, pp. 94-95.

74. Catling, *Cypriot Bronzework*, pp. 151 and 161.

75. One shows at the base of each handle three bull heads facing, with each contained in a looped oval-like handle pair. Above are three ewers and around the rim is a continuous circle of bulls at full gallop, being pursued by lions. A second one has a marine design at the base of each handle, and on the upper part of the handles appear four confronted pairs of Minoan Genii with their forelegs raised in adoration. Though both examples are very Minoan, Kantor points out that many similar things appear on the Greek mainland and assumes that the Cypriot examples come from there. See Helene J. Kantor, *The Aegean and the Orient in the Second Millenium B.C.* (Bloomington, Indiana: The Archaeological Institute of America, 1947), p. 94 and A. J. Evans, *The Palace of Minos* (New York: Biblo and Tannen, 1964), I, pp. 652-653. In connection with these metal vessels, it is interesting that virtually no vessels of bronze appear in Cyprus before the mid-thirteenth century, but only with the Aegean settlements come bronze vessels. See Catling, *Cypriot Bronzework*, p. 188.

76. It should be noted that these appear very late and seem to have been brought in by Achaean immigrants. See ibid.

77. This plaque, which comes from Lapithos, displays a Negro sleeping with his head resting on one arm, having his hair arranged in the Egyptian fashion and

wearing a long loincloth fastened with a belt. See Myres, *Handbook of the Cesnola Collection*, p. 517.

78. See R. D. Barnett, "Phoenician and Syrian Ivory Carving," *PEQ*, 71(1939): 1 ff and Åström, *Arts and Crafts*, pp. 136-143.

79. Åström, *Arts and Crafts*, p. 125.

80. Ibid., p. 124.

81. Paul Flossing, *Glass Vessels before Glass Blowing* (Copenhagen, 1940), p. 30. Dan Barag agrees that most Cypriot glass was of Egyptian derivation with slight local variation. He also concludes that all glass vessels found in Syria-Palestine in the Late Bronze Age are of Egyptian character and that there was no independent Syro-Palestinian production of core formed glass vessels. See Dan Barag, "Mesopotamian Glass Vessels of the Second Millennium B. C.," *Journal of Glass Studies*, 4(1962): 27.

82. Åström, *Arts and Crafts*, p. 121.

83. These included a female on a bull, two chariots and horses, a bull, three bulls with riders, a female figure of Ψ type, a figure of a bearded man with breasts, and two female figures of Φ type. See K. Nikolaou, "Mycenaean Terracotta Figurines in the Cypriote Museum," *OA*, 5(1965): 57.

84. The Swedish Cyprus Expedition at Ayia Irini alone discovered fifteen Rameside examples with the same representation on their base—a king in an upright or kneeling position with gods or goddesses in front of him. Thirteen of these are glazed, of white paste, and are exactly the same size. It is quite possible that these are a closed group of scarabs originating from the same workshop tradition and possibly of pure Rameside origin. Several Rameside scarabs also come from Tomb 7 at Amathus and Tomb 24 at Enkomi. See *SCE*, II, pp. 825 and 847 and Hall, *Catalogue of Egyptian Scarabs*, p. 235.

85. These names include Thutmose III, Amenhotep III, Queen Tiy (wife of Amenhotep III). See *SCE* II, pp. 626 and 845 and Hall, *Egyptian Scarabs*, pp. 195 and 274.

86. Gjerstad, *SCE*, II, pp. 848 and 850 and Arne Furumark, "A Scarab from Cyprus," *Op. Ath.*, 1(1953): 55.

87. Porada, "Cylinder Seals," pp. 180-181.

88. It is interesting that the stamp seal of conoid shape is purely Near Eastern but that the examples from Cyprus beginning before LB II C contained no discernible Near Eastern motifs. Strangely enough it is the Aegean influence, mainly from Crete, which exercised the main influence on the Cypriot stamp seals. Vassos Karageorghis, "Un Cylinder de Chypre," *Syria*, 36(1959): 113-115; V. E. G. Kenna, "Quelques aspects de la glyptique Chypriote," *Syria*, 44(1967): 111-117; V. E. G. Kenna, "Crete and the Use of the Cylinder Seal," *AJA*, 82(1968): 331; J. L. Benson, "Aegean and Near Eastern Seal Impressions from Cyprus," *The Aegean and the Near East: Studies Presented to Hetty Goldman* (New York: 1956), pp. 65-71; and V. E G. Kenna, "The Seal Use of Cyprus in the Bronze Age, III," *BCH*, 92(1968): 143-153.

89. This seal was found in Tamassos. It is gold with a semi-ovoid head and it has Hittite hieroglyphic characters within a decorative border of trefoil blossoms and triangles. This again is within an outer border of similar elements with the addition of daisy-rosettes and conventional trees. Although this seal comes from an unknown context, it appears likely that it should be dated between the fourteenth and thirteenth centuries. See D. G. Hogarth, *Hittite Seals: With Particular Reference to the Ashmolean Collection* (Oxford: Clarendon Press, 1920), p. 37 and Oliver Masson, "Kypriaka I. Recherches sur les antiquites de Tamassos," *BCH*, 87(1964): 204

90. Myres, *Handbook of the Cesnola Collection*, p. 274; Åström, *Arts and Crafts*, p. 144; and Karageorghis, *The Ancient Civilization of Cyprus*, p. 145.

91. It is known that such eggs were used as vases at Abydos in the Eleventh and Twelfth Dynasty graves and in shaft graves in Mycenae. See Åström, *Arts and Crafts*, p. 144; and Karageorghis, *The Ancient Civilization of Cyprus*, p. 145.

92. Catling, *Cypriot Bronzework*, p. 108. It should also be mentioned that Catling also thinks a leatherworking knife is of Egyptian origin. See p. 104.

93. This type sword apparently arose out of Europe and came into the Aegean just prior to 1250, and it is this type sword which is connected with the Achaeans as they moved into the East. In Cyprus these have been found at Enkomi, Idalion and Kaloriziki. It is characterized by a pommel with two wide-spread ears and no pommel spur, flanged handgrip, six to eight rivets in the haft, a hand-guard, a straight blade for most of its length tapering at the point and two blood channels. See H. W. Catling, "Bronze Cut and Thrust Swords in the Eastern Mediterranean," *PPS*, 22(1956): 102–124; H. W. Catling, "A New Bronze Sword from Cyprus," *Antiquity*, 35(1961): 115–122; Vincent Desborough, *The Last Mycenaeans and Their Successors: An Archaeological Survey c. 1200–c. 1000 B.C.* (Oxford: Clarendon Press, 1964), p. 196.

94. With the exception of this socketed spear from Ayios Iakovos, there are no Aegean weapons recorded in Cyprus between the Middle Bronze Age and 1200. All of the weapons which are discussed here appear after 1200. See Catling, *Cypriot Bronzework*, pp. 124 and 135.

95. Both the greaves and the shield come from LC III. Ibid., pp. 111, 140–141 and 146.

96. It is interesting that more double axes have been recorded in Cyprus than in all the eastern fringes of the Mycenaean world. Ibid., p. 89.

97. This seems to be a combination of the Near Eastern type and the Aegean 'Naue II' type. See Karageorghis, "Ten Years of Archaeology," p. 86.

98. *SCE* IV, p. 315.

99. This sherd belongs to a rather rare class of Hittitite pottery of buff color with red, burnished slip and ornaments in relief. See Sjövist, *Late Cypriote Bronze Age*, p. 184.

100. This ware appears in a form called spindle bottles, and their most unusual aspect is that many of these vessels have incised pot marks on their bases. Although

the origin of this pottery is obscure, it appears in rather small numbers in the Levant, the Aegean, Anatolia, and Egypt, as well as LB I sites in Cyprus. Most scholars, however, think that they probably originated in Northern Syria. In Cyprus they appear at Enkomi, Curium, Ayia Paraskevi, Katydhata, Klaudia, Maroni, Pigadhes, Hala Sultan Tekke, Pyla, Arpera Chiflik, Ayioa Iakavos, Dhenia, Stephania, Ayios Theodorus, Ayios Thyrsos and Tamassos. See Sjöqvist, *Late Cypriote Bronze Age,* pp. 85 and 184; R. S. Merrillees, "Bronze Age Spindle Bottles from the Levant," *Op. Ath.*, 4(1963): 193; Jean du Plat Taylor, et al, *Myrtou-Pigadhes: A Late Bronze Age Sanctuary in Cyprus* (Oxford, 1957), pp. 114–116; Vassos Karageorghis, "A Late Cypriote Tomb at Tamassos," *RDAC*, 1965, p. 19.

101. This is rather numerous at Tell el-Ajjul and Megiddo and in Syria at Ras Shamra, and there are even a few examples in Lower Egypt. In Cyprus these vessels appear in greatest amounts at Milia and smaller quantities in Kazaphani, Ayios Iakovos, Pigadhes, Akhera, Nitovikla, Enkomi, Stephania, Kourion, Ayia Irini, and Maroni. See W. A. Heurtley, "A Palestinian Vase Painter of the Sixteenth Century B.C. ," *QDAP*, 8(1938): 33; Karageorghis, "Ten Years of Archaeology," p. 528; Vassos Karageorghis, "Chronique des fouilles et decouvertes archaeologiques à Chypre en 1963," *BCH*, 86 (1964); 336; Paul Åström, *Excavations at Kalopsidha and Ayios Iakovos in Cyprus* (Lund: Berlingska Boktryckeriet, 1966), pp. 141–144; Claire Epstein, *Palestinian Bichrome Ware* (Leiden: E. J. Brill, 1966), pp. 130–133; J. B. Hennessy, *Stephania: A Middle and Late Bronze Age Cemetery in Cyprus* (London: Bernard Quaritch Ltd., 1963), p. 46; Vassos Karageorghis, "Chronique des fouilles et decouvertes archaeologiques à Chypre en 1962," *BCH*, 87 (1963): 246.

102. Of this ware there was found one jug in Tomb 10 at Milia, three jugs in Tomb 1 at Milia, others at Enkomi and Ayios Iakovos, a juglet from Stephania and a juglet from Tamassos. See A. Westholm, "Some Late Cypriote Tombs at Milia," *QDAP*, 8 (1938): 8; Sjöqvist, *Late Cypriote Bronze Age*, p. 184; Hennessy, *Stephania*, p. 53; Karageorghis, "Tomb at Tamassos," p. 15.

103. There are four examples from Tomb 10 and one from Tomb 11 at Milia. See Westholm, "Tombs at Milia," p.8. This vessel is also called the Tell el-Jehudiyeh Juglet.

104. This ware, which likely comes from Syria, presents itself in LC I Tomb 1 at Akhera (a bowl), in a LC I level at Kalopsidha, at Dhenia in Tomb 1 (a piriform jug), at Curium, in Tomb y and 19 at Enkomi, in Tomb 14 at Ayios Iakovos (two examples) and at Milia in Tomb 12 (eight examples). See Vassos Karagoerghis, *Nouveaux Documents pour l'Etude de Bronze Recent à Chypre* (Paris: E. de Boccard, 1965), p. 110; Åström, *Excavations at Kalopsidha*, p. 140; Paul Åström and G. R. H. Wright, "Two Bronze Age Tombs at Dhenia in Cyprus," *Op. Ath.* 4 (1963): 270; J. L. Benson, "A Syrian Krater from Bamboula at Kourion," *PEQ*, 92 (1960): p. 68; Westholm, "Tombs at Milia," p. 8.

105. This vessel is rather rare in Cyprus and occurs in small numbers at Pigadhes, Enkomi and Pyla. See du Plat Taylor, *Myrtou-Pigadhes*, p. 35.

106. Benson, "A Syrian Crater," pp. 66–68.

107. The jars have two handles and knob-bases. These vessels Wace identifies with

the grey Minyan ware found at Tell Abu Hawam and close in form to a crater from Minet el-Beida. See A. H. S. Megaw, "Archaeology in Cyprus," *JHS*, 73 (1953), p. 135.

108. In Cyprus, Minoan pottery has been found at Maroni, Kourion, Hala Sultan Tekke, Enkomi, Moulos, Pyla, Episkopi, Dhenia, Kouklia, and Nitovikla. See E. J. Forsdyke, "A Late Mycenaean Vase from Cyprus," *Essays in Aegean Archaeology Presented to Sir Arthur Evans in Honour of His 75th Birthday* (Oxford: Clarendon Press, 1927), p. 27; E. J. Forsdyke, "Minoan Pottery from Cyprus," *JHS*, 31(1911): 111–113; Evans, *The Palace of Minos*, IV, pt. 1, pp. 368–370; Catling, "Minoika in Cyprus," *BSA*, 53 (1960); 109–127.

109. The large Minoan stirrup jars, which are represented by ten whole or fragmentary examples, form the largest single class of Minoan objects in Cyprus. With their particular type of coarse, gritty clay together with the character of their surface finish, they are set apart from anything else on the island, while their normal decoration of octopods clearly distinguishes them from the coarse stirrup jars found on mainland Greece and Rhodes. See Catling, "Minoica in Cyprus," p. 121.

110. These early Mycenaean vessels and sherds appear at Arpera, Enkomi, Hala Sultan Tekke, Maroni, Milia and Nicosia. See Frank H. Stubbings, *Mycenaean Pottery from the Levant* (Cambridge: University Press, 1951), pp. 26–29; Catling, *Cypriot Bronzework*, p. 36.

111. This pottery appears at Akaki, Akhera, Angastina, Aradhippou, Arodhes, Ayia Irini, Ayios Epiktitos, Ayios Sozomenos, Ayios Theodoros, Ayios Thyrsos, Deklia, Dhavlos, Dhenia, Dhikomo, Dhiorios, Dhrousha, Enkomi, Erimi, Evreti, Galinoparni, Hala Sultan Tekke, Kaimakli, Kalavasos, Kalopsidha, Karmi, Katydata, Kazaphani, Kition, Klavdia, Kormakiti, Kouklis, Kourion, Lapithos, Larnaka, Larnaka-tis-Lapithou, Leonarisso, Limassol, Loutros, Lythrondhanda, Mantissa, Marathovouno, Memko, Morphou, Milia, Moulos, Nicosia, Palai Kythro, Pendayia, Pera, Phlamoudhi, Pigadhes, Polemidhia, Politiko, Pomos, Pyla, Sinda, Stephania, and Tamassos, See H. W. Catling, "Patterns of Settlement in Bronze Age Cyprus," *Op. Ath.* 4 (1963): 129–169; Karageorghis, "Chronique des fouilles et decouvertes archeologiques à Chypre en 1959," *BCH* 84(1960): 248; Karageorghis, "Ten Years of Archaeology," pp. 529–537; Åström, *Excavations at Kalopsidha*, pp. 70, 122, and 144; Einar Gjerstad, *Studies on Prehistoric Cyprus*, pp. 8–11; Åström and Wright, "Bronze Age Tombs at Dhenia," pp. 228–229; Kantor, *The Aegean and the Orient in the Second Millenium B.C.*, p. 100; Vassos Karageorghis, "Fouilles de Kition, 1959," *BCH*, 84 (1960): 529, 538, and 554; J. L. Benson, "Coarse Ware Stirrup Jars of the Aegean," *Berytus*, 14 (1961): 41; du Plat Taylor, *Myrtou-Pigades*, pp. 46–47; Megaw, "Archaeology in Cyprus," p. 135; Arne Furumark, "The Excavations at Sinda: Some Historical Results," *Op. Ath.* 6(1965): 105; Hennessy, *Stephania*, pp. 2, 4–5, 7, 12, 33 and 44; Karageorghis, "A Late Cypriote Tomb at Tamassos," *RDAC*, (1965), pp. 20–26.

112. Such scholars as Karageorghis, Sjöqvist, Stubbings, Furumark, Schaeffer, Myres, and Casson favor the idea that Mycenaean pottery was made in Cyprus, but others like Daniel, Immerwahr, Benson, and Catling think that all of this pottery was imported from mainland Greece. See Sjöqvist, *Late Cypriote Bronze Age*, pp. 92–96;

Stubbings, *Mycenaean Pottery from the Levant,* p. 108; Arne Furumark, "The Settlement at Ialysos and Aegean History," *Opuscala Archaeologica,* 6(1950): 267; Karageorghis, *Nouveaux documents pour l'etude du bronze recent à Chypre,* pp. 222 and 230; Claude F. A. Schaeffer, *Missions en Chypre: 1932–1935* (Paris: Librairie Orientaliste Paul Geuthner, 1936), p. 17; Stanley Casson, *Ancient Cyprus: Its Art and Archaeology,* (London: Methuen and Co., Ltd., 1937), pp. 46 and 52; J. F. Daniel, *"Problems of the Late Cypriote Bronze Age*—A Review," *AJA,* 46(1942): 289–290; Sara Immerwahr, "Mycenaean Trade and Colonization," *Archaeology,* 13 (1960); 12; J. L. Benson, "Coarse Ware Stirrup Jars of the Aegean," *Berytus,* 14 (1961): 41; H. W. Catling and A. Millett, "Composition Patterns of Mycenaean Pictorial Pottery," *BSA,* 60(1965): 214; Karageorghis, *The Ancient Civilization of Cyprus,* pp. 61–62.

113. These types of pottery were found at Enkomi, Kition, Sinda, Maa, Kourion, Pigadhes, Apliki, and Nicosia. See Schaeffer, *Enkomi-Alasia: Nouvelles missions en Chypre,* pp. 239 ff. and 415 ff.; Dikaios, "Enkomi in Cyprus," pp. 45–49; Furumark, "The Excavations at Sinda: Some Historical Results," *Op. Ath.,* 6(1965): 99–116; Desborough, *The Last Mycenaeans and Their Successors,* p. 622: Jean du Plat Taylor, "Late Cypriote III: In the Light of Recent Excavations," *PEQ,* (1956), pp. 22–37; J. F. Daniel, "The Achaeans at Kourion," *Philadelphia University Museum Bulletin,* 8(1940): 2–14; Karageorghis, *The Ancient Civilization of Cyprus,* p. 63.

114. Åström, *Arts and Crafts,* p. 150; Sjöqvist, *Late Cypriote Bronze Age,* p. 183. It should also be mentioned that Vassos Karageorghis related to the writer in a personal conversation that the many Egyptian-looking objects in Cyprus probably did not come from Egypt but rather from Palestine.

115. Karageorghis has pointed out that the quantity of Egyptian goods in Tomb 9 at Kition suggests that there were relations with Egypt from the thirteenth if not the fourteenth century. He likewise suggests that the copper which was smelted in Kition was mainly shipped to Egypt. See Vassos Karageorghis, "Excavations at Kition 1963," *RDAC,* (1963): 9.

116. See Furumark, "The Excavations at Sinda: Some Historical Results," *OA,* 6(1965): 110–111 and Einar Gjerstad, "Initial Date of the Cypriote Iron Age," *Opuscula Archaeologica,* 3(1944): 75 and 78; and Einar Gjerstad, "The Colonization of Cyprus in Greek Legend," *Opuscula Archaeologica,* 3(1944): 107–123.

Cypriote White Slip Pottery
in Its Palestinian Stratigraphic Context

Barry M. Gittlen

The Late Bronze Age witnessed a major influx of Cypriote pottery into Palestine. Archaeologists soon recognized these vessels as one of the major characteristics of Palestine in the LB. Following the work of Petrie[1] and Albright,[2] Cypriote pottery became a cornerstone of the relative chronology of Palestine. At the same time, Gjerstad[3] and Sjöqvist[4] relied on Palestinian contexts for the dating of this pottery in Cyprus. Recently, Cypriote archaeologists have begun to re-evaluate the typology and chronology of their Late Cypriote pottery.[5]

This paper investigates the nature of the relative sequence of Cypriote White Slip pottery in Palestine. The traditional nomenclature—the classes Proto White Slip (hereafter PWS), White Slip I (WS I). and White Slip II (WS II)—established by Myres,[6] Gjerstad,[7] Sjöqvist,[8] Benson,[9] and Popham[10] has been retained. The sample includes 486 bowls and bowl fragments and a single tankard which came from published reports.[11] I have subdivided the pottery in each class on the basis of rim frieze.[12] There is no type in Palestine which does not appear on Cyprus.

Several factors inhibit the usefulness of a quantitative approach to the White Slip pottery in Palestine and also make it more difficult to reconstruct its precise history there. Chief among these is the inequity from site to site in the size of the LB settlement and the extent to which it was excavated. At some sites, many LB tombs were excavated while at others none were found.[13] Finally, the amount of White Slip pottery chosen for publication varied from site to site[14] as did the information from which an accurate stratigraphic picture could be derived.

The comparative stratigraphy and relative chronology of the tombs and strata used in this study are based on each excavator's analysis and dating of the material at his site except where recent studies have necessitated revisions. In accord with current practice, absolute dates are given in the low chronology.[15]

Kathleen Kenyon has recently published a new reconstruction of the relative stratigraphy and chronology of Palestine in the Late Bronze Age.[16] Using a typological method, she isolates six consecutive key ceramic assemblages (Groups A-F) as the characteristic chronological stages of the LB. Onto this framework she ties the strata and tombs of nineteen Palestinian sites. Kenyon's theory that a ceramic break (equals population break) occurred at the cities Hazor, Megiddo, Tell el-Far'ah (N.), Gezer, Tell el-Far'ah (S.), and Tell Beit Mirsim following the campaign of Tuthmosis III and covering most of the fifteenth century B.C. is not completely convincing. It is precisely in this period that the records of Tuthmosis III, Amenophis II, and Tuthmosis IV make mention of those cities as do the Ta'anach Letters. Furthermore, the type assemblages for Groups A-B come from cities in the north of Palestine (Megiddo and Hazor) while Group C, separated from A and B by the campaign of Tuthmosis III, comes from a southern city, Lachish. It is only with Group D (c. 1350–1320 B.C.) that we have type assemblages from both the north and the south. Could there be an overlap in these groups, a regional variation which Kenyon's linear ordering of the groups does not recognize?

The chronology of Proto White Slip pottery in Palestine is inconclusive. The stratified context of one bowl at Megiddo has, however, been used as an important clue to the chronology of PWS pottery.[17] The bowl (Fig. 1:1) came from Locus 4021 in Area AA, attributed to Stratum X. Dated by the excavator c. 1650–1550 B.C., Stratum X represents the final phase of MB II in Palestine, paralleled by Tell Beit Mirsim Stratum D. This context argues for an early date for the development of PWS on Cyprus and, hesitantly, early trade connections between Palestine and western Cyprus.[18]

Room 4021 in Megiddo Stratum X can not be considered a reliable context. Most of the floors of the Stratum X building in Area AA had a paving of lime plaster but in Room 4021, where this crucial bowl was found, there was no indication of any sort of paving (or of any type of floor). While many of the Stratum IX floors were paved, the region above Room 4021 had no indication of paving. In one spot, the difference in absolute level between the "floor" of Room 4021 and that of Stratum IX was 45 cm. Only a meter or so away the difference dwindled to only one or two centimeters.[19] The two dipper juglets found in Room 4021 (which, together with the PWS bowl, make up the entire pottery assemblage from this room) typologically could have come just as well from Stratum IX as from X. The few small finds are similarly inconclusive.

The remaining PWS pottery in Palestine comes from late or problematic contexts. Included here is a sherd (Fig. 1:2) from Lachish. Though the publication regards this fragment as belonging to Temple II,[20] the notation "100 Shrine" on the reverse indicates that this sherd was discovered in the Houses 100 region. If so, the sherd is in an LB IIb stratigraphic context contemporary with Temple III.[21]

Three-quarters of the published PWS pottery come from Tell el-Ajjul, mostly from City II and Palace III (fifteenth century B.C.). These contexts offer no clear stratigraphic basis for the date of the introduction of PWS to Palestine. Though we can state that PWS was present in Palestine in LB I, there is no stratigraphic basis for a date early in that period and certainly not for a date at the end of MB II.

We have a clearer stratigraphic picture for WS I pottery in Palestine than was possible for PWS. The stratigraphic evidence indicates that, within the WS I class, no type preceded any other type to Palestine. Treating WS I as a whole, the clearest evidence of its early import comes from Hazor. In Lower City Stratum 2 were the vessels shown as Fig. 1:4, 5, and 6. The context is clearly LB I, prior to the campaign of Tuthmosis III, but whether the material belongs to the late sixteenth or early fifteenth century B.C. is unclear. Contemporary examples come from Tell el-Ajjul, Palaces II–III and City II: according to Miss Epstein's reconstruction,[22] this pottery would be assigned to Palaces II–IIIA and City IIA, all LB I,

Figure 1

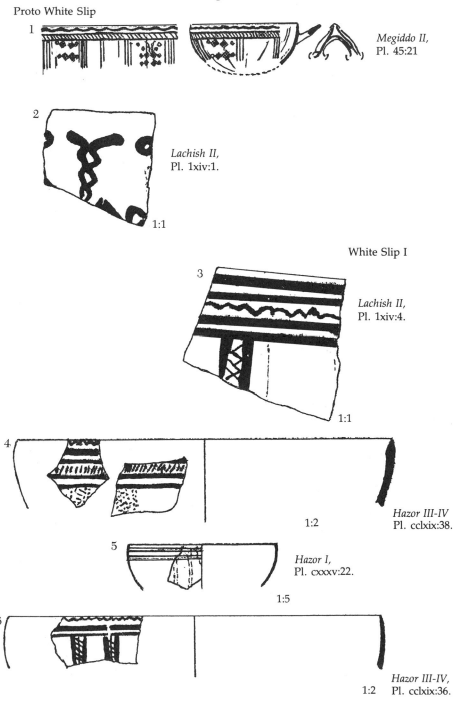

Proto White Slip

1   *Megiddo II,*
         Pl. 45:21

2   *Lachish II,*
         Pl. 1xiv:1.

1:1

White Slip I

3   *Lachish II,*
         Pl. 1xiv:4.

1:1

4   *Hazor III-IV*
                                         Pl. cclxix:38.

1:2

5   *Hazor I,*
         Pl. cxxxv:22.

1:5

6

1:2   *Hazor III-IV,*
         Pl. cclxix:36.

Figure 2

White Slip II

Megiddo Tombs
Pl. 49:23.

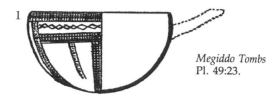

1:5

Lachish II,
Pl. xliii:155.

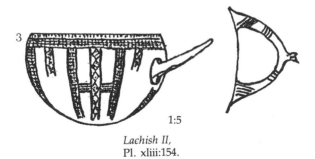

1:5

Lachish II,
Pl. xliii:154.

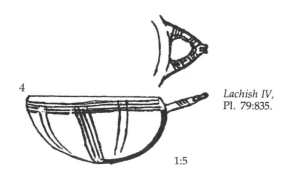

Lachish IV,
Pl. 79:835.

1:5

Figure 3

White Slip Pottery

in Palestine

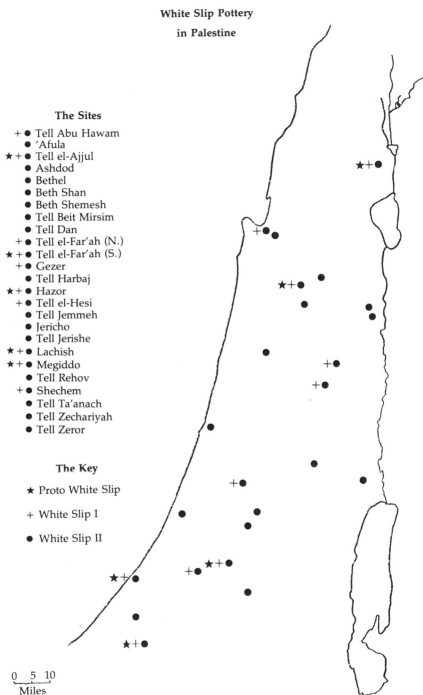

The Sites

+ ● Tell Abu Hawam
  ● 'Afula
★ + ● Tell el-Ajjul
  ● Ashdod
  ● Bethel
  ● Beth Shan
  ● Beth Shemesh
  ● Tell Beit Mirsim
  ● Tell Dan
+ ● Tell el-Far'ah (N.)
★ + ● Tell el-Far'ah (S.)
+ ● Gezer
  ● Tell Harbaj
★ + ● Hazor
+ ● Tell el-Hesi
  ● Tell Jemmeh
  ● Jericho
  ● Tell Jerishe
★ + ● Lachish
★ + ● Megiddo
  ● Tell Rehov
+ ● Shechem
  ● Tell Ta'anach
  ● Tell Zechariyah
  ● Tell Zeror

The Key

★ Proto White Slip

+ White Slip I

● White Slip II

0 5 10
Miles

some as early as the late sixteenth century B.C. (nearly half of the published WS I pottery comes from Tell el-Ajjul).

Stratigraphically, WS I appears simultaneously with PWS in Palestine in LB I (having demonstrated the unreliability of the Megiddo X context for PWS). Only a few examples appear thereafter: in Megiddo VIII, the first settlement at Tell Abu Hawam (indicating the ware was still being imported c. 1400 B.C.), and Hazor's last LB phase. The excavator's notation on the reverse of a sherd from Lachish (Fig. 1:3) indicates that it came from the Houses 100 region. It should not be taken as having come from Temple I, as the publication suggests.[23] I have demonstrated above (note 21) that stratigraphically this context can not be earlier than LB IIb.

White Slip II pottery was introduced into Palestine at least as early as c. 1500 B.C. It is stratigraphically contemporary with WS I and PWS. The WS II types represented by Fig. 2:1–3 come from LB I loci at Megiddo (Tomb 1145), Tell el-Ajjul (Tomb 1717), and Hazor (Lower City, Stratum 2). Though rare, vessels of this type also appear scattered through late LB II loci.

Following the campaign of Tuthmosis III through Palestine, many of the WS II types appear at the onset of LB IIa (c. 1450/1400 B.C.) in small quantities. At the beginning of the fourteenth century B.C. there is an increase in the WS II types represented and the quantity of pottery in each type. All the varieties of WS II in Palestine are present in LB IIa contexts and the ware reaches a numerical peak c. 1350–1300 B.C. No new WS II types appear in LB IIb (after c. 1300 B.C.), nor do any types degenerate in decorative style. All the more "careless" styles are in evidence in LB IIa contexts and their chronology in Palestine will not support any theories of their lateness. The type represented by Fig. 2:4 is usually regarded as a late, degenerate WS II type (Dikaios' WS III).[24] Yet it appears in Palestine as early as the rest of the WS II styles. This may indicate that we need to look more to regional traditions and market influences than to chronology along to explain the variations of WS II pottery.

On the sole basis of WS II pottery, it is not possible to differentiate an LB IIa assemblage from an LB IIb assemblage. The main difference between the two periods, as far as WS II pottery is concerned, is that there are fewer examples in LB IIb. A slow fade-out of WS II does not occur; rather, there is an abrupt cessation of finds c. 1225/1200 B.C., coinciding with the disruption of Palestine suggested by literary accounts to be the work of the invasions of Merneptah, the Israelites, and the Sea Peoples. The abruptness of this break in finds makes one wonder if trade between Cyprus and Palestine had not come to an end somewhat earlier.

There is no regional variation in the distribution of WS types in Palestine. No type or group of types is clustered exclusively in the mountains, plain, or coast, north or south (see Fig. 3). PWS, WS I and the earliest WS (Fig. 2:1–3) were unearthed at important sites along Palestine's main trade thoroughfare, the via maris (and at Shechem and Tell el-Far'ah (N.) situated on the important east-west route through the central mountains). By c. 1400 B.C., WS II had spread to out-of-the-way places such as Tell Beit Mirsim.

In the preceeding discussion of the Cypriote White Slip pottery in Palestine, I have tried to demonstrate that the evidence of Palestinian stratigraphy must be approached with caution. It does not provide any concrete support for the early appearance of Proto White Slip pottery. Moreover, given the present state of the evidence, it makes no chronological distinction between PWS, WS I, and certain types of WS II pottery. Cypriote archaeologists should not be looking to Palestine for answers to the problems of the chronology of White Slip pottery.

Perhaps a strict linear chronology is not what we should be looking for. Thorough analysis of clays together with stylistic analysis may lead to the discovery of which areas of Cyprus were producing the pottery which reached Palestine. We may discover that certain types were produced in quantity for the export market. Finally, we may come to understand the mechanism of the extensive trade between Palestine and Cyprus.

NOTES

1. W.F. Petrie, *Ancient Gaza I–IV* (London: Quaritch, 1931–1934), passim.

2. W. F. Albright, *Tell Beit Mirsim I–IA* (AASOR XII—XIII, New Haven: Yale University Press, 1932–33), vol I, paragraph 64; vol IA, paragraph 60.

3. E. Gjerstad, *Studies on Prehistoric Cyprus* (Uppsala: Lundeqvistska Bokhandeln, 1926).

4. E. Sjöqvist, *Problems of the Late Cypriote Bronze Age* (Stockholm: Swedish Cyprus Expedition, 1940).

5. Paul Åström, *Swedish Cyprus Expedition* IV:1c (Lund: 1971?). M. Popham, "The Proto-White Slip Pottery of Cyprus," *Op. Ath.* 4 (1963); 277–297. R. Merrillees, "Reflections on the Late Bronze Age in Cyprus," *Op. Ath.* 6 (1965); 139–148, and "The Early History of Late Cypriote I," *Levant* 3 (1971), pp. 56–79.

6. J. L. Myres, *Handbook of the Cesnola Collection of Antiquities from Cyprus* (New York, 1914).

7. Gjerstad, *Prehistoric Cyprus* pp. 194–200.

8. Sjöqvist, *Late Cypriote Bronze Age*, pp. 43–50.

9. J. L. Benson, "The White Slip Sequence at Bamboula, Kourion," *PEQ* 1961, pp. 61–69.

10. Popham, "Proto-White Slip Pottery."

11. The Proto White Slip class included 27 pieces, WS I included 41 pieces, and WS II included 419 pieces (including the tankard).

12. The typology used in the preparation of this study appears in my forthcoming Ph.D. dissertation, *Late Cypriote Pottery and the Chronology of Late Bronze Age Palestine.* *

13. There were no single inhumation tombs containing WS pottery. There were, however, 29 tombs which accounted for 42 examples of WS pottery (PWS—one tomb, one piece; WS I—two tombs, two pieces; WS II—27 tombs, 39 pieces). White Slip pottery was probably not important in Palestinian graves.

14. For example, there are many unpublished WS sherds from Lachish which may be seen in the Institute of Archaeology in London.

15. When referring to the history of Egyptian military intervention in Palestine, I have used the lower Egyptian chronology (accession of Tuthmosis III to the throne in 1490 B.C.). For the most recent position favoring the middle chronology for the Near East, see the paper by Dr. Muhly in this volume.

16. K. Kenyon, "Palestine in the Time of the Eighteenth Dynasty," *CAH*[2], vol. II chapter XI (published as Fasicle 69, 1971).

17. Popham, "Proto-White Slip Pottery," pp. 286–287.

18. The argument may be further strengthened by the presence of Tell el-Yehudiyeh juglets in Cyprus (cf. Merrillees, *Levant*[3], pp. 73–74) which probably preceded the import of Bichrome Ware, though the evidence on Cyprus does not seem to support this thesis (ibid.).

19. Cf. G. Loud, *Megiddo* II (Chicago: University of Chicago Press, 1948), Figs. 380–381.

20. Cf. O. Tufnell, *Lachish* II (London: Oxford University Press, 1940), Pl. LXIV:1.

21. The discussion of Houses 100 (Tufnell, *Lachish* II, p. 31) states that Loci 141–144, which contained pottery forms dating as late as LB IIb, were stratified

below the levels of Houses 100. Thus, Houses 100 can not be earlier than LB IIb and are likely to be late in that phase, contemporary with Temple III.

22. C. Epstein, *Palestinian Bichrome Ware* (Leiden:Brill, 1966), pp. 174–185.

23. Tufnell, *Lachish* II, Pl. LXIV:4.

24. P. Dikaios, *Enkomi* I (Mainz: von Zabern, 1969), p. 243.

* The typology used in the preparation of this study has since been changed to conform with that appearing in Åström, *SCE IV:1C*. Also, more pottery has been added to the sample under investigation. Substantive changes in the results reached in 1971 have been minor. The revised data will appear in my forthcoming PhD. dissertation, *Late Cypriote Pottery and the Chronology of Late Bronze Age Palestine.*

Early Phoenician Presence in Cyprus: Analysis of Epigraphical Material

Javier Teixidor

The Cambridge Ancient History, vol. II, ch. XXXIII (1966), asserts that "the beginning of Phoenician colonization in Cyprus and Sardinia cannot well be placed later than the tenth century and that a date after the ninth century is impossible." This has prompted me to examine the evidence upon which such a statement is based. The earliest Phoenician inscriptions from Cyprus have a significant bearing on the history of the Phoenicians because they partly reveal the kind of relationship that linked the island to the mainland, but at the same time these texts, studied within the framework of other northwest Semitic inscriptions, help the historian to define better the very origin of Phoenician colonization independently of the usual preconceived schemes.

The two earliest Phoenician inscriptions found at Cyprus are, first, the one published by A. H. Honeyman in 1939, and second, the inscription found by V. Karageorghis at Kition in 1969.

The Honeyman inscription dates from the first part of the ninth century B.C.[1] Its place of origin is unknown. The stone is badly damaged and incomplete. Seven lines remain visible but only a few words can be satisfactorily read. These lines indicate that the inscription was funerary and that some kind of warning was pronounced against those who would attempt to destroy the tomb. In line four the term *baal* is easily read but we do not know what it stands for.

The second inscription is incised in fragments of a votive bowl.[2] The archaeological context dates the object from the end of the ninth century, which is in agreement with the date assigned to the inscription on palaeographical grounds. A. Dupont-Sommer has published this inscription in "Mémoires de l'Académie des Inscriptions et Belles-Lettres," vol. II (1970), pp. 9–28, but his interpretation is unconvincing. He has practically forced the words to become a votive inscription whereby an individual by the name of ML offered his locks of hair to Astarte. Dupont-Sommer bases his interpretation on the appearance of the words *śe ʿâr* 'hair' and *gâlab* 'to shave' in the first line. However, the text is incomplete and the very presence of these two words in the inscription is far from being certain. As far as the name of Astarte is concerned the inscription has preserved only the last three letters: *t,r,t*. I am willing to accept Dupont-Sommer's reading of the name of Astarte, but one cannot say whether the name of the goddess appeared isolated or as part of a theophore. For the moment, a satisfactory understanding of the text, as it actually stands, seems to me to be a practically unattainable goal.

However inconclusive the interpretation of these two Cypriote texts may be, the fact remains that their script as well as their language make them genetically related to those inscriptions from Syria and Palestine which can be dated approximately to the beginning of the first millennium B.C. The ninth century inscriptions of Zenjirli and Karatepe[3] are, of course, obvious parallels, but other earlier inscriptions should also be taken into account, namely, the Byblian inscription of Ahiram ca. 1000 B.C.; the Gezer inscription in Palestine, from the tenth century; and the royal text of the Moab stele dated from the middle of the ninth century. All these inscriptions represent the last stage in the evolution of Canaanite.

In a prior stage we have texts inscribed on arrowheads found in Southern Palestine and Lebanon. They date from the end of the twelfth century. Rudimentary as they might have been, these inscriptions were already written in linear Phoenician characters. In fact, they belong to the period in which "the pictographic script evolved into the linear."[4] Thus, one can say that these arrowhead inscriptions furnish the link between the Proto-Canaanite texts from Sinai and the Canaanite texts from Ugarit and Palestine, on the one hand; and the above-mentioned group of inscriptions from Syria, Palestine and Cyprus, on the other.

The latter are known in our textbooks as either Phoenician or Old Hebrew inscriptions, according to the region from which they came. But this is inaccurate. These texts are unmistakably homogeneous, although peculiar grammatical features are noticeable here and there. Moreover, the style in which the events are narrated clearly manifests tastes and manners of a common culture. A comparison between the inscription of King Mesha in Moab and that of King Azitawadda in Karatepe illustrates this point clearly.

Even given this linguistic homogeneity the status of the two Cypriote inscriptions is not clarified, since the only trait in these inscriptions that can be evaluated is the article. The use of the article at this time, however, was flexible; for instance, it occurs in the inscriptions of Zenjirli and Karatepe while it is sparely used in the earliest Byblian texts. Therefore, on epigraphical grounds, it is unsound to speak of the people responsible for the early Cypriote inscriptions as having been Phoenicians. I would simply say that they were Levantine Semites.

By the end of the Second Millennium B.C. some Syrians must have been well established in eastern Cyprus.[5] We know that during the Late Bronze Age eastern Cypriote trade with Syria and Palestine increased considerably and, by then, some Syrians may have immigrated to the island. The oldest sanctuary of Kition, recently excavated by V. Karageorghis, is a Late Bronze II building strikingly similar to the temple of Lachish.[6] The ninth century temple of Kition, the so-called Phoenician temple,[7] also shows the influence of architectural fashions from the mainland.

All this archaeological evidence casts light indirectly upon the epigraphical material. Syrians established in Cyprus, and not a group of newcomers, must have been the authors of the two Cypriote inscriptions. They wrote in the language which was used by the Syrians and Palestinians of the mainland. It was most probably the "lingua franca" of the Levant during the tenth and the ninth centuries. When the Aramaeans succeeded in consolidating their realm in the Near East, this lingua franca was supplanted by Aramaic in some areas. In Zenjirli, for instance, Aramaic became the language of the eighth century dynasty of Panammu. The language of the littoral, however, held firm against the spread of Aramaic dialects from all over the Syrian inland and, finally, became the language not only of the coastal cities, but also that of their colonies in the West.[8] This confrontation with Aramaean culture must have helped Phoenicia develop the characteristics by which the region and its inhabitants were known to the Classical writers.

By the tenth century Tyre had certainly imposed her political supremacy in the littoral so much that the cult of Baal Shamem, the city god, acquired general acceptance as a god of cosmopolitan character. The spread of this theological conception may explain the religious innovations carried out by Solomon in Jerusalem.[9] The friendship of Solomon with Hiram, king of Tyre, and later on, the marriage of Jezebel, daughter of Ithobaal of Tyre, to Ahab, king of Israel, clearly emphasize the lack of religious or ethnic boundaries between the two kingdoms. Architects and craftsmen of Tyre worked in the construction of the temple of Jerusalem. They worked at Samaria where the archaeologists have uncovered walls of beautiful masonry assigned to the reign of Omri of Israel, i.e., to the first part of the ninth century.[10] The ninth century temple of Kition may be another example of the presence of Tyrian architects outside of their city. But as in the case of Samaria we do not conclude from the archaeological remains the existence of a Phoenician settlement, so in the case of Kition the recently excavated temple does not substantiate the idea of Phoenician colonization of the area in the tenth or even in the ninth centuries.

The political splendor of the Phoenician coast is not sufficient to exalt Tyre as a colonizing power at the beginning of the first millennium B.C. The two historians of this city, Dius and Menander of Ephesus, quoted by Josephus in his *Contra Apionem*,[11] fail to make such a statement. That quotation is introduced by Josephus as follows: "For very many years past the people of Tyre have kept public records, compiled and very carefully preserved by the state, of the memorable events in their internal history and in their relations with foreign nations" (I, 107). Dius does not record any colonizing activity of the city during the reign of Hiram (I, 113–115), and Menander only mentions the campaign of Hiram against some people called "the Utikians" (I, 117–121). Even if the reading *Itykaioi* were accepted it would not be enough reason to conclude that Menander was referring to the people of the Tunisian city of Utica, since the earliest tombs found there go back to the late eighth century only.

In summary, one can say that it is specious reasoning to argue in favor of an early Phoenician colonization of the Mediterranean by indiscriminately using Semitic inscriptions, archaeological finds from Cyprus, Sardinia, and Carthage, and Biblical passages and quotations from the Greek and Latin writers. Therefore, the statement made by *The Cambridge Ancient History* that the Phoenician colonization in Cyprus and Sardinia "cannot be placed later than the tenth century," is not based on solid ground.

The first text that truly mentions the Phoenician colonization of Cyprus is the inscription of the bronze bowls found at Mouti Sinoas, about 12 miles north-east of Limasol and 7 miles north of Amathus. According to the inscription, the bowls were dedicated by the governor of *Kartihadast*, the "New City," to Baal of Lebanon. The governor called himself "the servant of Hiram, king of the Sidonians."[12] This king is undoubtedly Hiram II of Tyre, who paid tribute to Tiglatphilaser III in 738 according to the Annals of the Assyrian king. Tyre and Sidon formed then a political unity. The existence of a city in Cyprus called "New City" is attested also in the Chronicle of the Syro-Palestinian campaigns of Esarhaddon. Here, *Kartihadast* is listed with some well known Cypriote cities. It is obvious that the name *Kartihadast*, "New City," points to the foundation of a city by people of Semitic extraction who had come from far afield, leaving behind their old city.

The precise site of this "New City" is unknown. Many scholars have identified the site of *Kartihadast* with Kition. But this assumption disregards an inscription of the fifth century B.C. found in 1869 at Kition itself.[13] It consists of a text written in Phoenician on both sides of a small limestone tablet. The reverse of it gives "an order of reward" and thereafter, in line 6, mentions Abd ʿabastis, *the Carthaginian*, i.e., a man from the "New City." By indicating the individual's native place this inscription indirectly excludes the possibility of identifying "New City" with Kition: epigraphical texts, always short and precise, never mention the home town of the individual when the inscription is written in that town. This is a well

established fact in northwest Semitic epigraphy of the first
millennium B.C.

Kition probably never changed its name in antiquity and it was
always known as such. Coins of Sidon of the second century B.C.
proclaim this Lebanese city as the "mother-city" of Came, Hippo,
Kition, and Tyre. How far back the name of Kition goes, is
impossible to say. In some Biblical texts the people of Kition, the
Kittim, passed for being the Cypriotes, which incidentally indicates
that the Kittim were the best known of the people from the island.
The Biblical texts, however, are not very ancient. The Table of
Nations of Genesis 10 in which the Kittim are listed belongs to the
Priestly tradition and could not have been incorporated into the
Biblical text before the fifth century, although the world picture
presented by the text may fit the historical circumstances of the
seventh century. The text of Isaiah 23:1, which speaks of the land of
the Kittim as the one from which the enemies of Tyre will come,
forms part of a collection of oracles against the nations only added
lately to the book of Isaiah. Thus the oracle against Phoenicia is not
to be dated before the middle of the fourth century. Other Biblical
passages mentioning the Kittim may well refer to the Macedonians
or even to the Romans.

To go back to the inscription of the governor of *Kartihadast*,
this is the sole document we have up till now to prove that Tyre
founded a colony in Cyprus. But we do not know whether this was
an isolated case. We are equally ignorant of the status of eastern
Cyprus under the Assyrians in spite of the military records of
Sargon, Sennacherib, and Esarhaddon dealing with the island. P.
Dikaios thinks that the effect of the Assyrian domination "was not
only political but also cultural, as it encouraged the influx through
Phoenicia of eastern influences into Cyprus."[14] However it may be,
the independence of Phoenicia was certainly threatened by the
advance of Assyria, and one is at a loss trying to explain the
foundation of *Kartihadast* in Cyprus at this particular moment. It is
equally difficult to explain how the colonization of Cyprus correlates
with that of the west Mediterranean. Justin, using a well informed
source, says that the Phoenician expeditions to Cyprus and Carthage
were concomitant. His information is probably correct. The
colonization of Sardinia must also have taken place at an early date.

The Nora inscription can reasonably be dated from the eighth century rather than from the ninth century as generally accepted. The text, however, is incomplete and, so far, unintelligible.

I find the scarcity of Phoenician inscriptions prior to the rise of the Persian empire a distressing fact. One of the perennial questions confronting a historian of the Phoenicians is the following: when does Phoenician history start? The answer can hardly come from occasional objects manufactured in the Near East but found in the Aegean or in the West Mediterranean.[15] Nor are late Biblical texts of great help when they mention the rise of Tyre as a commercial power in the tenth century. I believe that only new inscriptions and new literary texts can give the Phoenicians and their language the identity we are seeking. So far we have had to rely on the Greek writers, who present the Phoenicians as a well defined ethnic group. The *Iliad* (23:740 ff.) identifies Sidonians and Phoenicians and describes them as craftsmen and navigators. The Homeric references fit in with the eighth century culture. For Herodotus and Thucydides the term "Phoenicians" clearly stood for the people who vied with the Greeks for the exploitation of the Mediterranean markets. The late Phoenician inscriptions so far uncovered seem to corroborate the Greek sources. I find no conclusive evidence for a Phoenician colonization before the eighth century.

NOTES

* Thanks are due to the American Philosophical Society for partly supporting my visits to the various Phoenician sites and a first-hand examination of some of the epigraphical material mentioned in the paper.

1. H. Donner-W. Röllig, *Kanaanäische und Aramäische Inschriften* I (Wiesbaden, 1966) and II, 2nd ed., (Wiesbaden, 1968), no. 30.

2. V. Karageorghis, "Fouilles de Kition 1969," *CRAI* 1969, pp. 515–522 and *BCH* 94(1970): 251–258.

3. Donner-Röllig, *Inschriften*, nos. 24 and 26. For the date, see Teixidor, "Bulletin d'épigraphie sémitique 1971," no. 98, *Syria* 48 (1971).

4. See F. M. Cross, "The Origin and Early Evolution of the Alphabet," *Eretz-Israel* 8 (1967); 8*–24*.

5. Cf. R. S. Merrillees, "The Early History of Late Cypriote I," *Levant* 3 (1971), 56–79, esp. p. 77.

6. V. Karageorghis, *BCH* 95 (1971); 379–386.

7. See note 2.

8. Z. S. Harris, *A Grammar of the Phoenician Language* (New Haven, 1936), pp. 7–8.

9. B Mazar, "The Philistines and the Rise of Israel and Tyre," *Proceedings of the Isr. Acad. of Sciences and Humanities* 1 (1967), pp. 1–22; see especially pp. 19–20.

10. Cf. K. M. Kenyon, *Archaeology in the Holy Land*, 3rd ed. (New York, 1970), pp. 263–268.

11. I quote the English translation of H. St. J. Thackeray in Loeb Classical Library I (Harvard University Press, 1966), pp. 205-211.

12. Donner-Röllig, *Inschriften*, no. 31.

13. See now J. B. Peckham in *Orientalia* 37 (1968): 304-24. See also, Teixidor, "Bulletin d'épigr. sém.," *Syria* 46 (1969), p. 338, no. 86 and "Bull.d'épigr.sém.," *Syria* 47 (1970), pp. 369–370, no. 69.

14. Cf. P. Dikaios, *A Guide to the Cyprus Museum*, 3rd ed. (Nicosia, 1961), p. 47.

15. For these archaeological finds, see J. D. Muhly, "Homer and the Phoenicians," in *Berytus* 19 (1970): 19–64, esp. pp. 47–49.

Birds on Cypro-Geometric Pottery

Jack L. Benson

On several occasions[1] I have referred to the desirability of a closer study of the occurrence and stylistic development of birds on Cypro-Geometric pottery. It is a pleasure to be able to contribute the following observations on an assemblage of rather painstakingly collected materials[2] which, though not claiming the status of a corpus, must certainly be well representative of what can be known about this subject at present. Bird representations are not particularly numerous in the earlier part of the Cypro-Geometric period; even so, they compensate gratifyingly for the absence of same in the earlier Attic Geometric series. One rather substantial workshop, to be discussed presently, signals the later Cypro-Geometric period and heralds the continuation of the bird motif into the Cypro-Archaic period in a much broader stream. Several more workshops emerge for the latter period and will be the subject of separate studies.

For the purposes of this paper the relation of bird representations to other motifs, as well as their absolute meaning, will be left aside. Nevertheless, it is necessary to comment briefly on the status of the bird motif in Late Bronze Age Cyprus. The mere proposal to do so emphasizes at once the checkered history of the island. The native inhabitants at this time did not, in effect, have the habit of depicting birds on their pottery; yet they were in close contact with cultures which did, viz., the Mycenaeans (and even Minoans), Syrians and, ultimately, Philistines. In the historical process by which the culture

129

of the Mycenaean settlers amalgamated with that of the native population, the practice of adding birds to the decoration of vases apparently had its origin. For, to my knowledge, it was rarely if ever reflected in any truly Cypriote Bronze Age fabric,[3] not even Late Cypriote III Decorated ware which was open to foreign influence and occasionally admitted fish representations. It is never safe, of course, to draw categorical conclusions from the absence of something. Nevertheless, as of now, one can say that there was little or no interest in the depiction of birds on the part of native Bronze Age potters. The same is true of Cypriote coroplasts: although there was a long tradition of animal-shaped vases in Bronze Age Cyprus, animals other than birds figure most prominently in the Late Bronze Age, particularly bulls.[4] It is not until the inception of Proto-White Painted ware that bird vases (Pl. 1, Figs. 1-2) enjoy a certain currency in tomb groups, corresponding in their general format to Greek prototypes.[5] Further to the motif of birds in the Late Cypriote III period, it has been pointed out by Miss Porada[6] (Pl. 1, Fig. 3) that the glyptic worker adapts his birds from Egyptian sources when they are required by the theme.

If, then, there is no characteristically Cypriote bird type in the Late Bronze Age, we shall expect the birds which emerge at the end of this period to be at least as strongly under the influence of the Mycenaeans then arriving as were other facets of Cypriote ceramics at the same period. Moreover, we should not be surprised if some Syro-Palestinian influence[7] which had been operative on the typical native ware, Late Cypriote III Decorated, lingered on. Let us now examine these generalities in more depth.

It must first be emphasized that pictorial motifs are rare in both the Late Cypriote III and Proto-White Painted Wares. Indeed, until the last decade none in the latter fabric had been described in the published literature, to my knowledge, and even now there are perhaps only three instances, all with birds, two with other figures as well. Of the figures on the most elaborate of these, a kalathos[8] from Kouklia, it has been supposed that both Mycenaean and Syro-Palestinian influence are present. The "union jack" in close juxtaposition to the birds (Pl. 1, Fig. 4) makes the second part of this equation almost inevitable, despite the chronological gap involved, especially with Palestine Bichrome Ware; but the birds themselves show

Plate 1

several features which are not common, or are not commonly combined, in either milieu. These are reserved bodies, straight (i.e., unjointed) legs and what might be called "wire" tails—a grossly simplified version deriving ultimately from Minoan fan tails.

The first of these features seems definitely more related to the effect obtained on Syro-Palestinian birds (Pl. 1, Fig. 6) as does also body shape; the straight legs[9] occur infrequently in Mycenaean and earlier Syro-Palestinian, though at least one parallel from the latter (Pl. 1, Fig. 5) can be cited. This feature is not unusual, however, in the birds from Hama (Cimétière I: dated 1200–1075 by the excavator). Indeed, most of the features found on Proto-White Painted birds occur also in the Hama series, though in rather dissimilar combinations. In the bird of the upper left quadrant of our kalathos there seems to be amalgamation of an upper stroke (for a wing?) with two tail feathers; this may reflect a type of triple feather (wire-like) tail observable on Mycenaean and Syro-Palestinian prototypes (Pl. 1, Figs. 6-7) and even on an Egyptianizing flying bird of a Cypriote seal (Pl. 1, Fig. 10). But in none of these is there any confusion of wing and tail feathers.

My conclusion from this analysis is that the kalathos painter started with a rough impression of Syro-Palestinian bird types and proceeded very independently with more interest in decorative effect than in organic niceties. The interior X in the upper bird's body must have been inspired by the union jack; even the straight legs may have been an adaptation to this geometrical pattern; at any rate, it is important to notice that this became a consistent Cypro-Geometric feature. The tail can perhaps best be explained as a generalized reminiscence of Aegean conventions.

Fortunately, this analysis can be tested against two other instances of bird representations in the Proto-White Painted fabric, this time in connection with pots in the Michaelides Collection which have geometricizing decoration of Mycenaean (or perhaps better, sub-Minoan) type (Pl. 1, Figs. 9-10).

In both instances, the birds are entirely in silhouette, a feature perhaps less unusual in later Syro-Palestinian than in Aegean pottery. The bird on a jar (Pl. 1, Fig. 9a) has a very rudimentary indication of raised wings, a distinctly Aegean trait in itself, but a Syro-Palestinian derivation cannot be excluded.[10] The use of fringing for feathers seems vaguely Minoan.[11] There is a small symmetrical plume tail, probably derived from Aegean fish-tail types (Pl. 1, Fig. 8).[12] Again the legs are unjointed, as are also those of the bird on a krater-amphora (Pl. 1, Fig. 12a) which, however, has no indication of feet. Fringing is applied in this case to the neck and back. The wedge tail and indeed the whole shape of the body are so similar to a late Mycenaean type (Pl. 1, Fig. 11) that an accidental resemblance seems ruled out.

The conclusion from the foregoing analyses is that Proto-White Painted artists were influenced now by Syro-Palestinian, now by Minoan-Mycenaean prototypes and tendencies, but always maintained a certain independence which altered or even mingled these tendencies. This independent spirit fostered the emergence of a distinctly Cypriote type, clearly distinguishable from all others. It is characterized by a simplifying, unorganic and decorative approach to the bird shape, fluctuating between reserved and silhouette technique. Although the Proto-White Painted period may be contemporary with the sub-Mycenaean period in Greece, the creative process involved in pictorial representations can at present only be discerned in Cyprus, owing to a lack of mainland evidence (which may be accidental). In Cyprus, the problem was to select elements from contrasting cultures to achieve a new synthesis. This essentially implies a greater freedom on the part of the artist to seek variety, at least within certain limits. Let us see how this continued in the Cypro-Geometric I period.

First of all, it may be pointed out that there is considerable evidence for the earlier and the later parts of the Cypro-Geometric period (CG I and CG III). The intermediate period (CG II) is somewhat sparsely represented, which at present inhibits sweeping generalizations about the course of development. Even so, the statement may be ventured that there is some continuity, but also much experimentation at first, until an extremely assured type emerges in the later period, carried apparently by one principal workshop, from which then descend several very active and successful workshops in the Cypro-Archaic I period.

Just as in the Proto-White Painted category there were birds in definite panels and others tucked away among abstract ornaments, as it were, so a variety of positions occur in the first Geometric phase. A bird (near a snake) is inserted on a pyxis[13] from Kourion (Pl. 2, Fig. 1) in a free manner recalling the jar and krater-amphora in the Michaelides Collection. Birds on an amphora[14] from Lapithos (Pl. 2, Fig. 2) seem to be riding waves, perched at intervals along a triple wavy line in the handle zone (an idea derived from, or else passed along to, Cretan vase-decorators). However, on the neck of a krater-amphora[15] (Pl. 2, Fig. 3) from Kera, a bird is placed in a central panel-like space formed by flanking zones containing the butterfly design. The focal placement of the bird tends to produce a formal balancing of all the design elements, but at the same time the bird is a graceful creature of the air in full flight, with wings billowing and feet trailing behind.

A framed effect was even more specifically sought on a stemmed bowl (Pl. 2, Fig. 4) which has adorsed birds perched on branches of a clump of palm trees filling the entire panel.[16] The trees seem to reflect a Mycenaean motif.[17] At any rate, it can be seen that a panel style is from the beginning a feature of Cypriote pictorial decoration. Somewhat more freely disposed are the representations on a pilgrim flask in the Cesnola Collection (Pl. 2, Fig. 9). Probably to be dated toward the end of Cypro-Geometric I, it has a medley of birds interspersed with floral ornaments and quadrupeds.[18] The scheme of antithetic goats and tree should be, in this context, a Bronze Age reminiscence, possibly Aegean (see below).

The variety in the placement of birds demonstrated on the foregoing vases is matched by the variety of conceptions of bird form. Nevertheless, virtually all these conceptions remain consistent in two features: continuing the straight legs of the Proto-White Painted period and showing two wings with the addition of some type of fringing. As we saw, there is at least some slight precedent for double fringed wings on one of the Michaelides vases, (Pl. 1, Fig. 12a) but stronger and clearer confirmation of this would be desirable. Beyond this, the combination of features is quite free. The amphora birds are in bichrome technique with a barred outline (Pl. 2, Fig. 2b); this latter feature must surely be counted as a Mycenaean survival.[19] Nevertheless, the body shape, the neckless head, the wings rising like two boughs from the middle of the back, and the chopped, fringed tail are most unorganic. The bodies of the adorsed birds of the stemmed bowl (Pl. 2, Fig. 4) appear to be an even more severe, truly

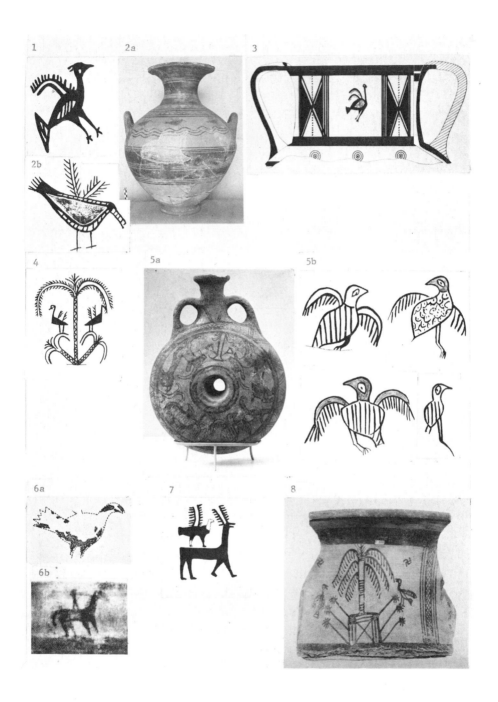

Plate 2

geometricized reduction of the rather triangular-shaped amphora birds; now in silhouette with wings rising parallel from the middle of the back. Yet the heads and necks are of normal type.

I have already described the bird of the krater-amphora (Pl. 2, Fig. 3). Its body is filled with open-work designs of a vaguely Mycenaean type. The bird of the pyxis (Pl. 2, Fig. 1), is a somewhat more severe version of the same type, with hatched body and more depressed wedge tail and with an unmistakable crest—a very rare feature of doubtful interpretation.[20] The birds on the pilgrim flask (Pl. 2, Fig. 5b) seem primarily to be reminiscenses of Late Minoan III birds[21] with displayed wings (presumably a variation of the downview flying pose seen on seals). The fringing of wings is more prominent and the drawing is altogether looser and fuller than in the preceding types, but hardly with any more regard for organic qualities; notice, for example, the bent back legs of the specimens on the left. The openwork decoration strongly recalls Mycenaean prototypes.[22]

It may be useful at this point to summarize briefly the impressions gained of the origins of Cypro-Geometric birds. These tell us of artists at first under the influence of Syrian and Mycenaean prototypes in the most formative stages, who then came increasingly to depend on the Mycenaean heritage with some occasional reference also to Minoan precedents. Yet at no time is there any question of *copying* prototypes, but rather of reducing and combining freely, in an unorganic way, selected features according to a generally accepted rule of parts. Thus, we seem not to be dealing with systematic continuity of previously established Mycenaean norms, but with a rather willful experimental spirit which remains in touch with Aegean precedents. Obviously I do not wish to generalize further until similar studies of more motifs, such as goats, have been made.

Descending in time, I must admit that I know of only one bird representation securely dated to the Cypro-Geometric II period, viz., a White Painted II bowl found at "Vathyrkaka."[23] The naturalistic quality of this bird, (Pl. 2, Fig. 6a) noted by the editor of the vase, seems related ultimately to Minoan fresco types and their immediate derivatives,[24] though it must be noted that a wing seems to emerge unorganically from the center of the back. Moreover, the so-called "horse and rider" on the opposite side of the bowl (Pl. 2, Fig. 6b) strongly recall the same motif on the Mouliana krater.[25] The probability that Minoan influence is present here is strong. On the other hand, previously-used bird types continue on a plate[26] in the Cyprus Museum (Pl. 2, Fig. 7) showing a bird alighting or else standing on the back of a quadruped. I must doubt that this can be later than Cypro-Geometric II, since the wings so strongly recall Cypro-Geometric I experiments.

Yet another piece[27] which may possibly belong to the Middle Geometric phase, or at least preserves some aspects of it, is the krater fragment C 859 in the British Museum. (Pl. 2, Fig. 8). It is obviously a derivative of the scheme of the adorsed birds, but I can make no authoritative contribution to the controversy over the nature of the object under the tree. The birds strongly recall the Kourion pyxis bird, although they show only one wing.

A sizeable group of vases which has been assigned to the late phase of Cypro-Geometric abuts on the preceding series rather harshly. Although one cannot speak of really close parallels with bird representations in other fabrics, there are perhaps some slight points of contact technically with Cretan[28] and Attic[29] bird types prevalent in the first half of the eighth century, viz., in the tendency toward the use of bent legs and outlined bodies. Nevertheless, a definite and uniform Cypriote manner—now vastly more consistent and assured than ever before—has announced itself so decisively that it is difficult to speak of specific influences with any confidence. Furthermore, there seems little possibility of discerning any significant development within the group. This fact, taken together with the close relationship the group has with Cypro-Archaic I workshops—which cannot be demonstrated here but nevertheless involves an unbroken continuity of stylistic phases—suggests that a date of just before 700 B.C., according to Gjerstad's chronology[30] should be postulated as the period in which these Cypro-Geometric III birds flourished. Indeed, this inference is strengthened by the fact that several vases which cannot be separated from the group presented here have been assigned independently to Cypro-Archaic I. Unfortunately, no examples appear to come from controlled excavations.

We are thus confronted, first of all, by a chronological anomaly for which I can suggest at present no solution: there are very few birds assignable to Cypro-Geometric II, which in any case ends at 850, according to Gjerstad. For the greater part of Cypro-Geometric

III (850–700) there is little to record until near its end, at which time
an entirely new bird type reflecting an assured sense of regular
volume, structure and decorative stability emerged. In fact, as far as
bird representations are concerned, we are driven to postulate a
decisive artistic maturation which rather precipitately brings Cypriote artists into the mainstream of Greek geometric schools. Again it
must be emphasized that this conclusion is tentative and must be
tested against analysis of other motifs.

It may be useful at this point to present some specific comments
on the group under discussion, prior to a summation of its connections and significance. The core of the new style is the depiction of
single birds, always with raised wing (or wings), usually facing right
and with bichrome bodies (center red). They are generally in panels,
though "free-field" placement can occur on jugs. Perhaps the most
characteristic shape is the stemmed bowl—recalling the examples
from the Cypro-Geometric I and II periods—with a lip defined by
either a painted or molded division (or both). Other shapes which
lend themselves to decoration with panels, such as krater-amphoras
and pyxides, also occur; but, as noted, jugs are not avoided.
Something of a hallmark of the group is the use of a reserved
quatrefoil as a decorative device and of swastikas sparsely placed in
the field. I propose to consider this group, which is linked together by
insoluble cross connections, a quite definable workshop which may
be called the NBB Workshop (for Nicosia Bichrome Bowls), because
three bowls in the Cyprus Museum display collectively most of the
tendencies referred to above.

NBB WORKSHOP

Two-handled stemmed bowls

(All birds, on all vases, face right unless noted and all have bichrome bodies with
red center.)

1. Nicosia, Cyprus Museum (hereafter CM) B1920 1935 Pl. 3, Fig. 1. No
provenience. Rim: reserved quatrefoils in barred panels alternating with a swastika.
Body: bird with reserved "bee wings" in middle of back (plainly inspired by
quatrefoil, but recalling wings of Lapithos amphora bird); outlined body solid inside,
with reserved segments at front and back; bent legs attached far forward; outlined
wedge tail. Swastika before bird. Panel defined by vertical lozenges outlining dot and
framed by vertical bars. Below frieze wide band outlined above and below by narrow
bands. Paint on foot. Same on obverse. Illustrated: *SCE* IV (2), Fig. *XXI*, 11.

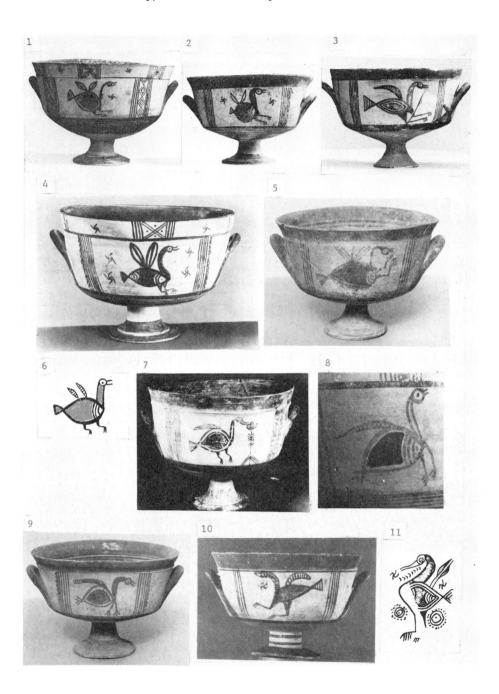

Plate 3

2. Nicosia, CM B1903 1935 Pl. 3, Fig. 2. No provenience. Rim: solid color. Bird like foregoing but less elaborate: wings lack central spine; body solid with segments only forward. Tail wedge-shaped, barred. Swastika before and behind bird. Panel defined by vertical bars, scalloped on the outside. Band under frieze has narrow lines above only. Paint on foot.

3. Nicosia, CM B493 1935 Pl. 3, Fig. 3. No provenience. Band on rim and single wide band under frieze. Bird has one wing, barred, solid body double outlined; barred wedge-tail. Panel set off by vertical bars.

The foregoing bowls show a progressive simplification in decoration and could represent a temporal succession—not, however, a significant one in type.

4. Once London, Spink and Son (probably earlier 1960s). Pl. 3, Fig. 4. Rim like No. 1 but doubled diagonal cross, with each interstice dotted, substituted for quatrefoil. Bird like No. 1 but not outlined, tail solid and segments have dots. Two swastikas before and behind bird. Panels like No. 2. Below frieze narrow lines bordered above and below by thick lines. Two bands around foot.

5. New York, Metropolitan Museum (hereafter MM) 74.51.513 Pl. 3, Fig. 5 L. Cesnola. *A Descriptive Atlas of the Cesnola Collection of Cypriote Antiquities in the Metropolitan Museum of Art, New York* (Boston and New York) Vol. II, 971 (hereafter *CesAt*); J. L. Myers, *Handbook of the Cesnola Collection of Antiquities from Cyprus* (New York, 1914), 84, no. 679 (hereafter *Hdbk*). Subsidiary decoration like No. 3. Wings of bird have become three parallel lines converging on center of back from which rises a straight line. Body and tail solid except for segments around dot forward. Legs attached just below neck (presumably because body was drawn too large to leave space for legs).

6. London, Institute of Archaeology KI 4/16. Pl. 3, Fig. 6. Purchased from Cyprus Museum. Subsidiary decoration like No. 3 with addition of band around foot. Two parallel barred wings in middle of bird's back. Body like that of preceding bird but neck wider, legs properly placed and widely spaced.

The following have single barred wings following flow of back and ending in a point unless otherwise noted.

7. Leiden, Nat. Mus. (hereafter NM) 1928/4.7 Pl. 3, Fig. 7. J. Brants, *Description of the Ancient Pottery preserved in the Department of Greek and Roman Antiquities of the Museum of Archaeology of Leiden* (den Haag, 1930), Pl. 11, 40 (hereafter *Description*). Band on rim and below frieze, two on foot. Panel defined by barred zones of vertical chevrons. Formula for bird's body like No. 3 with addition of forward segments; legs very like those of No. 6. Bird's beak touches trilobe flower in same technique as workshop quatrefoils).

8. Melbourne, Australian Inst. of Archaeology IA 3. 034 Pl. 3, Fig. 8. J. Stewart, *Handbook to the Nicholson Museum* (Sydney, 1948) 179 n.3. In rim, groups of vertical bars flanking horizontal zigzag (except panels defined by barred zones only. Two panels and two birds each side: single outlined, forward segments with dot. Tail formed by crossing of body lines to form a V, strengthened by an interior V. Feet attached under neck and almost straight (cf. no. 9).

9. New York, MM 74.51.514 Pl. 3, Fig. 9. L. Cesnola, *Cyprus* (New York, 1878)

405, Fig. 18; idem, *CesAt* II, 897; Myres, *Hdbk*, 84, no. 678. Auxiliary decoration like No. 2 but without narrow lines below frieze. Bird like foregoing minus segments, wing tip squared. By same hand as Nos. 3, 10, 20, 22-24 (Armidale Painter).

10. Boston, Museum of Fine Arts (hereafter MFA) 72.98 ex Cesnola Pl. 3, Fig. 10. A. Fairbanks, *Catalogue of Greek and Etruscan Vases* (Cambridge, Mass., 1928), no. 181, Pl. XIII (hereafter *Catalogue*). Subsidiary decoration like No. 3, but narrow band below rim, below base (without a wind band) and two on stem. Bird like No. 3 but with solid body and recersed in direction. Armidale Painter.

11. Cambridge, Fitzwilliam Museum 92.53 *CVA* Cambridge Fs. 2. IIc, Pl. IX, 4. Rim: at center, lozenge tipped with solid triangles flanked (in panels) by doubled X, 2 swastikas (vertically) and again doubled X. Handle zone divided into 2 panels by 3 zones of vertical zigzag. Both contain a bird like No. 2 except that body and tail are solid red. Wide red and narrow black band on lower part of vase.

12. Sydney, Nicholson Museum 52.66 Pl. 4 Fig. 1. Rim decorated with tangent quatrefoils. Frieze defined by vertical cross-hatched outlined lozenges barred vertically. Lower body like No. 9 plus two groups of two narrow lines on stem. Bird has square-tipped wing, solid body, V-tail, double curved neck and parallel curved legs: in the last named features it departs farthest from the workshop type.

13. Chambersburg (Pennsylvania), Wilson College V18 (formerly Pratt Institute) Pl. 4, Fig. 2. Rim: Central panel like No. 1, flanked by swastikas, then horizontal zigzag barred, then swastikas. At center of main panel: outlined X in a box with cross-hatched triangles based on outline of box in each interstice. Swastika in remaining zone defined by vertical bars. Band below frieze and on foot.

Barrel Jug

14. Toronto, Royal Ontario Museum C268 Pl. 4, Fig. 3. D. Robinson, C. Harcum, J. Iliffe, *A Catalogue of Greek Vases in the Royal Ontario Museum of Archaeology Toronto* (Toronto, 1930) 82, no. 248; *JNES* 20 (1961):84. Maltese cross at center of each side, bichrome zone, narrow lines defining main frieze. In axis of neck, two vertically placed tangent quatrefoils in barred zone. Flanking on each side, bird like No. 6 with single barred wing like Nos. 7–8, etc. For heraldic arrangement, cf. also Nos. 23–24. Obviously there was more use of this arrangement than I previously thought; yet it cannot be considered very common.

Trefoil oinochoe: a series of this shape is formally linked to the bowls by an elaborate example (No. 15) which displays the usual lip decoration in a special zone at the base of the neck, plus barrel hoops on the side (also on No. 16). The birds are of the types already encountered.

15. Nicosia, CM B1932 1935, Pl. 4, Fig. 4. Tall neck, spouted mouth with strainer, handle to mid-neck. Eyes on trefoil. On neck, narrow bands, a wavy line (cf. Nos. 14 and 24), narrow band. At base of neck, frieze defined above by horizontal chevrons. In frieze (opposite handle) vertical chevrons in barred zone, flanked by swastikas and zones of w's which continue onto shoulder and side, there interrupted by concentric circles, at right angles to handle. Thick band at base of neck. Two groups of circles at each side with Maltese cross at center. Ring of swastikas around shoulder and two on each side. Bird at center below spout: one wing with slightly curved rectangular

Plate 4

form. Body like No. 7 but tail and neck solid. Angle of legs sharp.

16. Once New York, MM (sold) Pl. 4, Fig. 5. *CesAtV*, 2 Pl. 126: 946. Rather unsatisfactory drawing suggests that this vase, both in shape and decoration, was a simplified version of No. 15. One-winged bird with outlined body and tail similar to No. 12. Other features solid. Swastika before and behind bird.

17. New York, MM 74.51.505 Pl. 4, Fig. 6. *CesAt* II, 953; *Hdbk*, 91, no. 723 "Free-field." Bird like No. 7 minus segments. Filling ornament of two dotted crosses before bird's neck. Eye rendered as circled dot.

18. Rhodes, Nat. Mus. No no. Pl. 4, Fig. 7. Description lacking. Bird like No. 3 with solid tail and an extra wing attached underneath and slightly behind the normal one.

19. Nicosia, CM B 794 1935 Pl. 4, Fig. 8. Ex Petrakides: "Free-field." Flower (a slight variant of that of No. 7.) flanked by single wing birds otherwise like No. 6.

20. Nicosia, CM (Neg. G 1290) Pl. 4, Fig. 9. "Free-field." Bird like No. 3. Armidale Painter.

21. Boston, MFA 72.96 ex Cesnola Pl. 5, Fig. 1. Fairbanks, *Catalogue*, no. 183, Pl. XIII. "Free-field," Single-wing bird otherwise like No. 6. Swastika before and behind bird.

22. Armidale (N.S.W.), University of New England 59.22 "Free-field." Bird like No. 9. Armidale Painter.

Krater-amphora

23. Nicosia, CM B 263 1935 Pl. 5, Figs. 2, 6. Provenience unknown. Vertical zigzag in barred zone dividing neck into panels with confronted birds like No. 9. Solid lozenges in three evenly spaced stacked triangles on shoulder. Heavily defined red band below handles; lower body solid color except for narrow reserved band above foot. Armidale Painter.

24. Boston, MFA 72.00 ex Cesnola Pl. 5, Fig. 3. Fairbanks, *Catalogue* no. 182, Pl. XIII. Horizontal wavy line at center of neck. Shoulder: tree with angular fringed branches in three tiers flanked by single winged birds, one like No. 9, the other like No. 11 (including swastika under neck and same orientation). Armidale Painter.

25. Nicosia, CM 1959 (XII-21/1) Pl. 5, Fig. 4. *Arch. Reports for 1961–62*, 38 and Fig. 14. Large central panel in neck containing bird like No. 4 with front segments, tail barred. Two "bee wings" in outline (cf. No. 2). Swastika before and behind bird. Vertical zones like central zone of No. 23 defining central panel. On shoulder, goat and stag(?), swastikas in field, various bands and lines on lower body.

26. Nicosia, CM RR 1542 1943 $\frac{\text{VIII–6}}{1}$ Pl. 5, Fig. 5. Fragment of panel containing bird like No. 6 (but with outlined body and solid wings). Swastika before and behind bird's head. Style rather practiced, even dashing.

Amphora

27. Paris, Louvre AM 659 RA 1899 I, p. 2; *CVA* Louvre Fs. 5 II Cb, Pl. 19, 5–7. Neck: bands above and below frieze, containing on each side 3 panels, 2 with birds

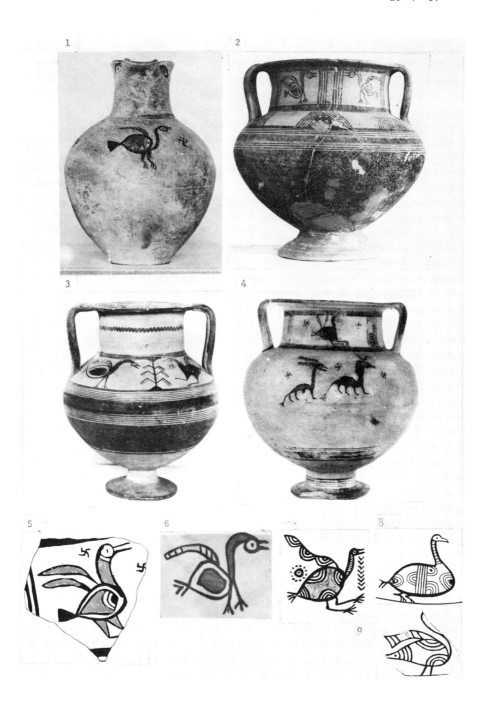

Plate 5

separated by zones each with a stacked lozenge and stacked triangle tangent above and below; the third panel with "wing" on this same motif. Birds like those of No. 14 except for wings matching those of No. 18. On shoulder vertical zigzag zone and cross-hatched outlined triangles. Handle zone: horizontal wavy line defined by 3 bands below; one band midway to base.

Tripod Pyxis

28. Larnaca, Pierides Collection, *JdI* 83 (1968) 88, no. 12, Fig. 16 d-e. Bull-protome handles. In panel formed by vertical lines with outer border of scallops: bird like No. 8 but with single line for neck and plain wedgetail; wings like No. 2.

In addition, the following vases seem to be attached loosely to the workshop for various reasons.

Stemmed bowl

a. Beirut, Museé National 1223 Pl. 3, Fig. 3. Provenience not known to me. Elaborate rim design of solid lozenge, filled lozenge at center flanked by horizontal chevrons, bars and an X with circled extremities. On each side, antithetic birds with double raised wings, separated by heavily defined zones of horizontal zigzag. Diagonal to these at either outer side of panels, heavily defined zones of chevron. These are more or less parallel to the sides of fringed, heavily outlined triangles, filled with solid lozenges, placed under each handle.

b. Leiden, NM 1926/4.8 Brants, *Description*, Pl. II, 41. Outlined latticed lozenge at center, awkwardly joined to tangent flanking zones like central zone of No. 23. Two-winged bird (right) in each of outer panels so formed. Bird very tall and simplified. Possibly later than other pieces listed but continues tradition of workshop.

Amphora

c. Paris, Louvre. *Mélanges Syriens offerts à Monsieur René Dussaud*, I, Haut-Commissariat de la République Française en Syrie et au Liban, Service des Antiquités. Bibliothèque Archéologique et Historique Tome XXX (Paris, 1939): M. Rutten, "Deux Vases Chypriotes du Musée du Louvre," 435 and Pl. I. Goat, bird and ram alternating with lozenges on neck. Cross-hatched triangles on shoulder. In heavily bordered handle zones: table, pots, lyre (?) on one side; goat; woman holding fish (?), bird and fish on other. Two bands on lower body. In publication dated tenth or ninth Century B.C. The bird type combined with vertical zigzag zones on body suggests close contact with the NBB workshop and requires a contemporary date, i.e., last quarter of eighth century B.C. For shape and general decorative scheme cf. *SCE* IV, 2, Fig. XXIII, 17.

d. Larnaca Petrakides Coll. *BCH* 91 (1967), 313 Fig. 101. Cross-hatched lozenge and X's in neck-frieze. On shoulder archer attacking a bird. Figure of man appears to derive from Attic painting. Bird is an adaptation of NBB type. For neck fringing, cf. also No. e.

Krater-amphora

e. Oxford, Ashmolean Mus. 1936. 596, Provenience unknown. Neck: "winged" lozenge consisting of subordinate latticed lozenges, flanked by two narrow zones of a checkerboard lozenge with checkerboard triangles vertically tangent. Background filled except for 2 reserved segments on each side. Shoulder: center zone like side zones of neck plus triple scallops. In resulting panels, confronted birds, doubled, outlined bodies with scale pattern, wings like No. 1, necks like No. 12, legs recalling Nos. 8 and 12. Neck pattern of vase: cf. *SCE IV*, 2, Fig. XX, 1 (White Painted III).

Tripod Pyxis

f. Nicosia, CM 1951 VIII–7 from Galathea Pl. 5, Fig. 7. Central zone like that of No. 23, heavily barred. Bird right in each panel; each has 4 groups of segments placed at right angles on body. Tail recalls those by Armidale Painter. Single wing like a line floating upward with 3 dependent concentric semicircles. Neck shaded. Vertical chevrons below bird's mouth; dotted circled dot behind bird. Wide and narrow bands below. The imaginative innovations and use of filling ornament relate this to No. a.

CHARACTERIZATION AND SUMMARY

The NBB workshop comprises the majority of known Cypro-Geometric III vases with bird representations. Even most of those not assigned to the workshop reflect some experience of it, as I have shown in the entries labelled a–e. In this respect, then, it furnishes a welcome reference point for the analysis of other facets of figural painting of the same general period. Two other vases with birds which are not connected with the workshop will be discussed shortly.

In discussing the NBB bird type so far, I have been cautious about attributing its origins to inspiration from other Greek Geometric schools, even though an awareness of them seems certainly to have been present. Gjerstad[31] has pointed out an instance of direct imitation of Attic figure style at this time and attributed the introduction of the swastika and chevron as filling ornaments to that source. To this may be added reserved quatrefoils, which might, in fact, serve as a direct link to Attic bird cups as a source of inspiration in the same sense that Rhodian Late Geometric bird cups may be so derived.[32] However, since the Cypriotes had their own tradition of bird painting—and even bird cups (!)—a mere nudge from the outside world may have sufficed to induce them to rejuvenate the motif on their pottery. At any rate, it must be emphasized that the rejuvenated conception does not adhere at all closely to previous Cypro-Geometric bird conceptions or to contemporary Greek bird types. In fact, apart from the consistent use of wings, it touches earlier Cypriote birds only at a few points where these had leaned exceptionally heavily on a revival of Mycenaean precedents, e.g., the use of bent legs and of segments at the breast (Pl. 2, Figs. 3, 5b). Even the insistence on bichrome technique (so rare in the earlier Geometric epoch) is possibly to be understood as a specific application of a mode prevailing in nonfigural vase-painting, though it might conceivably have owed something to the use of color on Philistine birds.

I should like to suggest the hypothesis that the sudden and distinct change in type of bird was owing to renewed contact on the part of the originator of the NBB workshop with Mycenaean prototypes—not discounting the likelihood that contemporary Greek bird types turned him in this general direction. On the whole, therefore, I believe that the governing characteristic of the NBB birds is what can, in approximative terms, be called a striving after pre-Hellenic or Aegean elegance and dash, although in no way literally copying prototypes of that epoch. The consistent use of an ovoid body, full to fat, in contrast to the earlier assorted shapes, is most likely from this source. Outlining of bodies could be either from the same source or borrowed from other Greek schools. But the core of the new style is experimentation with multiple segments at the breast and tail, a feature[33] present though not systematically exploited in Mycenaean birds, such as one on a jug found in Kouklia (Pl. 5, Fig. 8); here it becomes the key to a new style. Indeed, it is this very feature which can be used as an Ariadne thread to follow the development of important types of Cypro-Archaic I birds, as I hope to show elsewhere. At this stage, however, we seem to have to do with a recurrence of Bronze Age flavor as a starting point for a new style.

What I have been pointing to is a principal, indeed, an irresistible tendency. The proof of this lies in the occasional exceptions; at the moment I can cite only two, but that is enough to prove that the artistic process was in Cyprus, as everywhere, complex. The first is a pyxis[34] with a bird nestled under the horns of a bull's head handle. Despite its Cypro-Geometric III date, the bird continues the older series, and in fact, looks rather like a dessicated version of the bird previously noted on a plate (Pl. 2, Fig. 7) in Nicosia. Survivals of this kind must naturally be expected. The other example is an amphora[35] with confronted birds; the symmetrical deficiences of the composition are noteworthy. The shape of the bird's body points to influence from another Greek school, Attic at first glance.[36] However, the triangular wing seems to point to a Cretan or Corinthian component.[37] At any rate, we are confronted with the work of a painter who was not working in a typically Cypriote manner.

In summation, this study has demonstrated that the practice of bird representations inaugurated in Cyprus at the end of the Bronze Age never completely died out, although there are difficulties at present in documenting it in the earlier part of Cypro-Geometric III; and second, that a revitalization of the motif, apparently as much from retrospective as from contemporary Greek inspiration, took place in the latter part of the Cypro-Geometric III period in an energetic and influential workshop.

NOTES

1. *JNES* 20 (1961):75; J. L. Benson, *Horse, Bird and Man, the Origins of Greek Painting* (Amherst, 1970), p. 60, (hereafter *HBM*): in connection with the problem of continuity in Greek art.

2. I am under deep obligation to many colleagues for assistance in this, most particularly to Dr. Vassos Karageorghis for permission to publish vases in the Cyprus Museum, and to Professor Paul Åström.

3. Naturally I must exclude from this the so-called 'Rude Style' vases, the bird representations on which are purely and simply Aegean derivatives, and not necessarily painted by Cypriotes: cf. *AJA* 65 (1961):343.

4. E. Gjerstad, *Studies on Prehistoric Cyprus* (Uppsala, 1926) passim.

5. Compare, e.g., E. Vermeule, *Greece in the Bronze Age* (Chicago, 1964), Pl. XLII, B, with the specimen from Kourion here illustrated. The Cypriote coroplast tended to substitute a spout for the bird's head. But the close connection with Greece can be estimated by comparing a bull's head kernos from Lapithos (*RDAC*, 1965, Pl. X, 7) with a late mainland specimen: Vermeule, *Greece in the Bronze Age*, Pl. XLII, D. The bird of her Pl. XLII, B apparently derives from a Cypriote Middle Bronze Age type mentioned by E. Gjerstad, *Swedish Cyprus Excavations* (Stockholm, 1948) vol. IV, p. 2–294 (hereafter *SCE*) with bird's head, necked mouth, and handle on the back. A Proto-White Painted example found recently at Salamis (our Pl. 1, Fig. 2) illustrates the type fully, see V. Karageorghis, *The Ancient Civilization of Cyprus* (New York, 1969), Fig. 6; cf. also *RDAC*, 1965, Pl. VI: 11, occasioning some doubt as to whether any element of revival is involved.

6. J. L. Benson, *Bamboula at Kourion: The Necropolis and the Finds* (forthcoming) sub B 1630 (hereafter *Bamboula NF*).

7. I have reported on this factor in great detail in *Bamboula NF*, Ch. III.

8. V. Karageorghis, *Mycenaean Art From Cyprus* (Nicosia, 1968) p. 24 and Pl. 16 (with further bibliography).

9. Cf. A. Furumark, *The Mycenaean Pottery, Analysis and Classification* (Stockholm, 1941) p. 253, Fig. 30: o, Minoan bird flying (hereafter *MP*). Our Pl. 1, Fig. 8 would be difficult to interpret in this sense. For Syro-Palestinian bird types see C. Epstein, *Palestinian Bichrome Ware*, Documenta et Monumenta Orientis Antiquae 12 (Leiden, 1966) p. 37, Fig. 2; P.J. Riis, *Hama* II, 3 *Les Cimetières à Crémation* (Copenhagen, 1948) p. 97, Fig. 107.

10. A fragment from Ras Shamra: C. Schaeffer, *Ugaritica* II (Paris, 1949) Fig. 50:13 gives an apparently close parallel for the wing formation; this is seen occasionally also in the Hama birds.

11. See reference in note 9.

12. The fish tail occurs rarely in Syro-Palestinian (cf. Epstein, *Palestinian Ware*, Pl. IV, 3). In any case, the nearer temporal position of the Aegean prototypes makes these perhaps the more compelling choice.

13. Benson, *HBM*, p. 141. n. 62 (references).

14. *RDAC*, 1965, p. 84, no. 76; Pl. XIV: 13-14; cf. also Benson, *HBM*, p. 141, n. 56.

15. Unpublished. Drawing provided by Dr. H. W. Catling, formerly of the Cyprus Survey. The double wings of a bird in flight on this and on the Kourion pyxis might derive ultimately from Egyptian prototypes: cf. e.g., W. S. Smith, *Ancient Egypt* (Museum of Fine Arts, Boston, 1960) p. 88, Fig. 51 (MK).

16. P. Dikaios, *A Guide to the Cyprus Museum* (Nicosia, 1961) Pl. XI, 4; *RDAC*, 1966, Pl. III:8.

17. Furumark, *MP*, p. 279, Fig. 39:1 and 9. The ultimate source of birds-in-tree may, of course, be Nilotic friezes.

18. L. Cesnola, *Cyprus* (New York, 1878) p. 353; Myres, *Handbook of The Cesnola Collection* (New York, 1914), p. 70, no. 545. This vase has unusual features but its Cypriote origin is hardly in doubt. I hope to publish it more fully elsewhere.

19. Cf. Furumark, *MP*, 249, Fig. 29, Bird: 8. The same feature occurs in Cretan Early Orientalizing (J. K. Brock, *Fortetsa*, Cambridge, 1957, Motif 17 o) but hardly has any connection with the use being discussed here.

20. Cf. Benson, *HBM*, p. 141, n. 62.

21. Furumark, *MP*, 283, Fig. 30: m-o.

22. For scales on body, cf. Furumark, *MP*, 249, Fig. 29, Bird: 12 and *JNES* 20 (1961) Pl. VI, Fig. 3.

23. *RDAC*, 1964, 116, Fig. 2 and Pl. VIII: 2.

24. Furumark, *MP*, 253, Fig. 30.

25. V. Desborough, *Protogeometric Pottery* (Oxford, 1952) p. 269 f. On the motif, cf. Benson, *HBM*, p. 137, n. 29.

26. P. Dikaios, *Guide*, Pl. XII, 3. Dated without comment to Cypro-Geometric III. From the style of the decoration (cf. *SCE* IV: 2 Pl. XV:9) and particularly from the figures, not later than Cypro-Geometric II.

27. H. B. Walters, *Catalogue of the Greek and Etruscan Vases in the British Museum*, vol. I, pt. 2 (London, 1912) 173; *CVA* British Museum 2, IICc, Pl. 5, 4 (cf. also 5, 1); *JHS* 81 (1961) Pl. IV: 3.

28. Cf. J. K. Brock, *Fortetsa* p. 178: 17 k-m.

29. Cf. Benson, *HBM*, Pl. XXV.

30. H. G. Buchholz, "Östliche Herkunft eines griechish-geometrischen Gefässdetails" *JdI* 83 (1968): 58 ff. ends CG III at 720, passim.

31. *SCE* IV, p. 307 f.

32. For Attic, cf. J. N. Coldstream, *Greek Geometric Pottery* (London 1968) Pl. 10, b, c, f and j (jug). On Rhodian birds, see B. Schweitzer, *Greek Geometric Art* (New York 1971) p. 88 f. A closer study of exact interrelationship of this motif amongst the various fabrics would be useful. If the connection with Attic I have suggested is valid, this enhances the desirability of raising the date for the end of CG III (see note 30).

33. Cf. *RDAC*, 1967, Pl. VII, 3. Notice here also the bordering zone of vertical zigzag, similar to that used in our workshop. I am grateful to Dr. H. W. Catling for permission to publish the bird drawing provided by Dr. V. Karageorghis. Another similar Mycenaean bird representation found at Enkomi: P. Dikaios, *Enkomi* IIIa (Mainz-a-R. 1969) Pl. 81: 35(3394/1) is here reproduced in a drawing (Pl. 5, Fig. 9) by courtesy of Dr. V. Karageorghis.

34. *BCH* 89 (1965):239, Fig. 11; *Annual Report of Director of the Department of Antiquities, Cyprus*, 1964, Fig. 29; Benson, *HBM*, Pl. XVIII, 6.

35. *BCH* 89 (1965):241, Fig. 13.

36. Cf. *HBM*, Pl. XXV, 23 (or direct Mycenaean influence?: Pl. XXIV, 23).

37. Resp., Brock, *Fortetsa*, 178: 17 r; *BSA* 43 (1948): 28, Pl. 6.79, Fig. 16: motif not entirely clear.

The Cesnola Krater from Kourion
in The Metropolitan Museum of Art:
An Iconological Study in Greek Geometric Art

Peter P. Kahane

Modern archaeological research in the field of Geometric art has moved in three directions besides excavation:

1. In stylistic analysis and, using this as a basis, in the establishment of the development of the various Greek Geometric styles, mainly of the richest and most accomplished, the Attic. After about fifty years of intense excavations and research, we have now a standard work, *Greek Geometric Pottery*, N. Coldstream's book which covers the development of the ten main Greek Geometric Styles;

2. In the field of realia, i.e., on all aspects of daily life in the Homeric Age. Following Hilda Lorimer's *Homer and the Monuments* (1950), and Alan Wace's and Frank Stubbing's *Companion to Homer* (1962), the new German series *Archaeologia Homerica* (edited by F. Matz and H.-G. Bucholz, not yet completed) contains the most comprehensive collection of archaeological data on the Dark Age. What makes these booklets especially useful is the constant comparison of literary and archaeological material;

3. In the interpretation of representations in painting and sculpture on small objects. Research in this field lags far behind the research in stylistic analysis and the realia. There are good reasons for the slow process of iconographical and iconological research on Geometric pictorial representations: the pictorial language in a Geometric silhouette style is not given to an easy interpretation.[1]

A few examples will show the difficulty: a bronze group of "man and centaur" in New York;[2] "man struggling with a lion" on a four-legged terracotta stand from the Kerameikos;[3] the representation of a shipwreck on a vase in Munich;[4] "departure" or "abduction" on a bowl from Thebes in London.[5] Apparently, the Geometric style is so simple, so uniform, that it is in most cases impossible to distinguish between *individual* and *typical* scenes. To make some headway in this complicated field one has to concentrate on *typical* representations which repeat themselves again and again, perhaps with variations, on a good number of vases.

Before we turn to the interpretation of some Greek Geometric pictorial representations, I would like to point out that, with very few exceptions—which, by the way, deserve special consideration—Greek Geometric vases with figurative representations belong to the *Late* Geometric Period which, according to Coldstream and others, dates from c. 760 to 700 B.C., i.e., LG I A and B (c. 760 to 735), LG II (c. 735 to 700 B.C.). This means that the vase painters of the Protogeometric, the Early and Middle Geometric Periods—altogether from c. 1000 to 760 B.C.—refrained from pictorial representations. This fact in itself represents a remarkable phenomenon which is not easily explained.[6]

Let us now look at the pictorial representations on the centre piece of our iconological interpretation:[7] The krater was found in Kourion, a Cypriote site, and published by General Louis Palma di Cesnola [8] (Plate 1): it came, with its owner and his vast collection, to the Metropolitan Museum of Art in New York. According to Cesnola, the krater was found at the entrance of rooms called by him "Treasure Chambers of Temple at Curium." Altogether we are left somewhat in the dark about the exact provenance and therefore about the original function of the krater. Just one thing emerges pretty clearly from the find circumstances, coinciding with the fact that the bottom of the krater was left unbroken, namely that the Kourion krater did not serve as a tomb marker used also for fluid offerings to the deceased. One is first struck by the similarity of its shape (Ht. 1.15m) to the Attic Geometric tomb kraters[9] but on closer inspection there are also remarkable differences: the trumpet foot is, in proportion to the vase-body, smaller than on Attic kraters; the body is, compared with the wide Attic rims, rather closed, forming a beautiful egg-shape; a lid, here very fanciful, is altogether missing on Attic Geometric tomb kraters; in contrast to the two horn-shaped handles on Attic kraters, the Cesnola krater has four rather sophisticated band-handles.

This brings us to the painted decoration. The Attic two-handle arrangement allows a compositional variety in the wide handle zones: a near-symmetrical composite composition, combining central scene, frieze, and sometimes accompanying compartments or metopes with a frieze composition, usually on the second side of the krater. The narrow four-handle arrangement on the Cesnola krater, on the other hand, almost compelled the vase painter to a concentrated near-symmetrical field or metope compositon—a central scene is flanked by two almost identical metopes—altogether, a closed composite composition, repeating itself four times, in correspondence to the four handle zones. The remaining parts of the Cesnola krater are covered with figurative friezes; and with rows of ornaments of either dynamic (running) or static character.

Obviously, then, these mixed Attic and non-Attic elements in form and compositon indicate a local workshop under strong Attic influence. Turning to contemporary Attic Geometric workshops, it is the ex-Lambros Collection group which comes closest to the Cesnola krater, with regard to composition and ornamental repertoire.[10] This workshop can be safely attributed to LG IB, i.e., to the second part of that remarkably creative period 760–735 B.C. during which figurative scenes were generally introduced into Attic Geometric and thereafter into other Geometric styles.[11] Comparable too is an Argive jar with loop feet from Argos, of the same LG I Period.[12]

The surprise of the Cesnola krater is, however, its pictorial ensemble. If we compare the representations on the Cesnola krater with the stereotype theme on contemporary Attic tomb kraters,[13] the contrast is striking enough: here a social event, a burial scene, built around either prothesis or ekphora; there the animal world, carefully arranged, symmetrically, heraldically, suggesting some deeper, possibly symbolical, meaning. This leads to the question of the function of the huge vases: that the Attic kraters served as grave markers and at the same time as fluid offering-receivers—indicated by their deliberately broken bottom—is well known. There is no such opening in the Cesnola krater, and indeed, it was not found, according to Cesnola, in a cemetery but possibly in a sanctuary—that means it cannot be considered to represent a tomb vessel; its actual original function is, unfortunately, unknown to us.

N. Kontoleon's proposal to attribute the Kourion krater, together with a number of stylistically as well as iconographically closely related vases, to a Naxian workshop immediately found general acceptance.[14] But very recently Late Geometric pottery of the same style and similar decoration has been found in plenty in Euboea (in Lefkandi and Chalkis) and on Ischia (in Pithekusai, a Euboean colony); these discoveries, and also technical considerations, have prompted Coldstream to locate the workshop of the Cesnola Painter in Euboea and to infer that the products of this workshop were exported to emporiums and colonies in both the eastern and the western Mediterranean. The wide distribution of this pottery shows very clearly the intensive commercial and artistic connections of the Late Geometric period: on the one hand connections between Athens, Euboea, the Cyclades (Delos, Andros, and Naxos), Samos, Crete (Vrokastro), Cyprus and Al Mina (in northern Syria); on the other hand between Euboea and southern Italy (Cumae and Ischia).[15] More of these immensely important connections will be traced later.

Before we turn to the pictures on the Cesnola Krater, it seems appropriate to state two characteristics of Greek Geometric pictorial representations:

1. These Late Geometric vase painters do not always seem to care too much for a uniformity of pictorial representation on one and the same vase. Even on one of the earliest Geometric vases with figurative design—the epoch-making Attic tomb amphora NM 804,[16] chef d'oeuvre of the so-called Dipylon Master—we notice besides the dominant prothesis scene in the handle zone, friezes of grazing deer and resting goats. The "logic" of the Geometric vase painters is not ours. On other, smaller vases, the discrepancy is even more striking.[17] The mixing of subjects was, it seems, generally accepted.

2. Another principle, the *pars pro toto*, is, for obvious reasons, very often found on Geometric vases: on a small amphora[10] one cannot give a burial scene in toto, therefore only excerpts and abbreviations are represented which, however, do not usually leave much doubt as to the meaning of the representation and the funerary function of the vase.[18]

With these facts, stylistic conclusions, and some general observations on Greek Geometric vase painting, we have, to a certain degree, paved the way for an iconographical (descriptive) and then an iconological (more general) interpretation of the pictorial representations on the Cesnola krater.

Motif I: In the centre of each of the four handle zones, a sacred tree is flanked, in an almost heraldic position, by two deer rampant nibbling at the tree branches; underneath the deer, to the left, is a sucking kid. Above each of the two deer, a kid is resting with its head turned back. The position of the two kids conforms more or less to the heraldic arrangement of the two deer. There can be little doubt about the meaning of this motif: it is based on the Oriental concept of the fertility of the animal world.

Motif II: A frieze and a number of smaller compartments or metopes contain grazing animals, horses, and water birds, often combined. One is, a priori, inclined to connect this peaceful, almost bucolic animal scenery, with the fertility world of Motif I, but this remains to be seen.

Motif III: This consists of a horse, tied up, and a bird, neither of them feeding, with a double axe above. These objects seem not to belong to the same sphere of nature and fertility as the other two motifs, although the two metopes in which they appear are compositionally linked up with the central field. But, as we have just pointed out, such a compositional adaptation to the individual structure of a vase—here the zone between the handles—is a very common feature in Late Geometric vase painting: these painters liked symmetrical compositions (not rarely with slight but intentional aberrations); they favoured, no doubt, heraldic arrangements, known to them from countless Near Eastern small objects; such a compositon, it seems, meant something to them, even if not as straight subject matter.

Let us now turn to the iconological interpretation of Motif I: looking out for possible forerunners, our eyes turn automatically to the Near Eastern Lands, i.e., to the Canaanite-Syro-Phoenician cultural area, the Near Eastern gate to the Mediterranean. And, indeed, on a good number of pottery vessels, mainly double cone-shaped jugs, the same motif, down to details, is represented.[19] To our great surprise, the style is purely Geometric—note inter alia the triangular animal bodies. Of particular interest is the decoration of an amphora from Megiddo (Fig. 1-2): here we even have ornamental bands covering part of the vessel's body. The mother goats are jumping at the

Fig. 1-1
Late Bronze I

Fig. 1-2
Late Bronze II

Figure 1:   Examples of animal and plant motifs on pottery of the Late Bronze Age from
Canaanite cemeteries in Israel, especially Megiddo and Lachish. After Amiran, Pl. 50,
4.7–10.12, and May, loc. cit. (note 19), Pl. 40, B,F,G. Drawing by P. Jarden.

Late Bronze II

Fig. 1-3

Fig. 1-4

Fig. 1-5

Late Bronze II

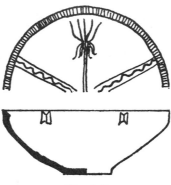

Fig. 1-6

Fig. 1-7

Fig. 1-8   Fig. 1-9

tree, followed by their kids. The tree is a date palm but it is characterized by water streaming down from it in wavy lines as a "sacred
tree" or "Tree of Life" symbol of fertility, well known from Oriental
monuments in art and literature. The majority of this class of vases in
Geometric style were discovered in Megiddo and Lachish, and can
be traced back from the Iron Age (c. 1200–1000 B.C., Fig. 2)—generally in a rather debased, abbreviated form—to Late Bronze II (1400–
1200 B.C., Fig. 1-2 through 1-9) and even LB I (c. 1550–1400 B.C.,
Fig. 1-1).[20] Forerunners are found on vases of "Bichrome Ware," a
class produced in quantities on the Canaanite coast (especially in
Ajjul and Lachish) as well as in Cyprus during the sixteenth to the
fourteenth centuries B.C. (MG IIC–LB IIA, Fig. 3).[21]

The connection between Bronze and Iron Age in the Near East
can be further demonstrated with the help of a good number of
cylinder seals having a representation of the sacred tree flanked by
animals: e.g., on a faience seal from Fosse Temple III at Lachish,
datable to the thirteenth century B.C.[22] The motif, especially the
detail of the animals' heads turned backwards, can be found again and
again on Near Eastern art objects (for example on a Bichrome vase
next to it on the same Plate) as well as on many Greek Geometric
vases—e.g., on amphorae and high-rimmed bowls from the Dipylon
Master's workshop—and on the Kourion krater itself.

The little circles on the drawing of the cylinder seal from
Lachish reflect the drill-boring technique, known from a class of
cylinder seals which are generally attributed to the Mitanni, an Indo-
European people whose empire extended from the Tigris to North
Palestine during the Period of the Amarna letters (first half of fourteenth century B.C.).[23] Another Mitannian cylinder seal shows the
same motif but, in addition, two winged genii in the attitude of adoration towards the tree;[24] these and the juxtaposed group of the fertility goddess, Ishtar, do not leave any doubt as to the original meaning of our Motif I. Dr. Edith Porada, in a study "Nomads and
Luristan Bronzes" (1964), connects the "tree-and-goats-rampant"
motif with an Elamite seal from Tchoga Zanbil of the thirteenth
century B.C. and with a Luristan cylinder seal from Surkh Dum of the
tenth to ninth century.[25] These small items are important as documents testifying to the wide distribution of our Motif I in Near
Eastern lands, its survival from the Late Bronze to the Iron Age, and

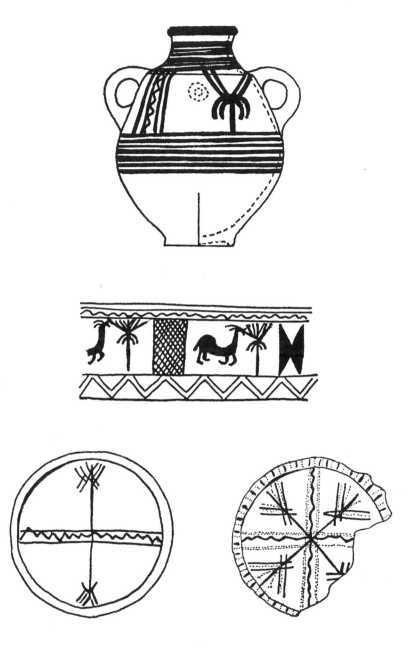

Figure 2:   Examples of animal and plant motifs on pottery of Iron Age I from Megiddo and
Gezer. After Amiran, Pl. 50, 123, and May, loc.cit. (note 19), Pl. 41. Drawing by P. Jarden

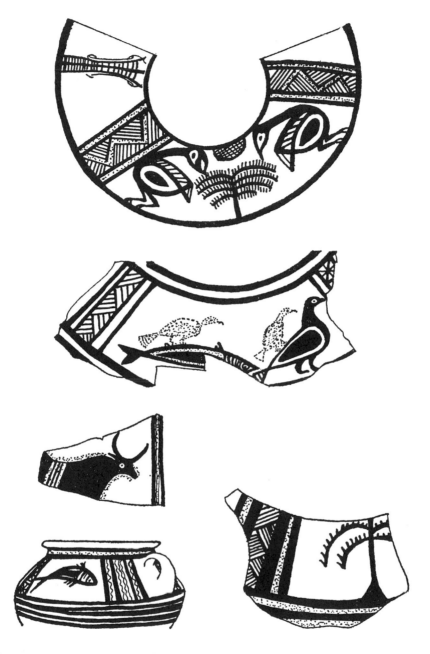

Figure 3: Examples of animal and plant motifs on Cypro-Canaanite Bichrome Ware of the Middle to Late Bronze Age, from Megiddo, Tell el-Ajjul, Minet el-Beida. After May, loc. cit. (note 19), Pl. 39. Drawing by P. Jarden.

to the trading of the motif in the southeast Mediterranean area.

Altogether, we move here on fairly safe ground. We may come to some wider reflections and conclusions concerning the class of Palestinian zoomorphic representations of the concept of fertility by looking at the masterpiece of the class, the Megiddo vase from Tomb 912D of LM IIA–B (c. 1400–1200 B.C., Fig. 4):[26] a group of animals of the earth (quadrupeds), the air (birds), and the sea (the crab), loosely arranged around a palm tree with two comparatively large ibexes near the tree, one jumping, the other apparently kneeling. The style, as on most other vases of this class, is strictly Geometric. What makes this vase so extraordinarily important is its iconographical *completeness*. Compared with this scene, the representations on other vases of this class seem definitely abbreviated, *pars pro toto*; the same principle as in Greek Geometric painting is here too at work. In this context, single animals or trees on some of the vases of this class could be easily explained by the *pars pro toto* principle; remnants, it seems, of a great pictorial concept of the fertility idea.

It is hardly incidental that a corresponding development can be observed in the Aegean. In search for representations of our Motifs I and II on painted vases from the realm of the Mycenaean Empire during LH III A and B (roughly fourteenth and thirteenth century B.C.), a few selected specimens found in Cyprus may suffice to make our point:

1. a LH IIB krater from Cyprus shows two bulls flanking a stylized sacred tree (Plate IV);[27]

2. a LH IIIB krater from Enkomi: a sacred tree heraldically flanked by winged male sphinxes wearing kalathoi, obviously an Orientalizing version of the motif,[28]

3. a LH IIIB krater from Enkomi: a frieze of grazing stags,[29]

4. a LH IIIA krater from Enkomi: a frieze of birds,[30]

5. on a LH III "chariot krater" from Enkomi: a frieze of animals, including bull, cow, and their calf, and various birds (Fig. 5).[31]

These examples, which could easily be multiplied, do not leave any doubt as to the popularity of our Motif I (tree flanked by animals) and Motif II (animal frieze) in Mycenaean III A and B, i.e. during the fourteenth and thirteenth centuries B.C. The *style* is Mycenaean, the *motifs* were apparently taken over from the Near East, an Oriental-

Figure 4: Canaanite vase from grave 912D in Megiddo, details. H. of the whole vase, 0.325 m. Chicago, Museum of the Oriental Institute, University of Chicago. After Guy, loc. cit. (note 26), Pl. 134.

Figure 5:   Animal motifs on Cypro-Mycenaean chariot-krater from Grave 18 at Enkomi in Cyprus, detail. After Sjöqvist, loc. cit. (note 73), Fig. 21, 1 (right half).

izing process. I do not intend to go into the intriguing problems of the Orientalization of Mycenaean vase painting.[32]

Corresponding to the decline of pictorial representations of Motifs I and II on Syro-Palestinian vases in the early Iron Age, a disintegration, stylistically as well as iconographically, of Late Mycenaean vase paintings can be observed on Cypro-Mycenaean pottery of Furumark's "Rude Style" Class which is dated, according to Dr. Karageorghis, to the late LH IIIB and early LH IIIC, i.e., to the second half of the thirteenth century B.C.:

1. a frieze of flying birds;[33] and
2. a sacred tree flanked by birds (Plate V).[34]

Of particular iconographical importance is a third group of pictorial representations on a good number of vases of a class termed by Desborough "Octopus Style Stirrup Jars."[35] These vases are decorated with a huge, highly stylized octopus on the outstretched arms of which all sorts of animals move about. The richest assemblage of animals, to my mind, is on a vase in the British Museum (Fig. 6) from the Island of Kalymnos (near Asia Minor, halfway between Rhodes and Naxos).[36] Here we see birds, deer, goats, hedgehogs, a crab, and scorpions—animals of the land, the sea, and the air, as on the Megiddo Vase. The Octopus Style Stirrup Jars can safely be dated between 1200 and 1000 B.C., covering the Mycenaean Close Style, and the sub-Mycenaean. In this connection we should remember the roughly contemporary sub-Mycenaean Philistine pottery of the 12th–11th centuries B.C., of which the various animal figures represent a late and distant survival of the rich Mycenaean repertoire.[37]

Of great interest is the geographical distribution of these stirrup jars. The types seems, according to Desborough, to originate in Crete (of course, in Mycenaean times), but its production centre was in the central and south Aegean, including Rhodes, Kos, Kalymos, and Naxos. Specimens were also found in Attica (Athens and Perati), in Delphi, occasionally in the Argolid Asine, a few pieces in Thessaly and the Aeolis (Pitane), one specimen in Tarsus, another in southern Italy. The quantities that were recently found in Perati (on the east-coast of Attica) and on Naxos betray close trade connections between Attika and the central and south Aegean in the sub-Mycenaean period. The class of the Octopus Style Stirrup Jars provides a rare example of motif-wanderings from the Aegean to the Greek mainland

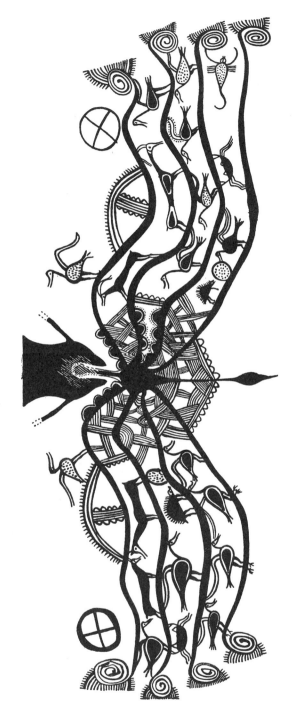

Figure 6:   Late Helladic Octopus Stirrup-jar from Calymnos, details. London, British Museum A1015. After Forsdyke, loc.cit. (note 36), Fig. 276.

in latest-Mycenaeañ and in sub-Mycenaean times.

The animal arrangement on the Kalymnos krater may furthermore serve as a bridge from Late Bronze to Iron Age animal friezes—
our Motif II. Without overstressing the point, in view of the numerous *pars pro toto* abbreviations of animal groups oŋ Late Bronze or
Iron Age vases and seal stones, it is noteworthy, iconographically,
that the tradition of the universal concept behind the countless representations on Bronze and Iron Age Near Eastern pottery, on Mycenaean and Geometric vases, etc. was, in one way or another, con-
sciously or not—who knows—kept up. In our context, the tradition of
our Motif II is of great importance indeed, for it was to represent a
most characteristic feature on Late Geometric vases all over the
Greek cultural area: the secondary figure frieze par excellence, the
"animal frieze": just one example out of hundreds, a small amphora
from the workshop of the Dipylon Master (LG IA),[38] who may have
introduced figure painting in a grand style into Greek Geometric.
Three animal friezes—grazing and reclining deer, and birds—
interrupt, at "strategic" points, the strict geometric design of the vase
in a most charming and enlivening way.

We cannot, to be sure, expect a clear cultural and artistic
development from the Mycenaean to the Geometric period, neither
on the Greek mainland nor in the southeast Mediterranean lands:
1400 the destruction of the Minoan thalassocracy (possibly as a result
of the Thera earthquake),[39] 1200–1100 the Dorian migration and the
end of the Mycenaean empire, 1200 the invasion of the Sea Peoples
and the collapse of the Old Hittite empire. There was hardly a region
in the Graeco-Oriental part of the Mediterranean which was not
involved in the catastrophic events which ushered in the Dark Age.

In view of the scarcity of archaeological material which could
help bridge the gap from Late Mycenaean to Geometric in the southeast Mediterranean, Dr. Porada's basic study in the Hetty Goldman
Volume (1956) of a stylistically and technically coherent group of seal
stones (mostly in the shape of scaraboids) of the late ninth and eighth
centuries B.C. is of considerable value. Out of fifty-four seals, twelve
are decorated with birds (birds flanking tree, single, and in frieze,
Fig. 7), and five with stags with or without birds, or with birds on the
back (Fig. 8).[40] Of great use for the establishment of cultural and
artistic relations between the southeastern Mediterranean lands, the
Dodekanesos, and the Greek mainland in the Iron Age is a statistical

Figure 7: Sealstones with bird motifs, mostly from the southeastern Mediterranean region. After Porada, loc. cit. (note 40), Figs. 32–40.

survey of the provenances of the fifty-four seals, including the seventeen with birds and stags: Syrian Coast (including Byblos), Zincirli (north Syria), Tarsus (Cilicia), Cyprus (Ajia Irini), Crete, Rhodes (Lindos, Kamiros), Chios, Delos, Aegina, Sparta, Thebes (in Boeotia). Statistically Rhodes dominates, and Dr. Porada favours Rhodes as the production centre; next comes Cyprus. The contact with the Syro-Phoenician Coast is maintained, contacts with the Greek mainland exist, though not as strong as one would expect. This, then, is the cultural area—the southeast Mediterranean, especially Cyprus and Rhodes—where the old traditions, the Near Eastern as well as the Mycenaean, in one way or another, survived well into the Iron Age.

Let me first quote from Dr. Porada's stimulating iconological interpretation of these and other representations of animals on those Iron Age seals:

> In conformity with ancient Near Eastern practice, we may assume that their designs (i.e., the designs on the amuletic seals) were meant to secure for the owner the protection of the deities whose symbolic animals or monsters . . . appear in the seal designs. The birds, for example . . . as well as the stags . . . could represent the deity who appears surrounded by them and other animals, riding a lion whose reins she holds, a specimen of the Class, probably from Greece (Fig. 9).[41] The representation suggests that the figure be linked to Syrian goddesses of fertility.

The goddess on this extraordinary seal is surrounded by quadrupeds and birds. Dr. Porada's iconological interpretation is, indeed, very suggestive. However, the question arises: why are there so many *zoomorphic* representations, as we have seen, with or without a sacred tree, entirely dedicated to the animal world? Without elaborating on this intriguing problem, it may just be suggested that one should distinguish between the *anthropomorphic* and the *zoomorphic* type of representation of the superhuman powers of nature and fertility. Generally, the anthropomorphic approach to nature and fertility is found in high cultures, royal or urban—a good and interesting example (Fig. 10) is the famous carved ivory pyxis lid of the thirteenth century B.C. from Minet-el-Beida (harbour of Ugarit-Ras Shamra)[42] which was, according to Helen Kantor,[43] made by Phoenician ivory craftsmen in imitation of a Minoan-Mycenaean representation of a seated Potnia Theron feeding two mountain goats—originally an Oriental motif. In contradistinction, the zoomorphic approach seems to have been produced in times of a cultural

Figure 8: Sealstones with deer motifs, mostly from the southeastern Mediterranean region. Porada, loc. cit. (note 40), p. 203, Figs. 25–29.

Figure 9: Sealstone with Potnia Theron motif. After Porada, loc. cit. (note 40), p. 201, Fig. 12.

Figure 10: Levanto-Mycenaean ivory pyxis lid from Minet-el-Beida. Paris, Louvre. H., 0.137 m. After Kantor, loc. cit. (note 42), Pl. 22J.

low, or by and for a farming society.[44] This explains the decided pre-
dilection for animal decoration of the painted pottery from the Syro-
Palestinian area, extending from the Late Bronze to the Iron Age.

Although the lion on the scarab we have just seen is a symbol for
power and does not exactly belong to the sphere of domesticated
animals whose proliferation is desired by the farmer, the combination
of two iconologically different motifs on Geometric pictorial representations is quite possible. Proof is a masterpiece of Late Geometric
pottery from Boeotia (ca. 680 B.C.).[45] On the front of the Boeotian
vase, a goddess is represented, heraldically surrounded by the
animals of earth (a bull's head and hind leg), air (the birds), and sea
(a fish), and two lions, evidently meant to represent the goddess's
symbolical animals. The powerful picture is framed on either side by
two snakes. We may call the goddess somewhat generally the πότνια
θηρῶν (the mistress of the animals), generally identified with Artemis
or Demeter, or we may give her a corresponding Oriental name,
Ishtar-Astarte, or name her, with Hesiod, Hekate.[46]

To sum up on Motifs I and II: our Motif I is, as far as we can see,
fully developed with the Megiddo Vase of the fourteenth–thirteenth
century B.C.; it continued with the Octopus Style Stirrup Jars of the
twelfth–eleventh centuries B.C., reappears on our Naxian Geometric
krater from Kourion at about 750 B.C. (in a somewhat abbreviated
form), and ends with the Boeotian Geometric jar about 680 B.C.,
where the sacred tree is, so to speak, replaced by the Potnia Theron.
With this change to the anthropomorphic representation of the
fertility idea we are at the very end of the Geometric style, on the
threshold of the high culture of Archaic Greece, ushered in by the
Orientalizing style of the seventh century B.C. This development
seems to leave no doubt as to the Near Eastern-southeast Mediterranean origin of Motifs I and II of the krater from Kourion.

We turn now to Motif III—horse tied to hook; bird underneath
horse; above, hanging double axe—within a comparatively narrow
but high field or metope. It appears eight times on the krater: in each
of the four handle zones twice, flanking symmetrically, almost
heraldically, the dominant central metope with Motif I.

The Naxian Cesnola Painter achieved compositionally such a
uniformity that one is first inclined to connect this motif with Motifs I
and II also iconographically. But such a compositional fusion, often
brought about by the formal conditions of a vase, is typical of a Late
Geometric vase painter: he had to fill the four handle zones as

harmoniously as possible. It is as if the two horses take part in the
central ceremony, enhancing its almost mystical power.

On closer inspection, however, there are clear indications that
these horses do not belong to the animal world in contradistinction to
all the other animals on the vase. These horses are tied-up domesticated animals; the double axes represent another human, though
possibly symbolical, element. With these two elements we leave the
animal world and enter the human, if not the divine, sphere.

Our first concern is to enlarge the body of evidence: Group A
consists of a number of vases by the Cesnola Painter himself or from
his workshop in Naxos or Euboea;[47] for Group B we turn from the
Cyclades and the Dodekanese to the Greek mainland, first to Attica:
Here a class of oinochoai (wine jugs), termed by Coldstream the
"Concentric Circle Group" of oinochoai, consisting so far of fifteen to
twenty specimens, has long since been recognized as manufactured
in Attica but of non-Attic appearance.[48] These jugs are, with rare
early exceptions (LG IB), painted on two sides with hand-drawn concentric circles—unheard of in Attic Geometric—and on the front
with various scenes, including contests (Plate VIII).[49] Some of the
vases have all the elements of our Motif III: the tied-up horse,[50] the
double axe,[51] and the horses, either flanking a tripod cauldron (Plate
VII)[52] or being held by a man in the attitude of a 'Potnios Theron';[53]
this actually corresponds to the two confronting horses of Motif III on
the Kourion vase. Could this doubling of the horse in both cases perhaps be explained as a *compostional* feature?

The dependence of this strange class of Attic oinochoai on an
Iron Age I and II Cypriote type of jug with concentric circles which
derives ultimately from Mycenaean prototypes, is well known.[54]
What makes this Attic type so important, is its combination of
Cypriote, generally southeast Mediterranean, elements—circle
decoration and double axe—with Greek mainland features—man,
tripod cauldron, contest scenes. We move, so to speak, from an
"Orientalizing" animal sphere to a human world, whatever it may
mean. Was it a "Cypriotizing" fashion on the Athenian potters'
market (the Kerameikos) during Late Geometric I B and II which
created this unusual class? Did it serve export purposes? But as far as
I know, such jugs have never been found outside Attica. Nor can we
be sure about the function of these vases. Representations of contest
scenes on them recommend their use as prizes in contests. Another
Attic oinochoe (Fig. 11), not of same class but of the same shape and

time, seems to confirm our suggestion,[55] as it bears on its shoulder a hexametric inscription—one of the oldest Greek inscriptions—reading from right to left: "Who of all the dancers dances most gracefully," hὸς νῦν ὀρχεστόν πάντον ἀταλότατα παίζει. The few letters that follow are disputed, but the meaning is clearly that the victorious dancer receives the oinochoe as a prize. Our short discussion of the two groups opens up all kinds of vistas, iconographically as well as culturally.[56] As we saw before, the products of the Cesnola Painter and his workshop are very widely distributed, from Cyprus and Syria to the west coast of Italy. The style of this pottery was probably influenced most by contemporary Attic Late Geometric I B, in spite of its marked southeastern Mediterranean iconography: it seems very likely that the Cesnola Painter and his school worked to order for customers in the eastern and western Mediterranean.[57] The Concentric Circle Group, on the other hand, mixed Cypriote with Attic features, style and subject matter, on one and the same vase.

Considering now the Attic elements of our Motif III—two horses flanking a tripod cauldron or two horses held by a man—it is certainly not limited to the Concentric Circle oinochoai. It is found on other oinochoai types, on amphorae (Plate IX), kantharoi, beakers, etc. And it appears in addition to Attica, on Boeotian and Argolid vessels.[58] Here and there secondary motifs are added such as the double axe (Plates X and XII), and the bird on the horse's back (Plate XI), or on the head of a man holding the horse.[59]

Special attention should be paid to the many *pars pro toto* renderings of the maximum form of Motif III. Altogether, one gets the impression that the Cesnola Painter incorporated the mainland motif—man holding two horses—into his Orientalizing animal world: the sacred tree flanked by animals, including also the two mainland horses (and the double axes). But the *geographical* distribution of Motif III in its full mainland-form, distinct from the abbreviated or integrated Naxian form, leaves hardly any doubt that Motif III originated on the Greek mainland.

We turn now to the question of meaning and specific origin of Motif III in its Greek mainland forms: (a) two horses tied to and flanking a tripod cauldron (or stand), (b) two horses held by a man. Actual bronze tripod cauldrons are found in great quantities in the sanctuaries at Argos (Heraion), Olympia, Delphi, Ithaka, Delos, Crete, and Cyprus.[60] On the basis of A. Furtwängler's *Olympia IV, Die Bronzen*, and subsequent research by S. Benton, E. Kunze, P.

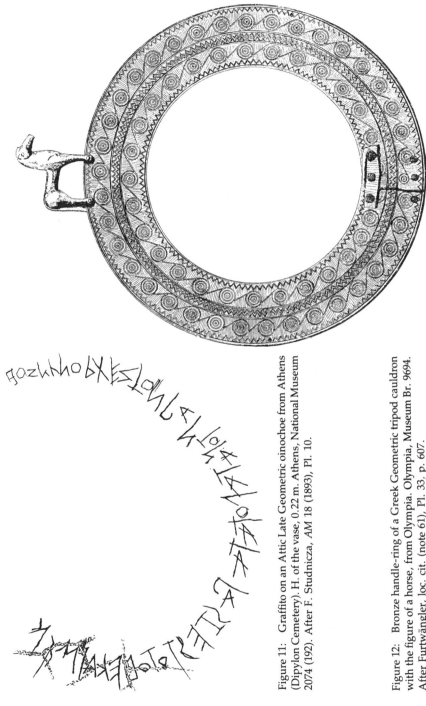

Figure 11: Graffito on an Attic Late Geometric oinochoe from Athens (Dipylon Cemetery). H. of the vase, 0.22 m. Athens, National Museum 2074 (192). After F. Studnicza, AM 18 (1893), Pl. 10.

Figure 12: Bronze handle-ring of a Greek Geometric tripod cauldron with the figure of a horse, from Olympia. Olympia, Museum Br. 9694. After Furtwängler, loc. cit. (note 61), Pl. 33, p. 607.

Amandry, F. Willemsen, and B. Schweitzer,[61] it is now quite possible to form an idea of the original appearance of the bronze tripod cauldrons from those sanctuaries. Some of them were richly decorated on top of their ring handles with figurines either of a single horse (Fig. 12), or of an (originally) armed man holding one horse (Fig. 13).[62] Since the epoch-making publication of the bronzes from Olympia, the meaning of the tripod cauldrons as prizes in the games and subsequent votives in the sanctuary has never been doubted.[63] Concerning the figurative decoration on top of a number of bronze cauldron-ring handles, one should not overlook the fact that, without exception, *one* horse only is found (with or without a man). In view of the "official" character of these prize-votives, this cannot well be incidental. If, then, one horse with one man would represent the original form of Motif III, we might consider the two horses on so many vase paintings as a doubling for compositional purposes, possibly influenced by Oriental heraldic motifs such as the Potnia or the Potnios Theron.

Before I pursue the enquiry into meaning and specific origin of our central motif, horse and man, I would like to say a few words about two secondary motifs, the double axe and the bird—not the bird as a charming fill-ornament underneath the horse (as on the Kourion krater), but in a more significant position, perching on a man's head (as on a Concentric Circle oinochoe).[64] Both motifs—I hardly need say—are closely connected with Minoan cults in Crete. The double axe was originally a sacrificial implement, then became a votive offering and cult object between the horns of consecration.[65] In Crete "it is never in the hands of a male god" (M. P. Nilsson), but always handled by women, especially in the service of nature goddesses. What it signified in Geometric times, on the islands (on the Naxian vases close to the Kourion krater), and on the Greek mainland, where it is represented on Attic, Boeotian, and Argive vases, is still a puzzle. Later I will mention one suggestion as to its possible meaning on the Greek mainland.

The bird, here a dove, appears on the heads of Minoan and Mycenaean figurines of a nature goddess from Middle to Late Minoan III times. Here the bird no doubt served as a symbolical animal of the deity, *her* animal.[66] But the meaning of these symbolical birds may have changed from period to period, from region to region. And a bird on the back of a horse cannot easily be compared with a bird on the head of a deity or a man. In a stimulating article in the Boston Museum Bulletin of 1943, Dr. Berta Segall tried to trace the motif "bird on back of horse" and its varieties from Luristan and Iran (Sialk) in the ninth century B.C. to Greece in the eighth or early seventh century B.C.[67] One Luristan bronze circlet shows the bust of a goddess, surmounted by a goat's head with long horns; an Iranian pottery jug of the ninth century B.C. from Sialk portrays a bird on back of a "horned" horse. Dr. Segall refrains from explaining the combination bird-horse. How did the Greeks understand and reuse this motif? *Non liquet!*

Let us come back to our *basic* Motif III elements, "horse and man." On the basis of the figurative decoration—horse, horse and man, and variations—on a good number of bronze tripod cauldron handles as well as on Attic, Argive, and Boeotian Geometric vase paintings, we feel almost sure about the agonistic character of Motif III.[68] This is confirmed by the descriptions of funerary games in Homer's Iliad XXIII, 257 ff. (for Patroklos), XXIII, 630 ff. (for Amarynkeus, as reported by Nestor),[69] and in the so-called Homeric Hymn to the Delian Apollo, where in addition to athletic contests, muscial games are mentioned. A dancing chorus is charmingly represented on an Atticizing amphora from the Artemision on Delos:[70] note the prize tripod! These three Homeric documents suffice to prove unmistakably that agonistic games did belong to (a) actual funerary ceremonies (krater fragment in the Louvre, Plate XIII),[71] (b) funerary ceremonies in honour of heroes, i.e., hero cult, and (c) cult ceremonies in sanctuaries of deities (krater in Delos). This wide range of agonistic games is amply corroborated by many representations on vases and by the finds of bronze votive tripod cauldrons in a number of sanctuaries all over the Greek world, but with the centre on the Greek mainland.

But even if we accept the suggested interpretation generally, there remain a number of questions and problems to be solved. Two questions come immediately to one's mind: what does the horse, and what does the man represent? Methodically, I suggest two ways to approach these questions—by "symbolical" interpretation, and by "realistic" interpretation. Either way has, admittedly, its pros and its cons.

Symbolically, the ensemble may mean "victory in an agonistic contest," or it may simply symbolize "agonistic games," or it may stand for "virtue (kalokagathia) of the victorious nobleman."[72] A quite different interpretation would perhaps identify the horse-holding man with the "Lord of the Animals" (Potnios Theron), a male counterpart to the "Lady of the Animals" (Potnia Theron), the ubiquitous fertility goddess of Oriental origin.[73] (The horse, however, did not play an important role in the religious concepts of the ancient Near East—indeed, wherever it appears in the east Mediterranean lands during the eighth century B.C. influence from the Greek mainland may be assumed).

By far the strongest arguments in favour of a symbolical identification of the horse-holding man with the god Poseidon are provided by the late Professor Bernhard Schweitzer.[74] Schweitzer's arguments are as follows:

1. He interprets the fish which appear on many Late Argive Geometric vases the horse below the horse (Fig. 14) as "determinatives," i.e., they determine or indicate the character of the figure *next* to them. In other words, the fish as the symbolical animal of Poseidon determines the Poseidonian character of the horse.

2. This identification of the fish (and with it of the horses) is corroborated by the find of a small early archaic bronze fish in the neighbourhood of the pre-Dorian Amyklaion in Laconia with the inscription (from *right* to *left!*) Pohoidanos (of Poseidon).[75]

3. A representation of double axe appears on an Argive Geometric sherd from the Heraion of Argos together with Poseidon's sons, the Aktorione-twins.[76] The double axe, weapon of Poseidon's sons, serves here again as a *determinative*, indicating the relationship to Poseidon of the twins whose heroon was, according to a legend, situated in Phlius near Argos.

4. Pausanias VIII. 42:3-4 describes the old cult image of Demeter of Phigalia in Arcadia as follows: the enthroned goddess was anthropomorphic except for the head which was that of a mare; in her right hand, the goddess held a dolphin, in her left a bird. Her consort was Poseidon.[77]

5. A last point is Schweitzer's mention of the famous horse-breeding in the Plain of Argos.

It goes without saying that Schweitzer's interpretation and method of argumentation must be taken seriously. His brilliant idea of using secondary motifs such as the fish and the double axe as *determinatives* leads, however, to a number of contradictions and problems which cannot well be taken lightly:

Figure 13:   Bronze handle-ring of a Greek Geometric tripod cauldron with the figures of a horse and warrior, from Olympia. Olympia Museum. Reconstructed drawing. After Kunze, loc. cit. (note 61), Fig. p. 9.

Figure 14:   Representation of a man holding two horses on an Argive Late Geometric krateriskos from Melos. H. of the vase, 0.20 m. Athens, National Museum 877. After Schweitzer, text-figure 20.

(a) One would be forced to distinguish iconologically between Argive Geometric vases painted with the motif *"man* between horses" and the motif *"tripod-cauldron* between horses. Such a distinction, however, seems problematic, inasmuch as these motifs, including the fish, appear together on a number of vases.[78]

(b) This would necessarily lead to a corresponding distinction between representations of these motifs on Attic Geometric vases, although there the fish does not appear at all within the framework of these two motifs.

(c) It would certainly be hair-splitting, should one differentiate between Argive representations of "man between two horses" *with* and *without* fish.

In view of the fact that the fish represents a standard secondary motif on Argive (not Attic) Geometric vases, I would, in full agreement with Schweitzer, consider the fish a local element of some importance. I would not, however, consider it a *determinative* which would establish horse and possibly also man as Poseidonian, or Poseidon himself.

A concluding remark by Schweitzer may, possibly, lead the way to a truly valid solution of the problem. He sees behind these Argive pictures a pre-Dorian religious stratum which one may vaguely define as belonging to the sphere of the chthonic Poseidon. Following this line of interpretation, I would, with all due reserve, suggest considering the fish as a rudiment of a pre-Dorian, local, Argive folk religon which worshipped nameless powers of nature, earth, sky, and sea—in the words of Herodot (II 52): "Formerly, in all their sacrifices, the Pelasgians called upon gods (this I know, for I was told at Dodona) without giving name or appellation to any; for they had not as yet heard of such."

It may well be that the pre-Dorian earth-god Poseidawon, whose name is known from the Late Mycenaean Linear B-tablets of the fourteenth century B.C. (from Crete and Pylos in Messenia), underwent a metamorphosis from an earth god to the supreme sea- and water-god; at the time he may have incorporated the fish— probably long since worshipped in the Argolid and in Laconia—as a cult symbol of his new domain.[79]

Any "realistic" interpretation of the vase painting-ensembles "man between two horses" and tripod-cauldron or tripod-stand between two horses" must take as its point of departure the very close connection with the bronze figurines of man and horse on the ring handles of the bronze tripod-cauldrons.

Within the agonistic framework one could, theoretically, suggest that the horse figure be considered (a) as symbolizing a prize in funerary games, following Iliad XXIII 259 ff. where besides cauldrons and tripods, horses and oxen etc. appear as prize items, or (b) as an indication of the category of contest in which victory and prize had been achieved. If we take the Homeric descriptions in Book XXIII of the Iliad as basic, only *chariot* races can be considered, for *horse* races were not practiced before the very end of the eighth century B.C. But if we consider the single horse and man on the tripod cauldron ring handles as representing a one-horse chariot race, another difficulty arises, because, according to Joseph Wiesner's research,[80] one-horse chariots were not used in that period—only two-, three- and four-horse chariots. It is, though, hardly possible to explain the single horse on cauldron ring handles as a *pars pro toto* abbreviation.[81]

The man appears generally, but not always, nude, with or without arms. We may call him an agonistic nobleman, i.e., the owner of the chariot and an expert charioteer—an *apobates* or warrior-athlete experienced in jumping from a fast-moving chariot in combat or sport.[82] As we have already said, either of our two ways of interpreting horse and man, the "symbolic" and the "realistic," has its strengths and weaknesses. Concerning the "realistic" interpretation, two points should be made: 1) the interpretation of the Olympian monuments is not conclusive, either from an iconographic or from a historical point of view, for the monuments of other Greek lands, including Attica, Boeotia, and Argos; 2) despite many basic similarities, the funeral games in honour of heroes, above all the Olympian games, cannot be identified a priori in iconographic terms with normal funerary usages as we know them from Attic cemeteries and ceramic representation.[83] Of the Eridanos cemetery in Athens Karl Kübler observed that there was no room for funeral games with chariots nor even for processions around the grave;[84] this circumstance has led many to reject a "realistic" interpretation of the Attic and Atticizing Boeotian vases depicting processions of chariots. But can we simply suppose that the friezes of chariots on the funerary vases are imaginary and inspired by corresponding scenes in epic poetry? Some experts have occupied a middle ground between the "mythological-symbolical" and "realistic" interpretations: K.

Schefold calls these scenes "archetypes of real life": i.e., under the influence of the Iliad, the scenes on Attic and other vases exalt an ordinary funerary custom—probably a traditional procession around the grave—to a heroic contest.[85] Another point of view, which also mediates between the two extremes described above, sees a profound artistic transformation of a motif which belongs equally to real life and to literature.[86]

We turn now to the final part of our discussion of Motif III—the origin and tradition of the funerary games.

In contrast to the uncertainty still prevailing concerning the survival of Mycenaean burial customs and hero cult in post-Mycenaean times,[87] there cannot be any doubt about the existence of a hero-cult in Geometric times and subsequent periods. With the conquest of Greece by the Homeric epics and other rhapsodic poems during the eighth and seventh centuries B.C., a number of hero-cults were established in various regions of the Greek world: e.g., the Agamemneion near the so-called Tomb of Klytaimnestra in Mycenae,[88] a Menelaion near Sparta,[89] an Odysseion on Ithaka.[90] Such cults were certainly not restricted to Homeric heroes, but comprised also other mythical figures such as Herakles and Theseus, and eponyms such as Pelops. Particularly popular as sites for hero worship were the powerful Mycenaean tholos tombs. In the dromos of such a Mycenaean tomb at Menidi (ancient Acharnai) near Athens quantities of pottery were found from Mycenaean times onwards, betraying the local cult of an (unknown) hero, extending from Geometric times to the Peloponnesian War.[91] The Geometric pottery from Menidi includes Attic Geometric tomb kraters of the eighth century B.C. with representations of funerary chariot games, early Archaic model shields (typical of hero cult), and about thirty fragments of early Archaic horse figurines (probably sub-Geometric) belonging to quadrigae and charioteers—altogether a very instructive example of local hero cult through the ages.

A welcome supplement to the Homeric reports on funerary ceremonies and games is provided by a number of Attic and Boeotian Geometric vase paintings (Figs. 15 through 17). They portray the following games: chariot racing,[92] sword combat, boxing, wrestling, and musical and dancing contests[93] (the latter mentioned in the hexametric inscription quoted above).[94] The numerous representations of funeral ceremonies and games are, with only rare exceptions (from the Cyclades and the Dodekenesos), from the Greek mainland,

Figures 15 and 16:   Scenes from the cult of the dead on fragments of Attic kraters from
Athens (Piraeus Street), ca. 700 B.C. Athens, National Museum 810. After E. Pernice, *AM* 17
(1892), Pl. 10 (above) and p. 226, Fig. 10.

especially from Attica, Boeotia, and the Argolid.

To round off our enquiry about the origins of Motif III, we have to ask two rather general questions which possibly fuse into one: (a) How to explain the apparently sudden emergence of figure-painting in a grand style on the Athenian grave amphorae and kraters and generally on Greek Geometric vases from about 760 B.C.? And (b) whence came the impulse to this epoch-making development? Our eyes turn almost automatically to Olympia, its funerary games and hero cult.

According to Greek tradition (lists of Olympic victors were collected in the fifth century B.C. by the sophist Hippias) the games were established in 776 B.C., i.e., only some fifteen years before the beginning of the Late Geometric figure style when colossal grave vases were decorated with representations of Athenian funeral ceremonies including chariot scenes and other kinds of contests. Most, though not all, scholars agree—I think rightly—that these Attic funerary pictures represent actual ceremonies held around the grave.

In contrast to these regular funerals in Athens and elsewhere in Greek lands, the Olympic games were, especially in early times, essentially permanent memorial cults in honour of the semimythical eponymous hero of the tribe of the Pelopes—Pelops being the father of Atreus and the grandfather of Agamemnon. And, indeed, the nucleus of the Olympian Altis consisted of a polygonal building, the Heroon of Pelops, or Pelopeion. Quantities of the bronze tripod cauldron votives, especially the earlier specimens, were found nearby; and the terracottas associated with the cult go back even further, to the Proto-Geometric period.[95]

All this seems to recommend strong Mycenaean connections, but the finds do not support such an assumption. For a long time, just *one* Mycenaean sherd was known to have been found in the sanctuary; later more pottery turned up (including LH IIIB and C-wares), together with some chamber tombs and remains of a settlement. But this hardly represents a link between Mycenaean and Geometric times. One has to wait for the results of the German excavations under Professor Emil Kunze, especially with regard to the dating of the Pelopeion I-structure which, according to Dr. Hans-Volkmar Herrmann,[96] should be dated "between Middle Helladic and Protogeometric, in other words: in Mycenaean times."

Even in case this could be verified, a hero cult at the Pelopeion in Mycenaean and especially in sub-Mycenaean and Protogeometric times would have to be established before we could accept a continued Mycenaean hero cult in Olympia.[97]

For an understanding of these scant Mycenaean and post-Mycenaean remains in Olympia, another, more general, explanation of the gap may be suggested: the Dorian invasion or, as the Greeks called it, the "Return of the Heraclidae."[98] In this assumption I feel strongly supported and supplemented by an important and most stimulating article by the Swiss ethnologist and Homeric scholar Karl Meuli.[99] The pastoral tribes and cattle-breeding nomads of the steppes, such as the Kirghiz and numerous other ethnic groups and peoples of middle and northern Asia, are organized, he says, in the form of clans (extended families), each with its own eponym. In the religious realm of these pastoral tribes the cult of the dead and ancestors plays an important role. Their funerary ceremonies with races, horse races, wrestling, etc. resemble those in the Iliad and Olympia to a surprising degree. And, just as in early Greece, their heroes, ancestors, and victors in games are praised and recorded in songs and hymns. Such feasts in honour of eponyms and other heroes are often repeated yearly with much pomp and numerous guests.

These funerary games developed, Professor Meuli suggests, from deadly (though strictly regulated) duels in prehistoric times to periodic games in Olympia with rich and varied athletic and artistic contests (the *agones*). Professor Meuli concludes that the phenomenon of the Olympic games can only be understood within the framework of the nomadic culture of cattle-breeders and warrior-shepherds. When the Dorians migrated to Greece from the northwest Balkans, their stage of civilization corresponded more or less with the stage of such shepherd-warriors. The general situation of Greece at that time can hardly be better described than in the words of Thukydides (I.12): "After the Trojan War Greece was in a state of constant movement and was being settled in a way that left her no peace to grow strong again. For the return of the Greeks from Troy took many years and brought many innovations, and civil wars happened in most cities, from which people escaped to find new places. . . . By the eightieth year after the War, the Dorians and the Herakleidai were in possession of the Peloponnesos."

Dating the Trojan War as Desborough does,[100] c. 1230 B.C., and the Dorian destruction and occupation of the Peloponnesos between

1200 and 1100, it would have taken 300 to 400 years before the hero cult at the Pelopeion, with its agonistic memorial games, could be established at Olympia (in Elis), perhaps as a result of the Dorian environment. There is, however, hardly a need to stress the *speculative* character of such suggestions and interpretations, including even Thukydides' statement. We know very little, indeed, about the local developments in the Peloponnese from the end of the Mycenaean Empire until the establishment of the Olympic Games in Elis.[101] It is only to be hoped that the excavations at Olympia may shed more light on Dark Age Greece and on the emergence of the phenomenon of the hero cult.

It seems that during the Dark Age the idea of the hero cult became popular in Greek lands. Its natural relationship and resemblance to the cult of the dead explains the iconographical similarity of Olympian figurines on votive tripod cauldrons with Argive, Attic, and Boeotian Geometric vase-representations. Looking once again at our Motif III and at the Cesnola Krater in general, one has to state that its iconography, together with its style, points definitely to Athens as the source of inspiration. One should refrain from fusing all these pictorial documents from the Greek mainland into one iconological unit! Each cult seems to have had its own origin and history, though all were possibly inspired by the Dorian spirit. In Book II, Chapter 50 of his *Histories*, Herodotus describes a general feature of Egyptian culture, in contrast to his own: "The Egyptians, however," he says, "are not accustomed to pay honours to heroes." What makes this statement of the great historian remarkable is not so much the Egyptian aspect as the Greek—the stress on the hero-cult as a typically Greek phenomenon. In Motif III of the krater from Kourion one may recognize a reflex of the Greek cult of heroes and of the dead, including funeral games. In this connection we must remember the role of Homeric poetry, both as a poetic or rhapsodic mediator of Mycenaean and Geometric culture and as the authorative "Classical" formulation of Greek heroism and hero-cult.

Three statements can now be made with reasonable assurance about the extremely complex Motif III of the krater from Kourion (Plates I and II): 1) it would be inconceivable without the two widely current mainland motifs which show a pair of horses flanking either a man or a tripod; 2) on the crater it has been artfully incorporated in the zoomorphic world of the fertility cult which originates in the lands east and south of the Mediterranean; 3) Motif III, like Motifs I and II on one and the same vase—and on other vases as well—form a striking testimony for artistic and cultural dissemination in the Mediterranean area, including Greece, in Late Geometric times: Oriental, southeastern Mediterranean, and mainland Greek elements are blended together, from the compositional, stylistic, iconographic, and iconologic point of view, to form a brilliant new unity. A striking example is furnished by the decoration of a Boeotian Late Geometric amphora (Plate XIV).[102] A warrior holds two horses flanking him in heraldic fashion; the areas below and above each horse are filled with a colt and kid respectively, the latter turning back its head.

Stylistically and iconographically the work stands so close to the school of the krater from Kourion that we must posit a strong influence from the European or Naxian workshop upon the Boeotian master: this is confirmed by a comparison with the representation of a tripod cauldron flanked by horses on a fragmentary amphoriskos of related style from the Samian Heraion.[103] What distinguishes the Boeotian scene from this work and from the whole production of the Cesnola Painter as it is known to us, is the "Classical" Late Geometric mainland motif of a man leading a horse, which is featured on the Boeotian vase; on the other hand, what connects the Boeotian vase with those of the Euboean or Naxian workshop is the profusion of animals and the atmosphere of the outdoors. The master of the Boeotian amphora was able to combine, in an astonishing degree, mainland elements with others from the Cyclades and the southeastern Mediterranean. And in this enterprise he stands very close to the Cesnola painter.

NOTES

A German version of this paper appeared in *Antike Kunst* 16 (1973), pp. 114-37, under the title "Ikonologische Untersuchungen zur griechisch-geometrischen Kunst: der Cesnola-Krater aus Kourion im Metropolitan Museum."

I am indebted to the following scholars for sending photographs and permitting me to use them here: Dr. Dietrich von Bothmer (The Metropolitan Museum of Art, New York); British Museum, London; Dr. Marie-Louise Buhl (National Museum, Copenhagen); the German Archaeological Institute at Athens; M. Pierre Devambez (Musée du Louvre, Paris); the French School at Athens; Elvehjem Art Center (Madison, Wisconsin); Dr. Vassos Karageorghis (Cyprus Museum, Nicosia); Dr. Barbara Philippaki (National Museum, Athens); Prof. Klaus Vierneisel (Staatliche Museen, Berlin). I also wish to thank Piri Jarden of Jerusalem for drawing the text figures 1-3.

The following abbreviations have been used in the notes to this chapter:

Amiran	R. Amiran, *Ancient Pottery of the Holy Land* (1969)
Andronikos	M. Andronikos, "Totenkult," *Archaeologia Homerica* vol. 3, chap. W (1968).
Coldstream	J. N. Coldstream, *Greek Geometric Pottery* (1968)
Coldstream, "Cesnola Painter"	J. N. Coldstream "The Cesnola Painter: A Change of Address," Institute of Classical Studies, University of London, *Bull.* 18 (1971), 1-15
Davison	J. M. Davison, "Attic Geometric Workshops," *Yale Classical Studies* 16 (1961)
Desborough	V. R. d'A. Desborough, *The Last Mycenaeans and Their Successors. An Archaeological Survey c. 1150–c. 1000 B.C.* (1964).
Hampe	R. Hampe, *Frühe griechische Sagenbilder in Böotien* (1936)
Hampe, *Gleichnisse*	R. Hampe, *Die Gleichnisse Homers und die Bildkunst seiner Zeit* (1952)
Hampe, *Grabfund*	R. Hampe, *Ein frühattischer Grabfund* (1960)
Matz	F. Matz, *Geschichte der griechischen Kunst 1: Die geometrische und die früharchaische Form* (1950)
Propyläen I	K. Schefold u.a., *Die Griechen und ihre Nachbaren, Propyläen-Kunstgeschichte* I (1967)
Schefold	K. Schefold, *Frühgriechische Sagenbilder* (1964)
Schweitzer	B. Schweitzer, *Die geometrische Kunst Griechenlands* (1969); English edition: *Greek Geometric Art* (1971)
Simon	E. Simon, *Die Götter der Griechen* (1969)
Wiesner	J. Wiesner, "Fahren und Reiten," *Archaeologia Homerica*, vol. 1, chap. F (1968)
Willemsen	F. Willemsen, *Dreifusskessel von Olympia, Olympische Forschungen* 3, (1957)

1. The interpretation of legendary scenes on Geometric vases is full of pitfalls and controversy. The following works are of general interest for the problem: E. Kunze, *Kretische Bronzereliefs* (1931); Hampe (see the list of abbreviations above); Schefold; Schweitzer; also P. Courbin, *La céramique géométrique de l'Argolide* (1966) pp. 445 ff., 478 ff., K. Friis Johansen, *The Iliad in Early Greek Art* (1967); Simon; K. Fittschen, *Untersuchungen zum Beginn der Sagendarstellungen bei den Griechen* (1969), with a critical discussion of the relevant scholarship.

2. Hampe, Pl. 30, 3a; Hampe, *Gleichnisse*, Fig. 17b; Schefold, Pl. 4a; Schweitzer, Pl. 185.

3. Schefold, Pl. 5a.

4. Hampe, *Gleichnisse*, Fig. 7-11; Schefold, Pl. 8; Schweitzer, Pl. 60 f.; Fittschen, op. cit. (note 1 above), p. 49., Fig. 13.

5. Hampe, Pl. 22; Hampe, *Gleichnisse*, Fig. 18b; Schefold, Pl. 5c; Schweitzer, Pl. 72; Fittschen op. cit. (note 1 above), pp. 51 ff., AA 1.

6. We cannot here take up the complex problem of the phases within Geometric (especially Attic Geometric) and in particular the disputed chronology of these phases, especially the date of the beginning of the Late Geometric phase. It is time to reconsider the formal separation of the Ripe Geometric phase and its classification as Late Geometric Ia-b carried through by E.T.H. Brann, "Late Geometric and Proto-attic Pottery," in *The Athenian Agora* 8 (1962), preface and introduction; Davidson, pp. 3 ff.; R.M. Cook, *Greek Painted Pottery*² (1966), pp. 17 ff.; Coldstream, passim, especially pp. 4 f., 29 ff., 53 f., and others. We must choose between a threefold division of Geometric which simplifies and even schematizes, and a fourfold division, which aims to do justice to the riches of Attic Geometric, and also of Argive and Boeotian. Four or even five stylistic phases of Attic Geometric vase-painting have been advocated by the author (*AJA* 44 [1940]: 464 ff.), and by the following, among others: G. Nottbohm, "Der Meister der grossen Dipylon-Amphora in Athen," *JdI* 58 (1943): 28ff.; E. Kunze, "Bruchstücke attischer Grabkratere," in *Festschrift Bernhard Schweitzer* (1954), pp. 56 ff., and "Disiecta Membra attischer Grabkratere," *Ephemeris* 1953–54 (1955): 168 ff.; J. Bouzek, "Die attisch-geometrische Keramik im Nationalmuseum in Prag und in den anderen tschechoslowakischen Sammlungen," Sbornik, *Acta Musei Nationalis Pragae*, Series A.; *Historia*, 13 (1959, 3), pp. 105-111 (a survey of the scholarship); *Propyläen* I, pp. 53 ff.; J. Bouzek, *Homerisches Griechenland*, Acta Universitatis Carolinae philosophica et historica, Monographia 29, (1969), especially pp. 147 ff.; Schweitzer, pp. 19 f.

7. Coldstream, "Cesnola Painter" (with references down to 1971).

8. Louis Palma di Cesnola, *Cyprus: Its Ancient Cities, Graves and Temples* (1897), pp. 259-277 (with plan on p. 262), especially pp. 273 ff. and Pl. 68. Cesnola's convic-tion that he had found the subterranean treasure vaults of a temple (263) may be dis-regarded; Coldstream ("Cesnola Painter," p. 11) is inclined to interpret the subter-ranean rooms together with the treasure (which included a Cypro-Phoenician silver bowl) as "the tomb of a princely patron with a strong liking for Oriental imagery." The bowl in question (New York, Metropolitan Museum, Cesnola Collection 4554) has in fact been classified as Cypro-Phoenician II and dated to the seventh century B.C. by E. Gjerstad ("Decorated Metal Bowls from Cyprus," *Opuscula Archaeologica* 4, Skrifter Svenska Institutet i Rom 12 [1946]: 10 ff., Pl. 7); thus the bowl cannot be contemporary with the Cesnola Krater, and the "treasure" is plainly not a unity.

9. E.g., Athens NM 990: Davison, Fig. 25; Coldstream, Pl. 8b; Schweitzer, Pl. 40. New York, Metropolitan Museum 14.130.14: Matz, Pl. 10; Davison, Fig. 26; *Propyläen I*, Pl. 166; Schweitzer, Pl. 41.

10. B. Schweitzer, "Untersuchungen zur Chronologie der geometrischen Stile in Griechenland II," *AM* 43 (1918): 138 ff, Pl. 2 f.; Coldstream, p. 44 ("The Lambros Workshop," Late Geometric Ib).

11. The classification is given with the reservation expressed in 6 above.

12. Argos, Museum c209: Courbin op. cit. (note 1 above), Pl. 100-104; Coldstream, Pl. 26; Schweitzer, Pl. 78.

13. See note 9.

14. According to E. Buschor, "Kykladisches," *AM* 54 (1929): 142 ff., Fig. 6, 7 (frag-

ments of a crater from Naxos with friezes of birds and horses with suspended double axes); N. M. Kontoleon, *Ephemeris* 1945–47 (1949) 1 ff., especially pp. 11 ff., Fig. 4-7; Coldstream, pp. 172 ff. ("The Cesnola Painter and Workshop"), who indeed has recently changed his opinion: see Coldstream, "Cesnola Painter." K. Schefold kindly referred me to the study of E. Walter-Karydi, "Geometrische Keramik aus Naxos," *AA* 1972, 386 ff. Kontoleon's attribution of the school of the Cesnola Krater to Naxos is here elaborated on the basis of further Naxian fragments. The proposal merits careful attention.

15. Coldstream, "Cesnola Painter," especially pp. 8 f.

16. Matz, Pl. 1.2; Davison, Fig. I; Coldstream, Pl. 2; *Propyläen* I, Pl. 164; Schweitzer, Pl. 30.

17. E.g., Cleveland Museum of Art 27.6; Matz, Pl. 187a; CVA 2 III Pl. 2; 3, 1. New York, Metropolitan Museum: Matz, Pl. 187b; Davison, Fig. 69a.b; *Propyläen I*, Pl. 165; Schweitzer, Pl. 50. London, British Museum 1936. 10-17.1: Davison, Fig. 55; Schweitzer, Pl. 55. Cambridge, Fitzwilliam Museum GR-I-1935: Coldstream, Pl. 3 e,f.

18. E.g. Athens NM 198: Matz, Pl. 187c. Athens NM 16011: Coldstream, Pl. 12d. Leyden, Archaeological Museum 1.09/1.1: J.P.J. Brants, *Description of the Ancient Pottery of the Museum of Archaeology of Leiden* (1930), Pl. 7,52; Coldstream, Pl. 11a.

19. H.G. May, "Material Remains of the Megiddo Cult," *Oriental Institute Publication* 26 (1935), Pl. 40, 41; Amiran, Pl. 50.

20. Note 19 above.

21. May, op. cit. (note 19 above), Pl. 39; Amiran, pp. 152 ff. ("The Bichrome Ware"), Photos 136 145, Pl. 48; C. Epstein, "Palestinian Bichrome Ware," *Documenta et monumenta Orientis Antiqui* 12 (1966).

22. O. Tufnell, Ch.H. Inge and L. Harding, *Lachish II (Tell ed Duweir), The Fosse Temple* (1940), pp. 72 f., Pl. 33 A.B. no. 43; Amiran, Pl. 50,2.

23. H. Frankfort, *Cylinder Seals* (1939), pp. 189 ff., ("Seals of the Mitannian Style of Kirkuk"), Fig. 45, 49, Pl. 31a; pp. 278 ff. ("The Popular Style of Mitanni 1700–1200 B.C."), Pl. 41 f, 42b-c, i, 1 : "The glyptic style which prevailed in the northern part of Mesopotamia during the middle of the Second Millennium B.C. cannot be understood in a purely Mesopotamian context. It came into being in North Syria, and spread within the boundaries of the ephemeral Mitannian Kingdom..." (182).

24. W. Culican, "The First Merchant Ventures" *Library of the Early Civilizations* (1966), p. 39, Fig. 32 (British Museum).

25. E. Porada, "Nomads and Luristan Bronzes: Methods proposed for a Classification of the Bronzes," in: *Dark Ages and the Nomads c. 1000* B.C. (1964), p. 15, Fig. I, Pl. 11.

26. P.L.O. Guy and R.M. Engberg, "Megiddo Tombs," *Oriental Institute Publication* 33 (1939), Pl. 134; May op. cit. (note 19 above), Pl. 40; Amiran 163, Photo 166.

27. F. Stubbings, *Mycenaean Pottery from the Levant* (1951), Pl. II, 2, CVA Cyprus Museum 1 IIC, Pl. 5 A 1647 (V. Karageorghis).

28. Ibid., Pl. 9,6: CVA British Museum IICb, Pl. 10 (Great Britain 22), I, C417 from Enkomi (A. H. Smith and F. N. Pryce).

29. Ibid., Pl. 9,8; CVA British Museum IICb Pl. 9 (Great Britain 21), 5, C408 from Enkomi (Smith and Pryce).

30. Ibid., Pl. 7,2; CVA British Museum IICb Pl. 9 (Great Britain 21) 4, C372 from Enkomi (Smith and Pryce).

31. Sjöqvist, *Problems of the Late Cypriote Bronze Age* (1940), Fig. 21,I (right half); E. Vermeule, *Greece in the Bronze Age* (1964), Pl. 32c.

32. The survival of the Mycenaean tradition in the post-Mycenaean period, especially in the southeast Mediterranean, and the mixture of Mycenaean with Near Eastern elements of a formal and iconographic character, are generally acknowledged, and have indeed been the subject of important pioneer works (above all Desborough, *Last Mycenaeans*); yet these phenomena require much deeper study. They are touched on several times in the following pages. Later traces of the Mycenaean artistic repertory are also studied by J. L. Benson, *Horse, Bird, and Man: The Origins of Greek Painting* (1970), especially ch. 5: "Tradition and its transmission."

33. CVA Cyprus Museum 1 IIC, Pl. 13, 5-7, A1750 from Enkomi, Grave 68 (V. Karageorghis).

34. CVA op. cit., Pl. 15, 1.2, A2020a + A2021a from Enkomi, Grave 96.

35. Desborough, pp. 271 f. (Appendix B), frontispiece and Pl. 6.

36. E. J. Forsdyke, *Prehistoric Aegean Pottery, Catalogue of the Greek and Etruscan Vases in the British Museum I*, I (1925) Pl. 15 and Text-fig. 276: A1015; A. Furumark, *The Mycenaean Pottery, Analysis and Classification* (1941), pp. 304 f., Fig. 49, no. 28 (Motive 21 Cuttlefish).

37. Trude Dothan, *The Philistines and their Material Culture* (1967, in Hebrew).

38. Munich, Museum of Ancient Art (1250) 6080 (H., 0.51 m): Matz, Pl. 8; CVA 3, Pl. 106; Davison, Fig.5; Schweitzer, Pl. 21.

39. On the controversy see P. Warren, *Gnomon* 45 (1973): 173 ff.

40. E. Porada, "A. Lyre Player from Tarsus and his Relations," in *The Aegean and the Near East; Studies presented to Hetty Goldman* (1956) p. 205, Fig. 32-40, Pl. 18 (bird); p. 203, Fig. 25-29, Pl. 18 (deer).

41. Ibid., p. 201, Fig. 12.

42. C.F.A. Schaeffer, "Les Fouilles de Minet-el-Beida et de Ras Shamra," *Syria* 10 (1929): 291-293, Pl. 56; H. Frankfort, *The Art and Architecture of the Ancient Orient* (1963), p. 155, Pl. 150; H. J. Kantor, "The Aegean and the Orient in the Second Millenium B.C.", *Archaeological Institute of America Monograph* I (1947); AJA 51, (1947): Pl. 22J.

43. Ibid., pp. 86 ff.

44. The complex problem needs a fuller treatment. To forestall any misunderstanding, let me observe in general terms that periods of collapsing civilization, as shown by many examples in the history of mankind, sometimes contain the seeds of "high cultures"—and the reverse.

45. Hampe, Pl. 17; Coldstream, Pl. 45d.

46. Professor Erika Simon now suggests the later date of c. 680 B.C. (instead of 700 as at Fig. 139 of her book), noting the relationship with the Cycladic relief pithoi. On the

Greek form of the Oriental Potnia Theron see Simon's chapter, "Artemis." Coldstream, pp. 202, 205, 208, 330, likewise commends a sub-Geometric dating.

47. See notes 14 and 15 above.

48. Coldstream, pp. 74-76, Pl. 13d, Pl. 56, 57; our Plates VII and VIII.

49. Schweitzer Pl. 56 (lower row).

50. CVA Frankfurt am Main I, Pl. 5, 2.3, VF 222 (K. Deppert); M. Collignon et L. Couve, *Catalogue des vases peints du Musée National d'Athenes*, Planches (1940), Pl. 13, 242 (193).

51. Athen NM 151: S. Wide, "Geometrische Vasen aus Griechenland," *JdI* 14 (1899): 212, Fig. 91.

52. Coldstream, Pl. 13d (London, British Museum 77.12-7.12); S. Benton, "The Evolution of the Tripod-Lebes," *BSA* 35 (1934–35): 104, Fig. 11a = Coldstream, P. 75, list no. 10 (British Museum, Manuscript Catalogue 2531). Athens NM 193 (see note 50 above) is perhaps better interpreted as a *pars pro toto* representation of the motif "tripod cauldron flanked by horses."

53. Schweitzer, Pl. 56.

54. *Swedish Cyprus Expedition* 4, 2 (1948), Pl. 34, 16b and Pl. 33, 6b (both "Bichrome IV Ware"). Cf. Coldstream, p. 75 with notes 2 f.; Schweitzer, p. 49 with note 68.

55. Athens NM 192 (2074): A Furtwängler, "Zwei Tongefasse aus Athen," *AM* 6, (1881): 106 ff., Pl. 3; F. Studniczka, "Die alteste attische Inschrift," *AM* 18 (1893): 225 ff., Pl. 10; J. Kirchner, *Imagines Inscriptionum Atticarum* (1948), Pl. 1,1; L. H. Jeffery, *The Local Scripts of Archaic Greece* (1961), p. 68, Pl. 1, 1; M. Guarducci, *Epigrafia greca I* (1967), pp. 135 f., Fig. 28 a,b; Coldstream, pp. 358 f. On the dating see T. J. Dunbabin in Jeffery op. cit., p. 68, 4; Davison, pp. 73 ff., Fig. 8, pp. 103-106 ("The Oinochoe Group"); Coldstream, pp. 32 f. ("Oinochoai"). The relative dating of Dunbabin—"the inscribed jug is stylistically rather later than Athens 152" (Kahane, *AJA* 44 (1940): Pl. 26, 1) "and I think typical poor Late Geometric"—is certainly acceptable, with the reservation that the oinochoe bearing the inscription is at the least very close, in respect of form and style, to the workshop of the Dipylon Master; i.e., according to Coldstream's chronological system it should be assigned to the late Geometric L. G. phase Ib, ca. 750–735 (Coldstream, p. 358 "around 740"). In this connection I must refer to the early dating for the transmission of the West Semitic alphabet to the Greeks, "about 1100 B.C.," proposed by J. Naveh: "Some Semitic Epigraphical Considerations on the Antiquity of the Greek Alphabet, "*AJA* 77 (1973): 1 ff.

56. On the definition of the concepts see E. Panofsky, *Meaning in the Visual Arts* (1955), ch. I, and *Studies in Iconology* (1967).

57. On the complex question of Greek trade connections in the eastern and western Mediterranean regions, see Coldstream passim, especially the chapters "Absolute Chronology" and "Historical Conclusions," on the emporium Al Mina (in northern Syria), ibid., pp. 384 f., and Coldstream, "Cesnola Krater," pp. 8 f. (list of the krater fragments from the workshop of the Cesnola Painter found at Al Mina, nos. 7 and 11).

58. *Attic Geometric:* e.g., Davison, Fig. 45 (Athens NM 18444), 51 (New York, Metropolitan Museum 10.210.7); Coldstream, Pl. 8c, d (Munich 8748), 13 c, f. (Cambridge, Fitzwilliam Museum GR-I-1935), 14c (East Berlin Civic Museum 31005);

192   The Archaeology of Cyprus

Schweitzer, p. 50, Fig. 16 (from Thera, Athens NM 13038), Pl. 29 (Athens, Kerameikos Museum 1306), 56 (from Aegina, West Berlin Civic Museum 3374), 59 (from Athens, Kerameikos, Copenhagen, National Museum 16280). *Boeotian Geometric:* e.g., B. F. Canciani, "Böotische Vasen aus dem 8. und 7. Jahrhundert," *JdI* 80 (1965): 26 (8), 67 f. Fig. 19 (Athens NM 236). *Argive Geometric:* e.g., Coldstream, Pl. 28-30; Schweitzer, p. 65, Fig. 20 (Athens NM 877), Pl. 77 (from Asine, Nauplia Museum 2248). Coldstream, p. 137 "The Schliemann Workshop" ii,6: a horse with man leading: Courbin op. cit. (note 1 above), passim.

59. E.g., Coldstream, Pl. 45a,44c (Boeotian); Schweitzer, Pl. 56 (Attic).

60. Apart from H. W. Catling, *Cypriot Bronzework in the Mycenaean World* (1964), pp. 190-223, we still lack a comprehensive survey of the metal tripod cauldron from the Late Bronze Age and Iron Age in the Mediterranean region. Along with the older works of E. Reisch (*RE V*, 2, [1905]: 1669 ff., Dreifuss) and K. Schwendemann ("Der Dreifuss," *JdI* 36 [1921]: especially 120 ff.), incidental details about the distribution of tripod cauldrons are to be found in the studies mentioned in the following notes (above all Benton op. cit. (note 52) especially pp. 92 f., 118 ff., 128 f.) and also in Willemsen, pp. 175 ff.

61. A. Furtwängler, "Die Bronzen . . . von Olympia," *Olympia* 4 (1890); Benton, op. cit. (note 52 above), pp. 74 ff.; E. Kunze, *Neue Meisterwerke griechischer Kunst aus Olympia* (1948), pp. 5-10, Pl. 1 ff.; Willemsen (with the agreement of S. Benton, *AJA* 63 [1959]: 94 f., Amandry, *Gnomon* 32 [1960]: 459 ff., and Schweitzer, p. 179: "it is improbable that the large decorative tripod cauldrons began before 800 B.C."); Schweitzer, pp. 178-198.

62. E.g., Williamsen, Pl. 78 (a single horse, from Olympia: Olympia Museum Br. 9694), Pl. 79 (a horse, from Olympia: Athens NM 7483), Pl. 80 (horse held by man from Olympia, Olympia Museum B2041) with a reconstructed drawing (18) on page 149, Pl. 86-89 (horse figures on ring handles, all from Olympia), Pl. 43, B 24 (man leading a horse on a ring handle, from Olympia); Schweitzer, examples of men leading horses on ring handles: Pl. 125 (from the Heraion of Argos: Athens, National Museum), Pl. 126 (from Olympia: Olympia Museum), Pl. 127 (from Olympia; Paris, Louvre), Pl. 136-139 (from Olympia: Olympia Museum), Pl. 132-135 (from Athens, Acropolis: Athens National Museum).

63. A comprehensive treatment of the related problems—chronology, development, function, style—is now provided by Schweitzer, ch.7: "Bronzedreifüsse und anderes Gerät," pp. 174-198. Also noteworthy are the supplementary, but in part divergent interpretations and comments of Andronikos and Weisner in the *Archaeologia Homerica*, and the latest studies of material from Olympia: H. V. Herrmann, *Olympia* (1927) especially pp. 66-79; A. Mallwitz, *Olympia und seine Bauten* (1972), especially pp. 41-46; W. D. Heilmeyer, "Frühe olympische Tonfiguren," *Olympische Forschungen* 7 (1972), passim; see also H. V. Herrmann, "Werkstätten geometrischer Bronzeplastik," *JdI* 79 (1964), 17 ff.; M. Weber, "Die geometrischen Dreifusskessel," *AM* 86 (1971), 13 ff. Very stimulating is W. Burkert's "Homo Necans. Interpretationen altgriechischer Opferriten und Mythen," *Religionsgeschichtliche Versuche und Vorarbeiten* 32 (1972), passim, especially pp. 108-119 ("Pelops in Olympia").

64. Schweitzer, pp. 55 f., Pl. 56. See also note 59 above.

65. On the Minoan double axe see M. P. Nilsson, *Geschichte der griechischen Religion*

I^2 (1955), pp. 275 ff. The ritual use of the double axe (as a sacrificial weapon in the bull-cult) emerges in the clearest possible fashion in the scenes on the sarcophagus from Hagia Triada (about 1400 B.C.); Spyridon Marinatos and M. Hirmer, *Crete and Mycenae* (1959), colour Pl. 27, 29; *Ant K* 8 (1965): Pl. 24,2. Further affinities are discussed by H. G. Buchholz, *Zur Herkunft der Kretischen Doppelaxt* (1959).

66. The bird on the head of Minoan goddesses is interpreted as their epiphany by Nilsson op. cit. (see note 65), pp. 290 ff.; F. Matz, "Göttererscheinung und Kultbild im minoischen Kreta," *Abh. Mainz* 1958, No. 7. Examples: the faience figurine of the "Snake Goddess" from Knossos (Middle Minoan III, about 1600–1580 B.C.), Marinatos and Hirmer op. cit. (see note 65), colour Pl. 24; female terracotta statuette from Gazi in Crete (Late Minoan III, 1400–1100 B.C.), Marinatos and Hirmer, op. cit. pl. 128, 129.

67. B. Segall, "Greece and Luristan," *Bull. Museum of Fine Arts Boston* 41 (1943): 72 ff., Fig. 1-16. See E. Porada, *Alt-Iran* (1962), pp. 69-83 ("Bronzearbeiten aus Luristan," 12.-7. Jahrhundert v. Chr.); pp. 96 f. ("Funde des ersten Jahrtausends aus Sialk").

68. Heilmeyer op. cit. (note 63 above), especially pp. 38-41, judges otherwise, supposing that a chariot was dedicated simply as the most costly possession of the nobility in the western Peloponnesus—"without reference to any particular journey or race." In my opinion, there must be deeper significance in the choice of these subjects—chariots, horses, chariot drivers, and men holding horses—for dedication at Olympia in the 8th century B.C.

69. The Homeric burial practices are compared with Hittite by O. R. Gurney, *The Hittites* (Pelican Book, 1954), pp. 164 ff. Naturally we cannot here take up the complex question of the early history of Greek funeral games and heroic contests in literary and archaeological contexts, although many substantial points require critical examination.

70. Ch. Dugas et C. Rhomaios, "Les vases préhelléniques et géométriques," *Délos* 15 (1943): Pl. 56.

71. On the fragment of a funeral krater: CVA Louvre 11 III Hb, Pl. 14, 8, A547 (F. Villard); Davison, Fig. 22. Note the two prize tripod cauldrons beside the bier.

72. According to K. Schefold, *Griechische Kunst als religiöses Phänomen* (1959), p. 20, the horse becomes the badge and symbol of a Greek hero.

73. See Weisner, especially pp. 79-92 ("Fahren ausserhalb des frühgriechischen Bereichs"). In this connection we ought to remember the special role which the class of Mycenaean "chariot-kraters" appears to play in Late Helladic III (14th-12th centuries B.C.). The numberous examples of the category from Cyprus allow an important distinction between Hellado-Cypriot and Levanto-Cypriot style: see E. Sjöqvist, op. cit. (note 31 above), pp. 71 f. The positon of this category of vase between the Near East and Greece urgently needs to be clarified; see Benson, op. cit. (note 32 above), passim.

74. Schweitzer, pp. 64 f. Fig. 20. Pl. 77; Coldstream, Pl. 29d-f., 30c-e. On the matter of the different iconographic interpretations of recurring motifs on Argive Geometric vases see Courbin op. cit. (note 1 above), pp. 445 ff., 478 ff.

75. E. Buschor and W. von Massow, "Vom Amyklaion," *AM* 52 (1927): 3, 37, Pl. 1.

76. Hampe, pp. 45 ff., Pl. 9, no. 10, Pl. 14, no. 28 and Pl. 34, lower left; Schweitzer,

pp. 45, 65, 146, 233 f., Fig. 13, Pl. 232. The identification is questioned by Fittschen op. cit. (note 1 above), pp. 68 ff., Fig. 15.

77. The goddess' all-embracing nature is symbolically represented by the beasts of earth, air and water. There is a clear kinship between the cult statue of Demeter of Phigalia as described by Pausanias and the Boeotian sub-Geometric vase painting of a Potnia Theron discussed above (our Pl. VI). I have already shown that she has precursors on a scaraboid seal-stone of the 9th–8th centuries B.C., perhaps from the southeastern Mediterranean (our text-fig. 9) and also on an ivory relief of the 13th century B.C. from Minet el-Beida at Ras Shamra in northern Syria (our text-fig. 10).

78. E.g., Coldstream, Pl. 29d-f, 30c.

79. J. Chadwick, *The Development of Linear B*² (1967), pp. 30, 114, 124, 126. On the early history of Poseidon one may now consult Simon's chapter on "Poseidon," which takes from L. Preller (*Griechische Mythologie I: Theogonie und Götter*, 1854) the thesis that "land and sea in the Aegean form an inseparable unity, which indeed is subsumed by the sea." Hence we must discard "the view, almost universally held today, that Poseidon originally ruled the land and was thereafter forced out to sea by Zeus..." (67).

80. Wiesner, passim, especially p. 136.

81. Dr. G. Beckel, Assistant at the Martin von Wagner Museum of Wurzburg University, suggested to me that consideration be given to the double occurrence of the horse, i.e., on each of the two ring-handles as also on the two side metopes on a number of vases (including the Cesnola krater). This could perhaps help to illuminate the dilemma posed by the representation of a single horse (with or without a man leading the horse) on the ring handles.

82. On the apobates see E. Reisch, *RE* I, 2 (1894), 2814 ff.; N. Yalouris, "Athena als Herrin der Pferde," *Museum Helveticum* (1950), pp. 19 ff., 50, 58-61; H. Metzger, "Recherches sur l'imagerie athénienne," *Publications de la Bibliothèque Salomon Reinach* 2 (1965), 69 ff.; A. Alföldi, "Die Herrschaft der Reiterei in Griechenland und Rom nach dem Sturz der Könige," in "Festschrift Karl Schefold," *Ant K*, Beiheft 4, (1967): 18 f.; Weisner, pp. 95 ff., 110; Andronikos, p. 126; Burkert, op. cit. (note 62 above), pp. 175 ff. The phenomenon of the apobates and the importance of the contest of apobatai for the origin of the Panathenaic Games were kindly brought to my attention by Homer A. Thompson, see *AA* 1961, 224 ff., and now H. A. Thompson and R. E. Wycherley, "The Agora of Athens," *The Athenian Agora* 14 (1972), pp. 121, 129. That depictions of apobatai already occur in the 8th century B.C. was demonstrated by R. Tolle, "Eine geometrische Amphora in Essen," *AA* (1963), 224 f., Fig. 1.2 (with a reference to the Homeric Hymn to Apollo, pp. 229-238, especially pp. 232 f.) Burkert op. cit. (note 63 above), p. 176 with note 94 mentions, without citing his source, another example from the Geometric period in Philadelphia (30.33.133).

83. Cf. Hampe, *Grabfund*, pp. 60 f. (with a discussion of the problem of symbolism or realism).

84. K. Kübler, "Die Nekropole des 10. bis 8. Jahrhunderts," *Kerameikos* 5 [1] (1954), 21.

85. E. Hinrichs, "Totenkultbilder der attischen Frühzeit," *Annales Universitatis Saraviensis* 4, (1955), 144 ff. Schefold op. cit. (note 70 above), p. 25. On the scholarly discussion of the three ways of approaching the problem see Andronikos, pp. 125 f.

86. On this important, but often neglected fourth point of view, see the interesting

comments of Hampe, *Gleichnisse,* passim.

87. On this vexed question, which culminated in the controversy between M. P. Nilsson and G. F. Mylonas, see Andronikos, pp. 126-128.

88. J. M. Cook, "The Agamemneion, Mycenae 1939–52, Part III," *BSA* 48 (1953): 30 ff.

89. A. J. B. Wace, M. S. Thompson and J. P. Droop, "The Menelaion, Excavations at Sparta," *BSA* 15 (1908–09): 108 ff.

90. S. Benton, "Excavations at Ithaca III," *BSA* 35 (1934–35): 54, Fig. 7.

91. P. Wolters, "Vasen aus Menidi, II," *JDI* 14 (1899): 103 ff., Fig. 17-19, 25-27.

92. On *Attic Geometric* grave kraters such as Athens NM 990: Davison, Fig. 25; Coldstream, Pl. 8b; Schweitzer, Pl. 40. New York, Metropolitan Museum 14.130.14: Matz, Pl. 10; Davison, Fig. 26; *Propyläen* I, Pl. 41. Athens NM 806: Kahane, *AJA* 44 (1940), Pl. 25; Davison, Fig. 18; Andronikos, Pl. 12. New York, Metropolitan Museum 14.130.15: Davison, Fig. 139. On *Atticizing Boeotian Geometric* vases such as the kantharos in the Archaeological Institute of Göttingen University 533h: Canciani, *JdI* 80 (1965). 42 f., fig. 7-9.

93. *Attic Geometric* kantharos from Athens, Kerameikos: Copenhagen National Museum 727: CVA III H, Pl. 74, 5a.b., 75, 2-6; W. Hahland, "Zu den Anfangen der attischen Malerei," in: *Corolla Ludwig Curtius* (1937), pp. 126 ff., Pl. 42, 43; D. Ohly, *Griechische Goldbleche des 8. Jahrhunderts v. Chr.* (1953), Pl. 18; Andronikos, pp. 121 ff., Fig. 10a,b., 11a-e. Fragments of a cauldron, Athens NM 810: E. Pernice, "Geometrische Vase aus Athen," *AM* 17 (1892), 226, Fig. 10, Pl. 10; Hampe, *Grabfund,* p. 50 f. Fig. 33-39; Andronikos, pp. 124 ff., fig. 11 f, g. *Boeotian Geometric,* e.g., a cup, Paris, Louvre: Hampe, p.23, Pl. 20, V. 6. Kantharos at Dresden: Hampe, p. 25 Pl. 23, V. 35; Andronikos, p. 124, Pl. 11a,b.

94. See the discussion above with note 55.

95. On the Proto-Geometric terracottas see Heilmeyer op. cit. (note 63 above). In this connection it is important to remember Heilmeyer's warning (pp. 3 ff.) that the location of the original finds of the tripod cauldrons in the sanctuary of Olympia cannot be determined.

96. H.-V. Herrmann, "Zur altesten Geschichte von Olympia," *AM* 77 (1962): 3-34.

97. On this complex problem, which is here considered only from a relatively narrow and local point of view, reference may be made to the comprehensive studies of Desborough, *Last Mycenaeans,* and Desborough and N. G. L. Hammond, "The End of Mycenaean Civilization and the Dark Age," *Cambridge Ancient History,* Revised Edition Fasc. 13 (1962). Many related questions will undoubtedly be clarified hereafter by the publication of the results of the German excavations of Olympia by Professor Emil Kunze and his collaborators.

98. E. Buschor, *Griechische Vasenmalerei*[2] (1921), pp. 31 ff.: "Although the Dorians did not develop the new style so brilliantly as other Greek peoples, yet it was the ferment caused by their arrival that produced the new mixture—the essentially Greek element which created, from the surviving traditions of the mainland and the diminished inheritance of Mycenae, a new style, a sure basis for a splendid development."

99. K. Meuli, "Der Ursprung der Olympischen Spiele," *Die Antike* 17 (1941): 189 ff.

100. Desborough, passim, especially pp. 244 ff. ("The Evidence of Dialect and the Oral Tradition").

101. We must not overlook Desborough's cautionary reference to "radical differences between the traditional account and the archaeological evidence" (pp. 251 ff, 287).

102. The amphora is now at the Elvehjem Center in Madison, Wisconsin; it was published by Professor Herbert Cahn, to whom I am indebted for knowledge of the vase and for a reference to the publication: *Art of the Ancients: Greeks, Etruscans and Romans* (André Emmerich Gallery Inc. New York, February 7-March 13, 1968) 3, no. 1.

103. Coldstream, "Cesnola Painter" p. 9, no. 12, Pl. 3d.

Figure 17:   Funeral games, etc. on an Attic Geometric kantharos from Athens (Dipylon Cemetery). H. including handle, 0.17 m. Copenhagen, National Museum 727. After Andronikus, text-figure 11 a–e.

LIST OF PLATES

Plate I

Plate II

Plate III

Plate IV

Plate V

Plate VII

Plate VIII

Plate IX

Plate X

Plate XI

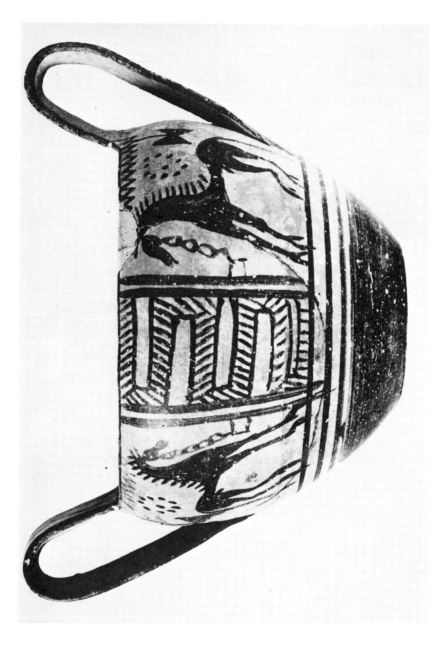

Plate XII

Plate XIII

Plate XIV

Excavations at Soloi

Jean des Gagniers

Less than forty miles from Nicosia, the modern capital of Cyprus, the ancient city of Soloi overlooks the western edge of the Bay of Morphou, on the northwestern shore of the island. The road from Nicosia, after crossing the Mesaorea, approaches the coast a few miles east of Soloi. It then runs through the quite recent agglomeration of Potamos tou Kambou whose first houses have been built on the archaeological site by the inhabitants of the neighbouring mountain village of Galini. The population of Potamos tou Kambou is composed of peasants, shepherds, day-laborers and a few mine workers. Cypriots call the people of our region Tylliri. They are the descendants of those Tylliri who, according to tradition, were brought by Saint Helena from Asia Minor, in an effort to increase the then insufficient population of the island. We recruit our workers amongst them. The Tylliri have a certain reputation for lust of gold, and the high prices they ask for their fields would make excavation difficult, were it not that years ago a large tract of archaeological land was acquired by the Department of Antiquities. The whole district is in fact controlled by this Department.

The Soloi region is of great archaeological importance. West of the city, at a distance of about 5 miles, the rock of Petra tou Limniti was the first Neolithic settlement to be found in Cyprus. High above this sea rock, at the top of a mountain, lies the fortified city of

Vouni, excavated by Professor E. Gjerstad and certainly one of the most impressive sites in the whole Mediterranean world. Owing to the copper mines, Bronze Age sites are numerous in that area. Amongst others, let me mention Ambelikou (where Dikaios has worked), Kathydata (excavated by Markides, the first curator of the Cyprus Museum), Apliki (where Miss Joan DuPlat-Taylor has dug), and Khalandrikas, which is now being excavated under the direction of Dr. James Carpenter of Kent State University. On these sites and on others, like Aletri, a tremendous amount of promising work remains to be done.

Soloi was built on the top and northern side of a hill which is a little more than two hundred feet high and whose summit is about 2500 feet from the seashore. The site has been very accurately described by Westholm in the third volume of the series published by the Swedish Cyprus Expedition. "Soloi was situated on one of the small hills in the region where the plain of Mesaorea, which occupies the centre of Cyprus, between the Kyrenia range and the Troodos mountains, is transformed into low hills before the high mountains of western Cyprus."[1]

This was indeed a very favorable situation, particularly on the eastern side, where Soloi overlooks the fertile and well irrigated plain of Morphou which even today is considered one of the best agricultural regions of the island; on this side, the site is surrounded by orange and lemon orchards. The narrow valleys of the Xeros and the Kambos rivers, which water the territory of Soloi, provide communication with fertile areas in the southern and western mountains. The city owed its prosperity to the presence of copper ore which, as early as the third millenium B.C., was extracted at Skouriotissa, a few miles southward; moreover, it possessed an excellent harbour. At the beginning of our era, it seems that this harbour silted up and, around the fourth century A.D., the partially exhausted mines ceased to be operated.

According to Plutarch, Soloi succeeded and replaced the more ancient city of Aipeia which Demophon, a son of Theseus, had founded on a neighbouring mountain. We read in the *Life of Solon* that on visiting his friend Philokypros, the king of Aipeia, the great legislator advised him to move his city closer to the plain and the sea. Philokypros did so and gave the name of Soloi to the new city in honour of his distinguished visitor. The story is only a legend, however, for Soloi already existed in the seventh century, long before Solon's time, when it appears under the name Si-il-lu in Esarhaddon's and Assurbanipal's list of Cypriot cities. One fact seems sure: the Soliots' sympathy was, if I may say so, oriented towards Greece. When Ionians rebelled against the Persians, Aristokypros, its king, died in the disastrous battle of Salamis. After this defeat, Herodotus writes that the city of Soloi was able to withstand a five months' siege by the Persians. This certainly means that it was already well fortified. Soon after its capitulation, a fortified palace was built a few miles to the west, at Vouni. Gjerstad infers that this fortress was meant to watch over the conquered city of Soloi.

After Cimon's attack against Marion, circumstances must have changed. The pro-Persian king of Marion was then replaced by a Greek king, and a Philhellenic dynast came to Vouni. It was he who transformed the oriental palace into a more Hellenic structure. However, Vouni's role was left unchanged: it kept watch over Soloi. This situation was to be radically reversed in 391–390, when Soloi, forgetting its alignment of 498, allied with Kition and Amathous and asked the Persians for help against Evagoras of Salamis, who sought to subjugate the entire island. Thanks to this change of policy, the Soliots then recovered some kind of independence and their king began issuing coins again.

The history of the city in the Classical period is not well-known. Though a vassal city, it was certainly an important one. It may have been the Soliots who after the alliance with Kition and Amathous burnt down the hateful palace of Vouni. Later, when Alexander the Great, returning from Egypt, celebrated sacrifices in Phoenicia, Cypriot kings acted as *choregi* and, according to Plutarch, the contest between the king of Salamis and the king of Soloi was close. Nikokles, a son of the king of Soloi, followed Alexander to India. Afterwards, relations between the city and Ptolemaic Egypt must have been close; at the end of the fourth century, Eunostos, the last king of Soloi, married Eirene, a daughter of Ptolemy Sôter and Thaïs, the famous courtesan.

Owing to its copper mines, Soloi was still a prosperous city in Roman times, as our excavations clearly indicate. It was

Christianized early by Saint Auxibius, whose story is told in the *Acta Auxibii*. The work was written rather late, probably in the fourth century A.D., but we know that its author followed an earlier version. Auxibius, having fled from Rome in order to avoid a marriage he did not want, no sooner landed on Cyprus than he met Saint Mark, who baptized him and sent him to preach the Gospel to the Soliots. He was to speak to them "tanquam infantibus" and he fulfilled his mission so well that he converted his first host, a priest of Jupiter. Auxibius was Soloi's first bishop, and he lived in the city for more than fifty years.[2]

In Auxibius' time, it seems that the harbour of Soloi had already silted up.[3] This must have been one of the main causes of the city's decadence after long prosperity. Another cause was the closing of the mines, which probably took place in the fourth century A.D. Soloi became an obscure town. It suffered from Arab raids, and must have slipped out of existence in the fourteenth century.

The city has often been mentioned since Medieval times. Etienne de Lusignan, who wrote during the sixteenth century, describes it as entirely ruined, though still inhabited as a village. Quite surprisingly, this author writes that the site is three miles from the sea, which is entirely erroneous. He also states that Saint Auxibius' tomb was still visible and highly venerated in his time; unfortunately, he does not say where this tomb could be seen. During the same century, Florio Bustrone in his *Chronique de l'Île de Chypre* describes the site as a "loco sicurrissimo ma aspero"; and from another author, Francesco Bustrone, Florio's brother probably, we know that the city was then also known at St. Estephio or St. Euxebius. During his voyage of 1738, the Earl of Sandwich saw nothing at Soli—either because his sight was bad or because he did not bother looking too carefully. Fortunately enough, the very same year, Pockocke wrote about the partially visible walls of the city and about another building which had Corinthian pilasters.

A century later, in 1843–4, Le Bas and Waddington wrote the following sentence: "Les ruines de Soli sont considérables et mériteraient qu'on y fît des fouilles" (there are important remains at Soli and excavations should be made there). A little later, before 1877, Luigi Palma di Cesnola found the theatre emplacement and did some work in this area. He also excavated or, rather, looted some tombs.

Considerable pilfering must have taken place between Le Bas's and Waddington's visit in 1843 and Hogarth's visit in 1888, since the latter saw "no single spot wherein to dig with profit." To this he gives the explanation that "the ancient buildings have been quarried to build Morphou and Lefka." The site was not excavated until the coming of the Swedish expedition under Prof. Gjerstad in 1926.[4] Since 1964, Laval University of Quebec has undertaken systematic excavations, whose results have been sufficient to justify the building of a Laval archaeological house on the site.

From still existing segments of its foundations, the Swedish archaeologists could trace a major part of the city wall which ran through the top of the hill and went down towards the sea. Its western side extended along the Kambos river. On the Eastern side, the wall can be followed for a shorter distance; today, the place of the Eastern city door is still marked by a huge heap of ashlars in a lemon orchard owned by a Turk inhabitant. This city wall, which reached the harbour, was more or less oval in shape. According to Westholm, the harbour installations, now invisible, must have been located not far to the right of the steel pier now used for loading copper ore on barges which carry it to seagoing ships at anchor in the bay.

At the top of the Acropolis, the Swedish found the remains of a very poorly preserved temple, and, a little lower, they excavated a Roman theatre. The temple must have consisted of three cellas (small rooms) opening on a court. But this plan is quite conjectural. Westholm has advanced the hypothesis that the royal palace was built on a lower terrace in the vicinity of this temple. The theatre, when excavated, had its *scaena* well preserved, but the steps of its *cavea* had been completely stripped of their stone casing.

This monument, which has been rebuilt by the Department of Antiquities, could accommodate thirty-five hundred people; it bears a resemblance to theatres of Asia Minor, North Africa and Arabia, and is usually dated to the second century A.D. In fact, the Swedish did their most intensive work west of the city itself, on the neighboring hill of Cholades. There, they excavated a series of temples covering an area of one hundred and forty meters by one hundred and thirty meters; these rubble-walled temples consisted of either one or several cellas opening on a court which, in some cases, was provided with porticos. They were dedicated to Aphrodite, Isis, Serapis, Eros and Canopus. In the excavation of this cult complex—which was in use for a very long time, from the third century before Christ to the fourth century A.D.—several statues were found, together with numerous fragments of sculpture which had been reused as building material.

We began to dig in Soloi in 1964; since then, there has been an expedition each spring.[5] A very large site was granted to us: it is not restricted to the city itself, but also includes the huge cemeteries on the sides of the neighbouring low hills. In these cemeteries, or necropolis, there are thousands of Geometric, Archaic, Classical, Hellenistic, Roman and Christian tombs. In most cases these tombs have been looted, but a few of them are still intact.

We have been working in the following sectors of this large archaeological field:

I.   Inside the ancient city wall, north of the theater, and close to the modern road which, as I wrote before, runs through the ancient city;
II. A little east of the first site, where we are excavating a Christian basilica;
III. Outside the city wall, south of the Acropolis, in the area of the necropolis;
IV. At the top of the Acropolis, where we have found the Hellenistic palace.

I

In 1965, in an effort to explore the city itself, we decided to undertake a series of trial pits, approximately 1000 feet north of the Roman theatre.[6] There was nothing visible there when we started but, knowing at least in part the perimeter of the town walls, we calculated that the area in question must have lain within the ancient city. In this we were right. By multiplying such trial pits, each of which is five meters square, we hope to learn the size of the city at its different periods. In fact, the trial pits undertaken in 1965

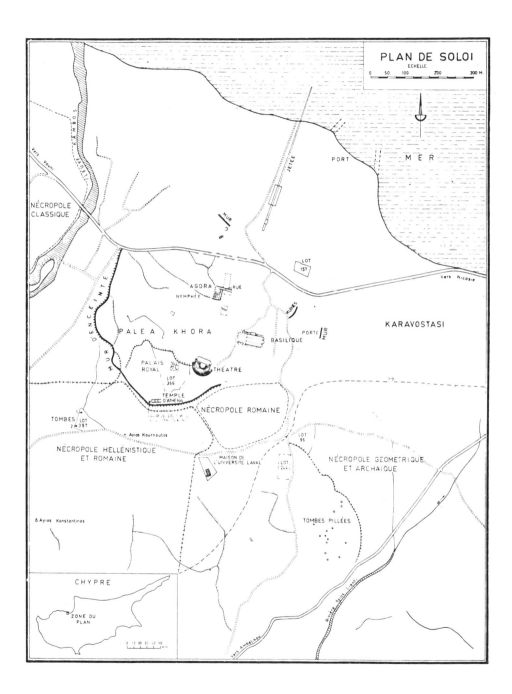

Figure 1: General view of Soloi

have now developed into a large working site, which verifies the fact that Soloi was already a town of some importance at the beginning of the sixth century B.C. In this area, we have gone 5 or 6 meters deep, and the numerous sherds enable us to establish rather easily the different levels of occupation and destruction. Under Byzantine debris, Roman rubble-walls appear. Mr. Ginouvès found that one of the Roman buildings is of large dimensions and consists of several rooms and courts. For a certain period, this building was used as an industrial complex and sheltered a glass-maker's shop (numerous fragments of bottles and drops of melted glass have been found in the southern pits), and a *fullonica* or dyers' shop (several waterproof basins with remains of dyes have also been found at a rather high level).

A remarkably well-preserved stuccoed Roman wall stands on the remains of a tidy building made of carefully trimmed limestone blocks. This building was probably erected circa 500 B.C. Up to the present time, only its northern angle has been excavated. We can affirm that its base is partly preserved, together with some of the wall-blocks, which consist of two facings of regular slabs enclosing a rubble core—a structural technique also used at the palace of Vouni.

Under this Cypro-Classical level we have found the thick foundation walls of sixth-century houses built of sun-dried brick. The style of these foundations—flat stones laid together with mud mortar—as also the numerous Cypro-Archaic sherds associated with them, make this chronology unquestionable. Moreover, a Corinthian sherd of the early sixth century has been found between two stones in one of these walls. It now appears that the sixth-century city was destroyed suddenly; this destruction might have followed the taking of the town by the Persians in 497. When the city was rebuilt in subsequent years, the primitive orientation of the houses and the streets was, for some reason, not maintained.

A little higher on the hill, southward of this first working site, a new system of trial pits was undertaken in 1968. There, remains of Hellenistic houses (later transformed into Roman houses) and, more recently, Archaic walls have been discovered. A beautiful male head in bronze was found lying directly on the floor of a late Roman house (see Fig. 2). Thanks to Professor E. Berger, this head has been graciously restored by Mr. Faltermeier at the Antikenmuseum of

Figure 2: Bronze head

Basel, and is now exhibited in the Cyprus Museum. Of exceptional quality, it reminds one of Classical Greek sculpture, especially that of the school of Polyclitus, but it is in fact characteristically Roman. It probably dates from the second century, and for some reason has been found out of its normal context.[7] Surprisingly enough, this area does not seem to have been important in Classical times; further work ought to enable us to verify this first impression. What we have learned from these two series of trial pits is that Soloi was already a rather large city in the Cypro-Archaic period, and that the city existed before Solon's trip to Cyprus.

In this area we excavated a paved street for a length of 20 meters. Running east-west, it was 4.85 m. wide, and had a covered sidewalk or portico on both sides. On the northern side the portico is entirely ruined, but on the southern side it is preserved well enough to allow restoration with the aid of the numerous architectural blocks which have been unearthed. This southern portico consisted of a colonnade resting on two steps. Three column bases and a fragment of a column shaft have been found. At the back of the portico were shops, as usual. We have a few fragments of the Corinthian column capitals. The entablature had three fasciae, a convex frieze and a cornice. Several architectural blocks have been found in the street. The inside of the cornice was decorated with many motifs, including theatre masks. Professor René Ginouvès dates this street to the third century A.D.

The style of the numerous fragments of architecture found in this area is related to Pamphylian and Western Syrian architecture. During the fourth or fifth century, the slabs of the sidewalk were removed and very poor houses were built inside the portico. Eastward, our street leads to a heap of ashlar blocks which probably indicates the site of one of the city gates. On the western side, it runs towards a wide paved area, of which 400 square meters have now been cleared, but which seems to be much wider. The quality of the stone pavement and the fact that a large street leads to it already suggested that we had discovered the Agora of the city; and this is now confirmed. The area so far uncovered forms the southeastern sector of the Agora, which was bordered by a retaining wall, preserved to a height of approximately 5 m. (see Fig. 3). The retaining wall on the east, which follows the downward slope to the

Figure 3: The southeast corner of the Agora

north, was bordered by a number of public buildings, opening on
the Agora. A street passed beside this complex of buildings, starting
from the colonnaded street and running uphill to the south. A
Nymphaeum was built against the southern wall. Although this
monument is not as yet entirely excavated, its plan is clear to us; it
had a large central basin and two projecting lateral ones. Several
important pieces of its marble decoration have been brought to
light: column bases, capitals, fragments of columns and of cornice,
etc., so that some of its elements can be restored later.

<h1 style="text-align:center">II</h1>

Since 1966, Professor Tran Tam Tinh has been excavating a
Christian basilica built on a partially man-made terrace, about 200
m. northeast of the Acropolis. The site of this building had
previously been occupied during the Hellenistic and Roman
periods. Even though the basilica is only partially excavated, it is
already possible to draw a tentative plan of the church, at the
moment of its largest extension. We know that the primitive basilica
went through two important changes, one of which must have been
contemporary with the acme of the church in Cyprus; the other
transformation must have coincided with its decline.

The first basilica can be dated of the end of the fourth century.
Coins of Valens, Gratian and Theodosius have been found in the
center of the sanctuary floor. This early building had three naves,
and only one apse; unfortunately, it is not yet possible to determine
its exact dimensions (see Fig. 4). It had a fine mosaic floor decorated
mainly with panels of interlaced figures, guilloches, and geometric
motifs (see Fig. 5).

In the middle of the central apse, there is an inscription set in a
tabula ansata which can be roughly translated: "O Christ, help the
one who gave [or dedicated] this mosaic." Written in black and red,
this inscription does not indicate the name of the donor, nor does it
shed light on the motives of the donation, as do the examples at
Mastichari or Aquilea. The short sentence is in the style of the
simple and moving invocations or prayers often found in Christian
papyri, from the second to the fifth centuries. Unfortunately for us,
the early Christians of Cyprus seem to have held anonymity in great

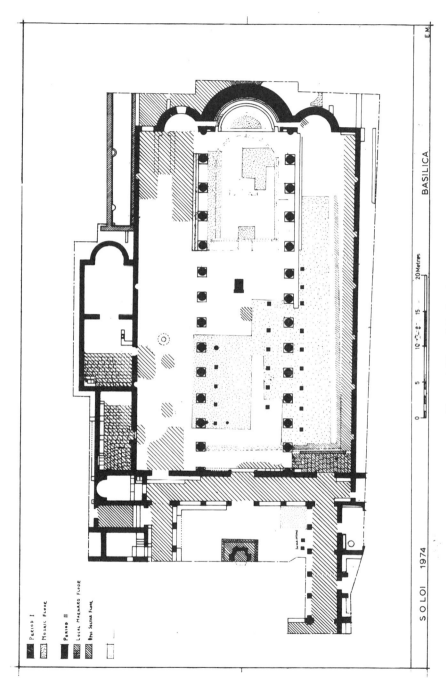

Figure 4: Plan of the Basilca

Figure 5: Detail of the mosaic pavement of the Basilica (Phase II)

esteem; we find the same discretion in an inscription of the fifth or sixth century, in the three-nave church of Shyrvallos, near Ktima.

During the fifth or sixth century, probably, three semicircular basins whose diameter is 1.70 m. were dug in the central nave of our basilica. Coated with waterproof pink stucco, these basins are connected with a water duct. For the moment, their function remains enigmatic: one basin found in the basilica of Emmaus has been identified as a *thalassidion* or *thalassa* by Father Vincent and Father Abel, but why three basins in our basilica? We hope to be able to answer this question in the near future.

The first transformation of the basilica seems to have been made in two phases. First, pilasters enclosing a chancel were placed directly over the mosaic floor, without cutting through it. In a second and much more important phase, the building underwent radical changes. Its central naves were widened and huge stone columns were set on rectangular bases which went through the mosaic floor. This second basilica received an atrium and a narthex and, on its northern side, an absidal parekklesion. The inside dimensions of the new building were 52 m. in length and 30.40 m. in width. It had two rows of twelve columns whose diameter was 1.10 m. The *opus quadratum* wall of its apse is preserved to a height of 2 m.

At the same time, the floor of the sanctuary was raised up 0.80 m. Luckily, this operation did not ruin the mosaic floor, but rather assisted its preservation by covering and hiding it. The new raised floor was paved with polygonal marble tiles set into panels.

In the middle of the northern apse, a door leads to a tiled area; there are also two other doors in this sector of the building, one in the north-east angle, the other on the side. On the western side of the basilica, three doors with marble sills lead to the narthex. Capitals and a fair number of marble facing-slabs have been found in situ; some slabs are decorated with astragals, Greek keys, and floral and animal motifs. This church, whose walls were adorned with mosaics (golden glass cubes have been found in several places close to the wall), was probably destroyed by the Arabs in the ninth or tenth century.

Arcade porticos were built on each side of the atrium, whose dimensions are 18.20 m. (N-S), and 15.50 m. (E-W). In its middle, we found a well-preserved hexagonal basin, set in a marble floor. Of remarkable craftsmanship, this *phiale* seems to belong to the first phase of the basilica and must have been preserved by those who undertook the transformation of the church.

On the southern side of the atrium, amongst numerous fragments of architecture, we found a long inscription dealing with the sufferings of the Cypriot Christians under Diocletian, and also giving details about the building of the church.

In the eastern part of the central nave can be seen the traces of a very late remodeling of the building. There, the floor was once again raised 20 cm. Largely reduced in size (it was only 14.50 m. long and 8.60 m. wide), the last church was a poor replacement for the ruined building over which it was raised, a witness to the decadence of the city. Inhumations under the floor, as well as outside, date this building tentatively to the twelfth century.

III

We resumed our work in an area of the necropolis occupying the side of a low hill which is separated from the southern slope of the Acropolis by a narrow valley, planted with olive trees.

The tombs excavated there are chamber tombs, a type used in Cyprus since the Bronze Age and still occasionally in use in Hellenistic times. We all know that one of the main characteristics of the culture and art of Cyprus is a surprising conservatism, of which the form of the chamber tomb is only one illustration. Our tombs are more or less circular in shape; they are about one meter high and their diameter varies between 2 and 5 meters. These chambers were dug into the friable rock, and their entrance was blocked by a rough wall built of undressed stones. A sunken dromos (passageway) with a few steps led to this underground chamber. In some cases, a dromos of larger size is used for more than one chamber.

While excavating the dromos of a tomb, we generally find sherds as well as intact vases. In one case, close to the steps of a dromos, we found a group of large vases which gift bearers had placed mouth downward. By chance, these vases had been overlooked by the men who, long ago, looted this tomb. Looting has

Figure 6: Christian burial east of the Basilica

been widely practiced in Cyprus, and it is generally estimated that only one tomb out of five is still intact. Some of the looted tombs were stripped bare: this was the case with the one mentioned, but its dromos had been overlooked. However, looted tombs can provide interesting information and even yield a few objects, since the looters were generally looking for precious material, like gold and silver jewelery, and were not interested in vases, which they often left unbroken. (This is not the case with present-day tomb-looters, since vases can now be sold to tourists.)

In tomb no. 6, for instance, which had been looted, we found more than 150 vases, several of them intact. Tomb no. 6—this is a common practice—had been in use at three different periods. The first was the very beginning of the sixth century B.C. Vases of that period together with bones, gold beads and small medallions, faience amulets of Egyptian style, lay directly on the rock floor. A layer of earth and rock splinters 0.15 m. thick separated this material from the second level. Of course, as will be easily understood, the looters were responsible for some disturbance in the levels. In the second period, which covers a part of the sixth and fifth centuries B.C., several bodies were buried in the tomb. They were surrounded with vases as well as with iron and bronze knives, mirrors, etc. Finally, above this middle stratum, the third level was Hellenistic. At that period, people entered the tomb through a tunnel which was dug on the side of the chamber; the only material belonging to this third occupation consisted of five large pointed amphorae.

Tomb no. 12 had also been looted and we found nothing in its chamber. However, while excavating its dromos, we had the good fortune to discover the skeletons of an ox and a goat which had been sacrificed at a funeral ceremony. Close to the bull's neck, we found the remains of an iron knife which had probably been used for the sacrifice.

One of the most interesting tombs emerged during the 1967 expedition. We first came upon a very simple grave with one skeleton buried under a disturbed row of stones. Nothing was found with that skeleton, and those who buried the man were most certainly unaware that there was a chamber tomb under the rough pit they had dug. In front of the entrance of this chamber tomb, we found two Attic lekythoi of the Hellenistic period and in the chamber, which had never been visited by looters, were two skeletons with fifteen plain vases and three beautiful jugs of a type yet unknown in Cyprus. The neck of these jugs is decorated with two figures of sacrificers, separated by a juglet used for pouring the liquid. An old man, clad in a himation or large mantle, holds a phiale and a bird. A young man, clad in a chiton or short tunic, seems about to sacrifice a sheep (?). The painted decoration has been preserved on two of the jugs. On one of them, it consists of two rows of red and green squares outlined with black. The decoration of the other is similar except that the panels are oval-shaped.

In 1969 and 1970, we dug east of this first group of tombs in a cultivated field which we had rented from its owner. There we found several Christian burials (see Fig. 6), one of which provided us with an amethyst necklace, beads of amber (the latter is very scarce in Cyprus), and also gold and bronze jewelery. Under these burials—and at so high a level that it is difficult to explain how the skeletons and objects which they contained could escape being crushed to dust by the farm tractors working in this field (they were found not more than one meter from the top of the soil)—we discovered a group of Geometric tombs containing ninth century, Cypro-Geometric pottery. This interesting find enables us to raise the date of Soloi about 200 years, that is to say to the ninth century B.C.

In 1970, eight almost intact Cypro-Geometric and Cypro-Archaic tombs were excavated. Like the previous tombs, they consist of small chambers with short dromoi. These burials contained several vases of good quality and one specimen of a ware with pictured decoration, a style which is very poorly represented in the north-western area of Cyprus. This is a kylix decorated with a fish.

IV

In 1973, Professor Kahil undertook new trial pits at the top of the Acropolis, north of the badly ruined temple which the Swedish had excavated more than forty years ago. The latter had dug a trench 100 m. long in the same area and had noticed "a great many walls, all belonging to the same rectilinear building." Although the trench had not been put on a plan, our trial pits revealed it very clearly, as well as the walls. Some of them are preserved at a height of more than 2 m. Most of them are rubble-built, but some are at least partially lined with well-trimmed limestone blocks, in a way which recalls the walls of the palace at Vouni. It is now easy to recognize two main phases in the construction of a large building which we regard as the Hellenistic palace of Soloi (see Figs. 7 and 8). Together with fragments of stucco mouldings and of painted plaster walls, we have found several terra-cotta figurines and, amongst other things, a beautiful bronze spearhead.

This is a very brief survey of the results of our excavations at Soloi. The programme for the future campaigns is now easy to define: we want to finish the excavation of the Nymphaeum and of the basilica with the numerous rooms adjacent to it, and finally, to bring the Hellenistic royal palace to light. We are confident that the excavation of these monuments will constitute an important contribution to Cypriot archaeology.[8]

NOTES

1. *SCE*, III, p. 399.

2. For an excerpt of the *Acta* relating Auxibius' arrival in Soloi, cf. *SCE*, pp. 408–9. See also A. Papageorghiou, *O Agios Auxibios*, Nicosia, 1969.

3. That was Oberhummer's opinion, followed by *SCE* I, p. 409.

4. Cf. *SCE* III, pp. 399–582.

5. For summary reports of our excavations, cf. Jean des Gagniers, Lilly Kahil, René Ginouvès, Tran Tam Tinh, "Trois campagnes de fouilles à Soloi," in *Report of the Department of Antiquities*, Cyprus 1967, pp. 50–8, with Pls. XII–XIV; J. des Gagniers, "Soloi, fouilles de l'Université Laval, Quebec." *Praktikon Tou Protou Diethnous Kyprologikou Synedriou*, Tomos A, Nicosia 1972, pp. 41–9; Tran Tam Tinh, "Rapport préliminaire' sur la fouille de la basilique de Soloi, Chypre," dans *Actas del VIII Congresso internacional de arqueologia cristiana*, Barcelona, 1972, pp. 501–85, with Pls. CCLIII–CCLVII; and also the following brief notices: *BCH* 90 (1966): 352–5; 91 (1967): 360–3; 92 (1968): 328–33; 93 (1969): 552–5; 94 (1970): 272–8; 95 (1971): 422–4; 96 (1972): 1074–7; and *AJA* 71 (1967): 403, 72 (1968): 376–7; 74 (1970): 75; 74 (1970): 396, with Pl. 104, Fig. 20; 76 (1972): 317, with Pl. 67, Figs. 40–1; 77 (1973): 58, with Pl. 8, Fig. 27.

6. The Laval Archaeological team is composed of Lilly Kahil (Université de

Figure 7: Walls of the Hellenistic Palace

Fribourg, Switzerland, René Ginouvès (Université de Paris-Nanterre), Tran Tam Tinh (Université Laval), Jean des Gagniers (Université Laval). The architect is Carlo Steffen (Geneva), and the draughtsman Elias Markou of the Cyprus Museum.

7. For a detailed study of this head, cf. Lilly Kahil's forthcoming article in *Antike Kunst.*

8. Laval University has contributed to the cost of the excavations since their beginning in 1964. In recent years, grants from the Canada Council have greatly helped our work in Soloi. The author of this article wishes to express his gratitude to both these institutions.

Figure 8: Floor levels within the Hellenistic Palace